Ramakrishna, The Nectar of Eternal Bliss

A Translation of the *Kathamritam* from the original Bengali

By
Shree Maa
Swami Satyananda Saraswati

Ramakrishna, The Nectar of Eternal Bliss

First Edition
Copyright © 2005 by
Devi Mandir Publications
All rights reserved.
ISBN 1-877795-66-6
Library of Congress Control Number: 2005901112

Ramakrishna, The Nectar of Eternal Bliss ,

Swami Satyananda Saraswati
1. Hindu Religion. 2. Goddess Worship. 3. Spirituality.
4. Philosophy. I. Saraswati, Swami Satyananda.

Published by
Devi Mandir Publications
5950 Highway 128
Napa, CA 94558 USA
707-966-2802
www.shreemaa.org

Preface

Shree Maa starts by singing a song about Ramakrishna. Swamiji translates.

Swamiji: Hey, all citizens of the city. Come and see, come and see! Ramakrishna has taken the form of the tree which grants the fruit of all desire. Come quickly and see. He is standing there giving blessings. Whatever desire you have in your mind, come quickly and tell Ramakrishna. Ramakrishna stands in the form of the wish-fulfilling tree. Come quickly and see!

The impact of the life of Sri Ramakrishna on spiritual evolution is still being felt around the world 120 years after his death. Even today in this modern age, people who never knew him, nor understood his language or his culture, find inspiration from his example of dedication and comfort in his philosophy of universality.

He demonstrated the meaning of devotion and achieved the epitome of its success to such an extent that it could be defined only by one word. In the Bengali language it was termed *Vyakulata*, sincerity, deep sincere longing, so intense that one can think of nothing else.

The majesty of his thoughts can be summarized in a few short statements:

There is One God of us all, who is called by many names in many languages.

As many as there are individuals, so many are the ways of worshiping the One God.

The point of religious experience is not to engage in intellectual debate, but to become submerged in the ecstasy of divine love through devotion to our path.

Immediately we can see the relevance of studying the life of such a great man! At such a time when we face the circumstances as we human beings do today, these simple propositions hold out perhaps the only promise of peace for a world beset with conflict.

Ramakrishna, who had practiced the basic tenets of the world's great religions, and personally verified the truth of each of them, that he could reach the same intensity of *Vyakulata* through the practice of each, stands today as a unifying example of mutual respect and reciprocal admiration, while many others of humanity are actually fighting over what to call divinity in a variety of languages.

He used to tell the story of the different stairs to the pond at his village, where the Hindus drew water and called it *jal*, the Muslims drew the same water and called it *pani*, and the Christians drew the same water and called it *water*. Yet it was the same to them all.

He said that every action performed with respect and attentiveness was a form of worship, so that every individual had his or her own way of honoring God.

And religious experience is not born of the mind. It occurs when we go beyond the mind, beyond all thought. Religious experience occurs when we become consumed by the ecstasy of intuitive cognition, when we fall in love to the extent that we forget ourselves.

And that is why Ramakrishna is called the wish-fulfilling tree, the form of the tree which grants the fruit of all desire. When we see him and listen to his words, feel his ecstasy, and practice his instructions, we go beyond the selfishness of the mind, and become enthralled with the dance of this Lover of Life, Lover of God!

Both Shree Maa and I have derived significant inspiration from Ramakrishna, and for at least the past twenty-five years we have been translating his stories and songs in sat sanghas around the world. Over the last few years we have been recording and transcribing these translations, and it is our joy to share with you our understanding of the book authored by Mahendranath Gupta, called *Kathamrita* in the original Bengali.

The book, first published in Bengali in 1887, is presented as a diary of Mr. Gupta's recordings of conversations and experiences in association with Sri Ramakrishna between March, 1882, and April, 1886, a few months before Ramakrishna's demise. In the text Mahendranath Gupta referred to himself as M., with all the humility of a true devotee who wanted to remain nameless, while sharing the wisdom of his guru.

In 1942 Swami Nikhilananda, presented his translation entitled, "The Gospel of Sri Ramakrishna." This book has served as a tremendous inspiration to acquaint devotees in the English-speaking world with the life and thoughts of Sri Ramakrishsna.

It is our desire to update the language of this tradition, and to reaffirm its relevancy for our times. Also we wish to convey even more of the inspiration of Ramakrishna and maybe present him as less of an intellectual and more of the ecstatic mystic that he was. With the music of Shree Maa's singing and the joy of our interaction in sat sangha, we hope to share the wonderful bhava Sri Ramakrishna has come to represent.

In Bengali *Katha* means words or story. *Amrita* translates as nectar, and moreover, immortal nectar, the Nectar of Immortal or Eternal Bliss. It is our desire to share this story about nectar. We want to try to communicate the eternal bliss, in a way that inspires devotees to go beyond the intellectual meaning of the words into the *Vyakulata*, into the love which takes us beyond the selfishness of the mind, into the ecstasy of pure devotion.

Ramakrishna once said to Mahendranath Gupta: A yogi is always looking towards God. His vision is always fixed on God. A yogi maintains inner silence and always looks towards God. If you see into a yogi's eyes, you will be able to understand this. Just as a bird sits on its eggs in the nest, the bird's mind is completely submerged in thoughts of the eggs, even while its eyes are staring towards the heavens above.

We wish to become those yogis. Ramakrishna wants us to become so. Shree Maa encourages us with her blessings, and with this understanding we share the Nectar of Eternal Bliss.

Shree Maa and Swami Satyananda Saraswati

Devi Mandir, 2005

Table of Contents

Ramakrishna, Thakur, The Master

Introduction

> Swamiji: Now we're going to talk about the birth of Ramakrishna.

Ramakrishna was born in the village of Kamarpukur in Hooghly District in the month of Falgun in the bright fortnight of February 22, 1836, in the home of a Brahmin priest. There are many opinions about the birth of Ramakrishna, which vary from historical to mythic. He lived in a human body for 52 years. His father's name was Khudiram Chattopadhyaya, who was an extremely disciplined and great devotee. His mother was Chandra Devi, who was a simple lady filled with compassion. The family lived three miles away from the village of Kamarpukur.

> Swamiji: Khudiram's landlord was the richest man in the area. He was contesting a case in the local court. He asked Khudiram to tell a lie to support his case. Khudiram refused to lie to the judge, and instead told the truth The landlord lost the case and was very angry, so he took away Khudiram's property. Khudiram then moved his family to Kamarkupur.

As a child Ramakrishna's name was nicknamed Gadadhar, who wields the club. Gadadhar was sent to the local village school to learn how to read and write. His father became the pujari of a temple of a form of Rama called Raghuvir, the hero of the Ragus.

Gadadhar didn't like learning in the village school, and after a very elementary education consisting of reading and writing, Gadadhar became the pujari of the Raghuvir temple. He used to sing his own songs and had a beautiful voice. Gadadhar would see a drama one time and learn every song in the play.

His childhood was spent in complete bliss, and everyone in the village loved him. Near the family house was the home of the Laha family, beside which was a guest house in which visiting sadhus would reside. When the sadhus used to stay there, Gadadhar would go to perform some small errands for them. When any of the sadhus would recite the Scriptures, he would listen with great intent. In this way he memorized many passages from the scriptures, from the Ramayana, the Mahabharata, and the Bhagavata. He knew all the stories by heart.

One day, when he was eleven years old, he was walking across the fields to a nearby village called Anurgram. Ramakrishna later described the scene personally.

Ramakrishna: Suddenly I saw a great aura of light, and I became unconscious. People said that I had moved into bhava samadhi, the attitude of perfect communion.

After the death of his father Khudiram, Ramakrishna went to live in Calcutta with his older brother, Ramkumar. His age then was about 17 or 18. In Calcutta, Ramakrishna became the assistant to his older brother who was the priest in the house of Govinda Chatterjee. The two brothers traveled throughout the neighborhood from house to house performing family pujas.

Rani Rasmani bought land in Dakshineswar about five miles from Calcutta, in order to establish a Kali temple. She employed Ramkumar as the chief priest of the temple. From time to time Ramakrishna went to visit the temple, and he began to officiate at the worship ceremonies. His age was about 21 or 22. By then Ramakrishna's middle brother, Rameshwar, also became a priest at the Kali temple. Rameshwar had two sons named Ramlal and Shivaram and a daughter named Lakshmi Devi.

After several days of performing worship in the Kali Temple, Ramakrishna became filled with divine love. He began to spend the entire day sitting in front of the image in the temple. Day after day he would spend sitting in the temple with the deity. Seeing this condition, his relatives decided to try to make him more worldly. They thought that there was nothing that would change a man quicker than marriage, and this is what they proposed.

About four and a half miles from Kamarkupur was the village of Jayrambati. Ramachandra Mukherjee lived there. He had a daughter named Saradamani.

In 1859 she was married to Ramakrishna. At that time Ramakrishna was 30 years old and Saradamani was 6.[1]

After the marriage Ramakrishna went back to the Kali temple in Dakshineswar. He began to worship Kali with even greater fervor, and some days later he had Her darshan in many forms. He would perform arati[2] to the deity, and the arati had no end. He would sit for puja, and the puja would go on and on. He would put a flower on his own head and sit there for hours completely still. Ultimately, he couldn't perform the worship at all, and people thought that he became like a crazy man.

The son-in-law of Rani Rasmani, Mathur Babu, thought of Sri Ramakrishna as a great soul, and he began to serve him and fulfill his needs. Mathur put another Brahmin in charge of the pujas at the Kali temple, Hriday Mukherjee, who a cousin of Ramakrishna, and gave him the responsibility of caring for Ramakrishna.

Now Ramakrishna neither performed the pujas, nor did he enter into a worldly relationship with his wife. Day and night he would just call "Mother, Mother." He sometimes sat like a stone or a doll. Other times he was like a madman or

a little child. He never cared for money. He saw people who
were beset with many thoughts and many cares, and he would
run away from them immediately. He would only talk about
God. He didn't like to talk about anything else. And all the
time he would say "Mother, Mother, Mother."

Sadhus, saints, and sanyasins all came to the Kali temple.
One such sadhu was named Totapuri. Totapuri stayed in
Dakshineswar for eleven months, and taught Advaita (non-
dualistic) Vedanta. One day he was describing many points
about Vedanta, when Ramakrishna went into nirvikalpa
samadhi.[3]

One woman Sadhu named Brahmani Bhairavi came to
the Kali temple. She had performed many types of tantric
sadhanas. Others sadhus came also to teach Ramakrishna
about the Koran, the Gaurimath Sampradaya, and Sri
Chaitanya. When the Brahmani saw that Ramakrishna was
learning non-dualism from Totapuri, she warned him to be
careful of Vedanta. She said to him, "Don't listen to Advaita
Vedanta. If you study Vedanta, your bhava and devotion will
become dissipated."

There was a pundit named Vaishnavacharan, who was a
teacher of Vaishnava philosophy. He used to come every day
to the Kali temple, and often took Ramakrishna to the
Vaishnava Society, where he would sing the songs of Lord
Chaitanya. Ramakrishna became submerged into the bhava
of Chaitanya. Vaishnavacharan was the main teacher of that
congregation. He said to Mathur Babu, "This crazy man isn't
ordinary at all. He's mad with love. He's crazy for God."

The Brahmani and Vaishnavacharan said that
Ramakrishna was filled with mahabhava.[4]   Sometimes
Ramakrishna remained completely oblivious to the entire
external world, and he was submerged in samadhi. At other
times he was so totally unaware of what was happening out-

side that he would remain crying "Mother, Mother." He talked only about God. He took orders only from the Divine Mother. He used to say to Her, "Mother, I'm only going to listen to you. I don't know anything about scriptures or teachers of scriptures. If you instruct me, I'll have faith in what you say." Ramakrishna felt this completely, and he used to act in this way.

Ramakrishna: She is the Supreme Divinity, the unlimited, unqualified Sat-Chit-Ananda.[5] She is the Mother of the Universe.

Ramakrishna (to the Mother of the Universe): You and I are one. Your will is manifest everywhere and is only for the good of all embodied beings. All the devotees will come to you. You don't have to call them. Even the most pure devotees with the purest desires are going to come. They're all going to come.

One day at the time of arati, Ramakrishna began to cry with a loud voice, "Hey, devotees, where are you? Come quickly!"

He always saw his mother, Chandramuni, as a form of the Divine Mother. He used to worship her in that way. When his older brother, Ramkumar, left his body, Chandramuni became ill. Ramakrishna brought her to the Kali temple at Dakineshwar. Ramakrishna visited his mother daily and bowed down to her feet.

Ramakrishna went on pilgrimage to various sites of India two times. The first time he took a train to Benares along with his mother, Ram Chaturjee and Mathur Babu. During this journey, Ramakrishna went in and out of Samadhi frequently. They visited Baidyanath, Kashi, and Allalhabad. During his second pilgrimage in 1868, he traveled with Mathur Babu and his wife, Jagadambe, and Hriday. They went to Benares, Prayag, and Vrindavan.

Swamiji: Mahendranath is explaining the different saints of this era whom Ramakrishna met.

In Benares, Ramakrishna went into samadhi at Manikarnika Ghat, the famous cremation grounds of the city. After having a very intense darshan of Vishwanath, the principal deity of Benares, Vishwanath gave Ramakrishna the name Tarak Brahma. At that time he was introduced to Trailanga Swami. In Vrindavan, Ramakrishna fell in love with Radha. Also he would talk to the river, Ganga, like She was an embodied being.

The respected Keshab Sen along with many devotees meditated in the garden at Belgharia. Ramakrishna, along with Hriday, went to see Keshab Sen at Belgharia in the year 1875. There was a captain in the Napalese army whose name was Vishwanath Upadhyaya. He used to come often to see Keshab Sen.

When Ramakrishna went to see Keshab Sen, many devotees came to see him. Between 1879 and 1880, the inner circle of Ramakrishna's devotees started to congregate. When they came to see Ramakrishna, he used to become crazy with devotion. Ramakrishna remained like a child, and he would often become silent. Often he remained completely submerged in samadhi and at other times in bhava samadhi. After he came out of samadhi, he would be in a state of intoxication. At other times he acted just like a 5-year-old child. He would just say "Mother, Mother, Mother," time and again.

Shree Maa related this story about Ramakrishna:

When Thakur was 5 or 6 years old he loved to stay with women, like his Auntie. He easily made friends with all women and he loved to listen to the women gossiping.

In olden times the women covered their heads. They never showed their faces. The village women go to the pond to get water throughout the day. There was a group of women sitting together near the pond gossiping. One day when he was 15 or 16 years old, he wore a sari and he covered his face, so that no one could tell that he was not female. He went to the pond and sat down with the women and was listening to their gossip. That gossiping, you know, is women's nature. Sorry to say that this is women's nature — but they talk about everything: how much they have, what their husband told them, what their mother-in-law said, blah, blah blah. Then Thakur opened his cover and said, "Now I'm going to tell everybody everything!" Constantly he used to tease the women and teach the women to be "real mothers".

Thakur's village had a theater. One time when he was 6 years, somebody was scheduled to perform the role of Shiva in a play at the theater. That person became ill. The people thought that the play could not be performed because there was no one to play the role of Shiva. Everybody started talking, "Gadadhar will do it, Gadadhar will do it!" Thakur was very happy to play Shiva in the drama. They made him up into a beautiful Shiva with a trishul, and they took him onto the stage. The drummer began to play, and Ramakrishna went completely into samadhi. Everybody began to question, "What is going on? He became Shiva. Where is His play?" Thakur became a stone, and nobody could do anything.

Another day during his youth, he was walking and a thunderstorm came. At that time he saw a big light and he fainted. He was always divine. Everywhere he looked, he saw God. From his childhood he always showed respect to the whole of creation.

Thakur told me to respect your actions all the time, and you'll get me. It is true! If we respect our actions, we'll know who we are.

One day Thakur went to someone's kitchen room in the village, and saw that rice was boiling in a pot on the stove. It was making bubbles and a gurgling sound. He told the house wife, "Look, the rice is boiling. That is like your ego: boiling, bubbling and gurgling! Afterwards, when the dish will be cooked, it will be calm and quiet. That means your ego is gone." In a patient way he taught the village people. You can watch boiling rice yourself. When it is done, it is calm and quiet, completely silent. He explained relationships in a simple way but with a big meaning.

---

1 Such marriages are really betrothals, to be consummated at a later time.
In Ramakrishna's case, it would never be consummated.

2 Evening worship.

3 State of consciousness beyond all relativity where even divine forms are left behind.

4 The highest degree or the culmination of devotional practice.

5 Pure Existence, Pure Consciousness, Pure Love.

Chapter 1

The Master and Mahendranath Gupta

March 1882

Calcutta

Swamiji: Now we're going to discuss the first meetings of Mahendranath Gupta (known as M.) and Sri Ramakrishna.

The temple of Dakshineswar is on the bank of the Ganga. The first meeting between Mahendranath Gupta and Sri Ramakrishna occurred at the temple of Mother Kali during the spring of 1882. Just after Ramakrishna's birthday Keshab Sen and Joseph Cook went to see Ramakrishna. On that day M. was also present. This was his first visit.

Dakshineshwar Temple

M. saw that the Master's room was full of people who were sitting silently and listening to the nectar of immortal bliss from the words of Ramakrishna. The devotees were sitting spellbound. M. was taken aback and looked at the scene with wonder. He understood immediately that it was actually Sukadeva, the son of Vedavyasa, who was expounding the scriptures with devotees. It was as if all of the holy places were present in the room. Then he looked again and saw that it was actually Sri Chaitanya sitting there singing the glories of God.

Ramakrishna: When you sing the name of God even once with devotion and bhava, if you shed tears, then know for certain that all the rituals of worship are completely fulfilled. Then actions are renounced of their own accord. Karma leaves us, and only the name of God remains. Then it will be enough if you listen to the Om inside. The sandhya dissolves into the Gayatri, and the Gayatri dissolves into Om.

M. had gone with one friend named Sidhur to Baranagore. They walked through the garden of Prasanna Bannerjee. It was the twenty-fourth of February. Sidhur told M., "There is a beautiful garden on the bank of the Ganga. Will you come with me to see this garden? There's a great soul living there." M. agreed. They entered into the Dakshineswar temple garden and they met Ramakrishna, who was living there.

M. was surprised, and he began to think to himself, "What a beautiful place. What beautiful people. What beautiful words. I don't want to move from here." After a few moments he thought, "I'm going to see this place first and then come back to sit down."

When he again approached the door of the house with his friend Sidhur, he heard the sound of arati coming from inside. He heard the ringing of brass bells and cymbals. Along with the ringing of the bells and cymbals came sweet tunes and harmonies.

M. was amazed and thought to himself, "Can you imagine? I was walking along the Ganga, and I find myself listening to such beautiful, melodic music?" The moon was shining. Ramakrishna began to dance in all directions in ecstasy.

M. visited all twelve of the Shiva temples, the Radhakanta temple, and the Bhavatarini temple in the Dakshineswar complex. He listened to the worship ceremonies and watched the aratis being performed in all of the different temples.

Sidhur (to M.): Is this the temple complex that Rani Rasmani has established? I see that all the Gods are worshiped here. The two men talked as they walked towards Sri Ramakrishna's room. They arrived at the door to Ramakrishna's room. Just at that time someone had filled the room with the fragrance of incense and closed the door.

M. had been educated in English manners, and he thought, "Well, maybe we should not enter Ramakrishna's room just now." Next to the door was a female servant, and he asked her, "Is the sadhu inside the room?" The maid servant replied, "Yes, he is in the room."

M: How long has he lived here? Does he read many books?

Maidservant: Books? He has no need of books. All the books come out of his mouth.

M. was a college graduate, and he was amazed that Ramakrishna didn't read books.

M: What do you mean this sadhu doesn't read books? Is he going to perform the evening worship? Can we go enter the room now? Please find out and let us know.

Maidservant: Go inside, go inside.

Then they entered the room and saw there was no one inside except Ramakrishna, who was seated on a wooden cot. Incense filled the room. All the windows and doors were closed. M. bowed down to the Master who sat on the cot and engaged them in conversation.

Ramakrishna: Where do you come from? What do you do? You came from the big city. Why did you come here?

M. gave his full introduction. M. saw that from time to time Ramakrishna seemed distracted. Later he learned that this is called "bhava." It is like a fisherman who watches his hook as he catches a fish. The fisherman remains fully attentive. When the fish grabs onto the hook, then the fisherman can't hear words that are spoken to him. Ramakrishna's mind was like this.

Ramakrishna would go into this bhava during evening meditation. Sometimes he was completely oblivious to the external world.

M: If you are going to do your worship, we will leave you alone.

Ramakrishna was full of bhava. He said, "No, no, no. I have no need for formal worship. All that I do is worship." After a few more words, M. again bowed down and took his leave.

Ramakrishna: Come again.

When M. was leaving, he began to think, "This man is so simple. I have a strong desire to see him again. Is it really possible that he does not read books? He's not a great scholar, and yet he's so engaging. This is very incredible and surprising. I have a great desire to come again. He did invite me to come again. I shall come either tomorrow or the next day."

Mahendranath Gupta - M.

M.'s Second Visit

The next day at eight o'clock in the morning, Ramakrishna went to be shaved. It was a little bit cold, so he was wearing a shawl. He saw M. standing there and asked, "You came again? Very good, sit down here." This meeting occurred on the south side of the veranda. The barber arrived and started to trim Thakur's beard. While the barber was shaving him, M. started a conversation. Ramakrishna stuttered a lot because the barber kept pulling the hairs on his chin.

Ramakrishna (to M.): Where is your home?

M. replied that he lived in Calcutta.

Ramakrishna: Well, why are you staying here?

M. replied that he came to visit his elder sister at Ishan Kaviraj's house in Baranagore. Ishan Kaviraj was a great devotee of Ramakrishna.

Ramakrishna: Oh, you're staying at Ishan's house? How is Keshab Sen? He was sick recently.

M: I've heard that he is all right now.

> Swamiji: Ramakrishna had offered a coconut to Kali on behalf of Keshab so that he could be blessed with good health.

Ramakrishna: Very late at night I went to Kali's temple and prayed to Her on behalf of Keshab. I cried in front of Mother. I said, "Mother, you must make Keshab better. Relieve him of his illness. If Keshab doesn't live, then what will I do when I go to Calcutta? Who will I talk with?" That's why I gave Her a coconut. Do you know if a man named Mr. Cook has come to Calcutta? I heard that he gives lectures. Keshab took me on the steamer one time, and Mr. Cook was there also.

M: I heard something similar. I've never heard his lectures. I don't know anything about him.

They began a discussion on the duties of a householder and the duties of a father. Pratap's brother was staying with Ramakrishna for several days.

Ramakrishna: Pratap had told me, "I'm going to stay here." So he took his whole family and put them at his in-laws' house and came here to become a sadhu. I scolded him very much. I told him that you've given birth to sons, daughters, and a whole family, and you've left their responsibility with somebody else? I gave him a serious scolding. I told him to get out of here and look for some work.

Swamiji: Now the next subject describes how M.'s ego was cut to pieces.

Ramakrishna: Are you married?

M: Yes.

Ramakrishna (excitedly standing up): Oh, you've already gone and tied the knot.

M. lowered his head like he had committed a great wrong. He started to think, "Is getting married such a fault? Did I do something so bad?"

Ramakrishna: Do you have any children?

M. (heart beating fast and trembling): Yes.

Ramakrishna (with great contempt): You have sons and daughters, too?

M.'s ego began to dissolve.

Ramakrishna (after a few minutes and with great love): Look, your signs are very good. I'm looking at your forehead and eyes, and I see that you are a man of great vision. Tell me about your family. Are they spiritual, or are they under the spell of ignorance?

M: They are ignorant, Sir.

Ramakrishna: What? And you have knowledge? You live in your head and have no heart! Right now you don't know what is knowledge and what is ignorance. Do you think that books and education can bring wisdom?

> Shree Maa: M. was an overlearned man. He could not believe that Thakur knew everything. M. thought that if you want to earn wisdom, you have to read lots of books. His ego dissolved that day.

After hearing these words, M.'s false perception was put aside. He now understood that knowing God is wisdom, and not knowing God is ignorance.

Ramakrishna: And you are a man of knowledge?

M.'s ego had been profoundly shocked.

Ramakrishna: Do you believe in a God with form or God without form?

M. was completely surprised. He said to himself, "If you believe in God with form, how can you believe God is without form? If God is without form, if you have this faith, then how can you believe in God with form? Is it possible that both of these could be true at the same time? If something is white like milk, could it be black at the same time?"

M: I like to think of God as formless.

Ramakrishna: All right. If you have faith in either, that is enough. If you believe in the formless, then that's very good. But never think that is the only truth, and everything else is false. Remember that God without form is true, and God with form is just as true. Whichever one you have faith in, hold on to that, and move towards God.

Hearing that both were true, M. was filled with wonder.

M. thought that this kind of teaching cannot be learned from books. "How can both things be true at the same time?" Then his ego was shaken for the third time, but it wasn't demolished. He began to argue again.

M: I can understand that God has form, but do you think it is that of an image made out of clay?

Ramakrishna: Why couldn't it be made out of clay? It is the image of the Infinite Consciousness.

M. couldn't understand what he meant by the image of Infinite Consciousness.

M: For those who worship these images made out of clay, is it not necessary to remember that these are not God? It's not appropriate to worship a deity made out of clay thinking that the clay image is God.

Ramakrishna became greatly agitated.

Ramakrishna: You people from Calcutta all have the same attitude. You only give lectures and talk. No one ever stops to get the light himself. Who are you to give lectures to others? She who has created this entire perceivable universe will understand. She has created this entire universe -- the sun, the moon, the planets, stars, human beings, and plants. She has made provisions for the nourishment of all people. In order to protect the young, She made mothers and fathers. She gave them love, devotion, and attachment to their children. She will understand. She has made so many methods of attainment. Will She not teach us the way of attainment? If it's necessary for us to understand, She will teach us. She is within us. If there's any mistake in worshiping an image of God made out of clay, will She not know? We are invoking Her through these deities. Do you think She wouldn't explain to us if it were wrong? She is

pleased through this worship. You don't have to trouble
yourself with these matters. You should try to gain
knowledge and cultivate devotion yourself. That will be
enough for you.

This time M.'s ego was shaken to its depths. M. began to
think, "What he is saying is true. What is the need for me to
explain to him? Do I know myself? Am I arguing against
devotion? Do I know God? I don't know and I don't
understand. I should be ashamed to try to defeat someone
who's more accomplished than me. Without understanding it
myself, I am trying to reason with someone who has great
understanding. He is not a man of little attainment. This isn't
mathematics or history. It's not necessary for me to explain
to him as though he were my student. This is the principle of
God. What he has said, I really appreciate."

This was M.'s first and last argument with the Master.

Ramakrishna: You were talking about worshiping an
image made of clay? Even though it is made of clay, worship
is appropriate. God has created various forms of worship.
He has created this entire universe and provided various
practices by which people can attain knowledge. Whatever
path an individual takes, is the most suitable one for that
individual. The Divine Mother has arranged different paths
for different individuals. Look, a mother had five children.
She brought home a fish to eat. She began to cook it in
different ways. For one individual she made fish pulao. For
another she made fish soup. For someone else she made
baked fish with vegetables. Another got fried fish. Each one
liked the fish that they got, just to their taste, to their
satisfaction. Do you understand?

M: Yes.

Swamiji: Ramakrishna talks about the path of
devotion.

M. (with a very humble attitude): How can we fix our minds on God?

Ramakrishna: You have to sing the name of God always and contemplate Her qualities. Seek out sadhus and devotees and have sat sangha. Whenever possible come together for sat sangha. If you stay all the time in samsara, this world of objects and relationships, and with worldly thoughts, it's very difficult to remember God. Every now and then when you get the opportunity, go to a quiet place, and meditate on God. If you can't sit in solitude now and then, it will be very difficult to lead your mind into meditation. When a tree is small, you put a fence around it. If you don't put a fence around it and protect it, the goats and the cows will come and eat it. In the same way, you should withdraw and meditate in solitude or go to the forest. Always contemplate spiritual ideals. God is truth. God is eternal. Everything else is transient and temporary. Discriminating in this way, one can renounce transient things from the mind.

M. (with a humble attitude): How should we live in this world?

Swamiji: Now Ramakrishna is going to
explain the spiritual path for householders.

Ramakrishna: Perform your duties, but keep your mind on God. Remember that it is a privilege to serve your family and parents, but they are not your own. Know that they don't belong to you.

In the home of a wealthy family, there is a maidservant who does the household work, but her mind is always thinking about her own home in her own village. She serves the children of her master's house as though she were serving her own children. She calls them "my Rama," "my Hari," but in her heart she knows that they are not her children.

The tortoise floats around the lake on top of the water, but where is the mind of the tortoise? There, on the shore with her eggs. Wherever she's placed her eggs, that's where her mind is, even though she's floating on the surface of the lake.

Do your work in the world, but keep your mind at the feet of God and leave it there. If you perform your activities in the world without first contemplating God, you're going to fall into worldliness. The burden of responsibility and worldliness will become unbearable. The more you contemplate worldly attachments, the more your energy becomes weaker by the day. Before you cut open the jack-fruit, cover your hands with oil. The jackfruit is extremely sticky, and without oil your hands will become stuck together. Just so, rub your mind with the oil of devotion to God. Then you can perform your worldly duties.

In order to achieve this kind of devotion, it's important to spend some time in a secluded place. To get butter, you have to churn yogurt. When you are making cream, if you keep stirring the milk, it won't congeal into cream. You have to set it in an isolated spot to rise to the top. Therefore, in order to make the cream of devotion, you have to meditate in solitude in a secluded place. Then you can churn the cream into the butter of mature devotion.

Again, as you practice in this way, you develop divine wisdom. If you dwell on the world, your mind will go to a lower state of attachment. In the world your mind is always attracted to desires and to the means of fulfillment of those desires. The world of objects and relationships is like water, and the mind is like milk. If you put the milk in the water, then the milk and water will become one. It's very difficult to separate the milk from the water. If you turn the milk into cream and churn the cream into butter, you can then take that butter and put it in water and it will float. That's why it is necessary to spend some time in solitude, and then you can obtain the butter of devotion and wisdom. Then you can put that butter in the water of the world and it will float.

Please think about this very deeply and very intensely. There are many forms of desires and many forms of what is required to fulfill them. They are all transient. God is the only true reality. What do you get with money? When you have money, you get rice, clothes, and a place to stay. You don't get God with money, so money cannot be the goal of life. This is called discrimination between the real and the unreal. Do you understand?

M: Yes. There is a Sanskrit play called *Prabodha Chandrodaya*. This play is about discrimination.

Ramakrishna: Look, neither wealth nor a beautiful body is permanent. Think about this. Even beneath the beautiful body, there is only bone, meat, urine, and waste. Why do humans think about these things and forget God?

M: Can one get darshan of God? Can one see God?

Ramakrishna: Yes, you certainly can see God. From time to time, sit in a secluded place. Sing the names and glories in worship of God. One must use all these means.

M: In what circumstances can one get the vision of God?

Ramakrishna: When you cry to God, cry with the deepest sincerity. People cry with such intensity for money, wealth, their children, or their families. How many of them cry for God? You have to call for God with a real sincerity.

Saying this, Ramakrishna began to sing:

> Call, oh my mind, with a real cry.
> If you do, can the Divine Mother, Kali,
> stay far away?
> How will She stay far away from a
> true devotee?
> How can She stay away from someone
> who calls with sincerity in their heart?
> If your mind is in a lonely place,
> exclusively devoted to Her,
> and in your heart you are placing
> hibiscus flowers and sandal paste at
> Mother's feet,
> Mother cannot be far from you.

Ramakrishna: When you call with sincerity, She must come and pay attention. When the morning dawns, first the light begins to radiate, and then you see the sun. Sincerity is the key to the vision of God.

M.'s Third Visit

Narendra, Bhavanath, and M. were present. Ramakrishna saw the 19-year-old boy, Narendra, and was filled with delight. He began to tell many stories. Narendra was studying in school. He regularly visited the Brahmo Samaj meetings where Keshab Sen spoke. Every one of his words was precise and exact. His eyes were filled with light, and he had the look of a devotee of God. The Master entered into a deep spiritual mood.

Master: Narendra, what do you say? We worldly people talk, often disparagingly, about spiritual devotees. Look, when an elephant walks, various other animals make so many noises at it, but the elephant doesn't even look back. If people speak ill of you, what do you think? Is it of any value?

Narendra: I will think that the dogs are barking. (Ramakrishna began to laugh.)

Master: No, my beloved, it's not quite like that. (Everyone began to laugh.) God is within every atom, and he mixes very well with good people. But when you're in the company of bad people, then you need to discriminate. In the tiger there is also God, but even knowing that God is within the animal, still you don't want to hug the tiger. (All began to laugh.)

If you know that God is within the tiger, then why would you run away? God is also within those who say, "Run away. Flee to a distance." Why won't you listen to their words?

Listen to a story. There was a sadhu who lived in the forest. He had many disciples. One day he gave instructions to his disciples, "God is within every object of creation. If you understand this, then you must bow down to everyone."

One day a disciple went into the forest to gather wood for the sacred fire. Suddenly there was a great noise and a rustling in the forest. There was a cry from the forest, "Everyone flee, flee! There's a mad elephant running loose." Everyone ran away. The disciple did not run. He remembered that God is also in the elephant. He asked himself, "Why should I flee?" Thinking thus, he stood still. He bowed and began to sing hymns to the elephant.

At this time the caretaker of the elephant was running and screaming, "Flee, flee! Get out of the way!" The disciple didn't move at all. Ultimately, the elephant grabbed him with his trunk, picked him up, and threw him to the side of the road. The disciple lay unconscious and seriously injured. Hearing the news of the injured disciple, the guru came with all the disciples to the location of the injured disciple and carried him back to the ashram. They began to treat his injuries with medicines.   After some time he regained consciousness. Then someone asked him, "When you heard that the elephant was coming, why didn't you run?" The disciple replied, "Our teacher gave us the instruction that God is within all manifestation, including all that lives. That's why, when I saw the elephant coming, I didn't want to run." Then the guru said, "True, the elephant was coming in the form of God, but the caretaker of the elephant was also in the form of God calling to you to move out of the way. If everyone is God, then why didn't you believe in the words of the man who told you to get out of the way? The caretaker was the form of God that asked you to move out of the path of the elephant." (Everyone began to laugh.)

God is in your every breath. Water is a form of God. Some water is appropriate to offer to God. Some water is appropriate for you to bathe in. Some is appropriate for you to wash your utensils and clothes, but the water that you use to wash your dishes and your clothing is not appropriate to drink. In the same way, God resides in every heart -- sadhus, devotees, and those who are unholy. With the unholy and unrighteous, you have to discriminate as to what kind of behavior is appropriate. You should keep to a distance from them. You may talk with some, but with others you should stay away entirely. In this way, you must discriminate as to how you will behave with different people.

Devotee: Is it appropriate to remain inactive when you see someone committing an evil act?

Master: When you are in the company of evil people, occasionally it is appropriate to show some tamas or darkness to protect yourself, but you don't have to return violence for their violence. Listen to a story.

Once there was a field where a cowherd raised his cows. In that field there was a very dangerous snake. Everyone who came there was terrified of the snake, and they all took great care to cross that field without disturbing the snake. One day a brahmachari was walking across the field. The cowherd boys ran to where the brahmachari was walking into the field and told him, "Don't enter this field. A very terrible snake lives here." The brahmachari said, "That's all right, don't worry about me. I have no fear of snakes. I know mantras to protect me." So saying, the brahmachari proceeded on his way. The boys were terrified, and none of them walked with him into the field.

Meanwhile, the snake began to hiss and foam and came slithering towards the brahmachari. As he was approaching the snake, the brahmachari began to recite a mantra, and the snake stopped and lay down at the feet of the brahmachari, who asked, "Why are you terrifying all of these people with your evil intent? I will give you a mantra. By repeating this mantra, you will become a devotee of God. You will attain God realization and eliminate your violent behavior." In this way, the brahmachari initiated the snake into spiritual life. When the snake received the mantra, he lay down at the feet of the guru and asked of him, "Respected Sir, in what way shall I perform sadhana?" The teacher replied, "Repeat the mantra and do not harm anyone." As the brahmachari was about to leave, he said to the snake, "I will come again." Several days passed. The cowherd boys saw that the snake wasn't coming to hurt them anymore. Then they became courageous and began to throw stones and sticks at him. The snake didn't respond or protect himself. One day, one of the cowherd boys came near the snake and grabbed it by the tail and threw it far away. Blood came out of his mouth, and he became unconscious. The snake didn't move at all, and the cowherd boys thought that it had died. Thinking thus, they all went home.

Late that night the snake revived. With difficulty he slowly moved toward his hole and went inside. He didn't have the energy to move his body. After many days of not eating, he shriveled up and became very thin. Then late one night he came outside looking for something to eat. He didn't come out in the daytime because he was very afraid. He continued to repeat the mantra and gave up doing harm to others. He lived on leaves or whatever fruit fell from the trees.

One year passed and the brahmachari returned. He walked into the field and began searching for the snake. The cowherd boys said, "That snake died a long time ago." The brahmachari didn't believe them. He knew that as long as the snake repeated the mantra, he could not leave his body until he had attained the fruit of the mantra. The brahmachari searched everywhere for the snake and even began to call him loudly by name. When the snake heard the sound of his teacher's voice calling, he crawled out from his hole. With great devotion he lay down at the feet of the guru. The brahmachari asked him, "How are you?" The snake said, "I'm fine." The teacher asked, "How did you get so thin?" The snake replied, "Revered Sir, you told me not to cause injury to anyone. That's why I've been eating leaves and fruit. That's how I lost so much weight." The snake was filled with truthfulness. He had no anger or malice towards anyone. He even forgot that the cowherd boys had beaten him and almost took his life.

The brahmachari replied, "Could you have gotten into this condition just from not eating? I'm sure there is some other reason." The snake began to remember and said, "One time the cowherd boys did cause me injury. Respected Sir, now I remember. One day those cowherd boys ferociously beat me. They are ignorant and didn't know that I had changed my behavior. How could they know that I wouldn't bite any body anymore? They didn't know that I had renounced violence." The teacher replied, "Are you that stupid? You couldn't even protect your own self? I told you not to bite anyone, but I didn't tell you not to hiss at them. If you would have hissed at them and instilled fear in them, they would have left you alone. You must hiss at evil people so that they don't try to injure you, but never injure them or inject your venom into anyone."

There are various forms of life in God's creation -- men, animals, and plants. Some animals live in the trees. Among the animals some are very gentle and some are dangerous. Animals, like tigers, can cause injury. Trees give nectar and fruit, yet there are other trees that give poison. Similarly, among human beings, there are the good and the evil-doers, the holy and the unholy. There are the worldly people and those who are devotees of God.

There are four classes of men: the bound, the spiritual seekers, the free, and the eternally-free. Narada is in the class of the eternally-free who live in the world for the welfare of others to teach mankind spiritual truths. The bound soul lives with attachment and forgets God. Not even by chance would a bound soul think of God. A mumukshun[6] desires liberation. Among this class, some may attain liberation, and others may not.

Liberated souls are not bound by desires and attachments. Their minds are free from attachments. They are always meditating on God.

In fishing, some fish are clever and never get caught. They are like the eternally liberated souls. But most of the fish get caught in the net. Some try to get out. They are like the seekers of liberation, the mumukshun. But not all of the fish can escape from the net. A few of them are able to free themselves. Then the fisherman says, "A big one got away!"

6 One who desires liberation.

Those who are caught in the net have no way to escape. They don't even try. Even though they are caught, they swim towards the bottom of the pond and hide in the mud thinking, "There's no fear here, we are safe." But the fisherman will pull them up in the net and drag them out. These are like the bound souls.

Ramakrishna: The people of the world are bound by attachments and the means of fulfilling their desires. Their hands and feet are bound, as it were. They believe that these desires, if fulfilled, will bring joy, pleasure, and comfort, and that by fulfilling all their desires, they will live without fear and anxiety. How seldom do they think that these things are transient, that all of this will pass away. When bound souls leave this earthly plane, their families say, "You left us. We have lost so much." Their worldly lives are bound by illusion.

When a bound soul is departing from this life, he says, "Oh, the lamp is too bright. Don't waste oil, make the wick shorter." Thus, ever thinking of the world, death comes to him. Bound souls do not think about God. They live in maya. Even as life draws to a close, they continue to gossip about worldly matters. They say, "I can't remain still, that's why I'm making a fence." When time hangs heavily on their hands, they begin to play cards.

Swamiji: Next comes a discussion of the means of attaining faith.

As the Master was speaking, one devotee thought to himself, "Then we who are in the world have no means to escape from the world."

Master: Certainly there is a means to escape from this world. When you have the opportunity, seek out holy men, and from time to time sit in a quiet place and contemplate

God. You must always discriminate between God, Who is Real and Eternal, and this world, which is a passing dream. You must pray to God, "Give me faith and devotion." Once you have faith, you have all. There is nothing greater than faith.

Master (to Kedar): It is written in the Puranas that Rama, who was actually the incarnation of Narayana Vishnu, in order to get to Lanka, had to construct an immense bridge. But Hanuman, who was a true devotee always singing the name of Rama, by his faith in Rama alone, just sang the holy name and jumped across the ocean in one leap. He had no need for a bridge. (Everyone began to laugh.)

Vibishana was the brother of Ravana and a great devotee of Rama. One time he wrote the name of Rama on a leaf, and he took that leaf with Rama's name written on it and tied it in the corner of the cloth of one of his friends. He said, "With this you will be able to fly across the ocean." He told his friend, "Be fearless, have faith, and cross the ocean. But watch out, don't fall into doubt. If you begin to doubt and your faith wavers, you will sink under the waves." The man took his leave and at once began to fly across the ocean. But as he was flying, he began to think, "What did Vibishana put in my cloth that I am able to fly so easily across the ocean?" He had a great desire to know what was there, so he carefully untied the knot and found only a leaf with the name of Rama written on it. He thought, "What is this? It's only the name of Rama," and immediately he sank into the ocean and drowned.

He who has faith in God, even if he were a great sinner, even a murderer, if he calls out to God with full faith, even the greatest of his sins will be destroyed. If he were to say, "I will never perform such behavior in the future," he will be free from all fear. (Ramakrishna began to sing.)

If I die repeating the name
Durga, Durga, Durga,
all my days of ignorance will be destroyed.
I have now come to know
You Who are the Divine Light of Goodness.
You destroy even such great sins
as slaying a brahmin or drinking wine.
All these sins will be destroyed,
and I will come to the feet of God,
if only I can pass away repeating,
Durga, Durga, Durga.

> Swamiji: Now the story is about Narendra and
> the bird.

Master (pointing to Narendra): Do you all see this young man here? He acts this way here. When a young boy sits near his father, the father hugs him with great delight. But when the boy looks at the moon, he's a different person. Individuals such as Narendra are eternally perfect. They are never bound by the world. When they grow to maturity, their spiritual consciousness awakens, and they immediately go toward God. They come into this world of objects and relationships only to teach and to be examples to other people. They are not attached to anything in this world. They never deplete their energy by indulging in worldly attachments and desires.

In the Vedas, there is the story of the homa bird. The mother bird lives high up in the sky. There she lays her egg and the egg begins to fall. It is at such a height that it takes many days to reach the earth. While the egg is still falling, it cracks open and the little bird continues to fall. As it falls toward the ground, its feathers begin to grow and its eyes open. Then it is able to see that it is falling and that if it reaches the ground, it will die. At once the young bird flaps its wings and flies upwards toward its mother. Together they rise up into the sky.

Swamiji: Ramakrishna is speaking about Narendra.

In Sri Ramakrishna's room there was sat sangha. Kedar, M., and many others were present.

Master: Look, Narendra is very good at singing, playing musical instruments, school, work, and he gets good grades. That day when he was arguing philosophy with Kedar, each time Kedar would speak, Narendra would reply in such a way that Kedar's every argument was cut in two. (Everyone laughed.)

Master (to M.): Are there any books on debate in English?

M.: Yes, in English there is a book on logic.

Ramakrishna: Oh, that's very good. What is it like? Explain it to me.

M. (embarrassed): It's a way of reasoning from the simple to the more complex. "All men die. Pundits are also men, therefore pundits will die." It's sort of like that. Reasoning in this way will give the truth in most cases.

Here is another form of reasoning. "This crow is black. That crow is black. All the crows that I see are black. Therefore all crows are black." But if you reason in this way, you can make a mistake. What happens if you search very thoroughly or come to another country and find a white crow? Here's another example. "Whenever there is rain, there is a cloud." Reasoning in this way, you would conclude that where there is rain, it comes from a cloud. And here is yet another example. "This person has thirty-two teeth. That person has thirty-two. All the people that I have seen have thirty-two teeth. Therefore, every human being has thirty-two teeth." In this way, there are many books of logic written in English.

Ramakrishna listened silently. As he listened to these words, he went into a spiritual mood and seemed to lose all interest in the subject.

When the congregation left, the remaining devotees began to discuss among themselves. M. walked to the Panchavati, the grove of five sacred trees. It was about five in the afternoon. He returned and went to Sri Ramakrishna's room where he saw on the north veranda of his room a marvelous sight. The Master was standing completely still. Narendra was singing. There were two, three, or four other devotees. M. came near and listened to the song. He became mesmerized by the beauty of the song. Other than Sri Ramakrishna's singing, M. had never heard such a sweet voice.

Panchavati

Suddenly he looked at Sri Ramakrishna and was startled by what he saw. Sri Ramakrishna was standing completely still. His eyelids didn't move. There was no evidence of his breathing. One devotee said, "This is called Samadhi."

M. had never seen this before nor had he ever heard of it. He was completely surprised and taken aback and thought, "By thinking about God, is it possible for one to become so motionless and free from thought? How much faith and devotion must be required to attain such a state!"

Chapter 2

October 1882

Sri Ramakrishna is in the Kali temple. It is Friday the twenty-eighth of October, and tonight is the Lakshmi Puja, which falls on Ashwin Purnima, the full moon night in the month of Ashwin.

Sri Ramakrishna is sitting on the eastern side in a room at the Kali temple talking with Vijay and Haralal. A Brahmo disciple of Keshab Sen approaches the Master and makes pranams. He says, "Great Sir (Mahashay), will you please come and meet Keshab? Keshab is waiting to greet you. He sent us to bring you to the boat." It was about three o'clock in the afternoon. Sri Ramakrishna went to the dock on the Ganga and climbed aboard the boat with Vijay. No sooner did he sit down than he went into samadhi. M. was also seated in the boat nearby. He looked at Ramakrishna in samadhi, and he was astounded by the scene.

At four o'clock in the afternoon the boat arrived in Calcutta. M. had a great desire to witness this meeting between Keshab and Sri Ramakrishna. He wanted to hear their blissful conversation. He wanted to hear the subject of their discussion.

Keshab regularly gave profound lectures which captivated and inspired the minds of all who heard them. Many of the young people who came and listened to Keshab would give their hearts and souls to him. Keshab was an ardent student of English. He was also familiar with the English versions of philosophy and logic, and he had no faith in the worship of Hindu gods and goddesses. M. thought, "Is it possible that these Brahmo devotees, who have no faith in gods and goddesses, have faith in Sri Ramakrishna? Is it really true that they would actually come and bow down to him? This is something unthinkable! How could this occur? How could such an attitude of devotion arise within them?" M. greatly desired to discover the secret of how these people became so enamored of Ramakrishna.

Ramakrishna moves into the realization of nirvikalpa, and then he moves out into the worship of that which has form. He thinks of the Infinite Beyond Conception, and then again he sits in front of all the images of the gods and goddesses. He puts sandal paste on the flowers and offers the flowers to the deities. He is always singing. He sits upon his wooden cot. He wears a red-bordered dhoti and a shirt, socks and shoes, as well. He wears the clothes of a gentleman, but he is not a worldly person. His inner mood and attitude is that of a sannyasin. That is why people call him a *paramahamsa*, a great soul. Keshab Sen, on the other hand, is a worshiper of the formless aspect of God. He is married with children and deeply involved in the affairs of the world. He gives lectures in English, edits a newspaper, and is always in his mind.

The Brahmo devotees in the boat arrived at the dock in front of the Dakshineswar temple. When they ascended the steps from the landing on the Ganga, they saw the twelve Shiva temples. These are the temples containing the twelve Jyotir Lingams.

It was a beautiful autumn day with a blue sky. They all went to the Bhavatarini Mandir of Mother Kali, the central temple of the Dakshineswar compound. To the north was the Panchavati, the garden of five sacred trees where Sri Ramakrishna had done so much of his sadhana. To the south side of the Kali temple was the Nahabat Mandir, the music chamber. Between the Nahabat and the Kali temple was the Udhyan garden where many flowers were growing for offering in the temples. The many flowering bushes were covered with blooms. The outer scene was altogether lovely, and the hearts of the devotees were filled with bliss. Experiencing the beauty and divine presence of the temple compound, these Brahmo devotees, devoted to the exclusive worship of the formless God, felt overcome with devotion.

Above was the clear blue sky and to the rear was the sacred river Ganga. Anyone who sits quietly on the bank of the Ganga will easily enter into meditation. And here in the midst of all this beauty was the Great Soul Sri Ramakrishna Paramahamsa, the manifestation of spiritual perfection. It is not written in the fate of many human beings to behold as beautiful a scene as seeing Ramakrishna sitting in Samadhi, but the heart of anyone fortunate enough to do so would be filled to the brim with peace, devotion, and longing for God.

Swamiji: The soul is never destroyed.

The boat was arriving, and everyone was eager to see Ramakrishna. Keshab was trying to whisk Ramakrishna safely away from the crowd. Ramakrishna was in samadhi. With great difficulty Keshab took the Master to his room on the boat. Ramakrishna was filled with bhava. He was leaning on the shoulder of one devotee. His feet could hardly move. He entered the room very carefully. Keshab and his devotees all bowed down to Ramakrishna. He had no sense of anything. In the room there was a table and a few chairs. They seated Ramakrishna on a chair. Keshab also sat on one, and Vijay sat on another. Some devotees took their seats on the floor. Many other people did not have places to sit, but stood at the door straining their necks to get a peek inside.

Ramakrishna was still immersed in samadhi. He was totally oblivious to the outside world. Everyone was looking at him with one-pointed attention. In the middle of the room, Keshab saw Vijay, who began speaking to various members of the Brahmo Samaj. When Keshab saw all this activity going on and Ramakrishna sitting there in samadhi, he felt very uneasy. He was sitting with one-pointed focus on Ramakrishna, whose samadhi was very deep. His bhava was intense.

Master (in a very unclear way): Why did you bring me here? Can I be bound within the fence of all this activity?

Ramakrishna saw that worldly people are bound within a fence. They can't break out of that fence. They can't conceive a life outside. Their hands and feet are bound. They can only see the things that are inside the fence. They think that the objective of life is to be comfortable, and they think about their attachments and desires. That's why Ramakrishna was saying "Mother, why did you bring me here?" Thinking and talking in this way, he gradually became more aware of his surroundings.

In Ghazipur, there is a holy man named Pavhari Baba. One Brahmo devotee said to the Master, "Oh, Great Sir (Mahashay), Pavhari Baba has your photograph in his house."

Ramakrishna (pointing to his own body): He put only the image of this outer form in his house. This body is nothing but a pillow case.

Third Discussion

Swamiji: The yoga of wisdom, yoga of devotion, and yoga of action.

There's a pillow and a pillowcase. There's the wearer of the body and the body itself.

Ramakrishna: The body is transient. It is not indestructible. The wearer of the body is indestructible. So what gain will Pavhari Baba have by putting a photograph of this body in his house? This body is a transient thing. If you love the body, what will happen? What gain will you get? He who knows the God who is within, knows that the same God resides in the hearts of all living beings. Such beings are worthy of your worship.

Ramakrishna (in a very relaxed way): There is another side to the story. The heart of the devotee is filled with love for God. God is present in all existence. You can know that presence tangibly in the heart of a devotee. It's just like a rich landlord whose authority extends throughout all his land, but he stays in one particular house which is his personal estate. People will speak like this, "That the heart of a devotee is the special residence of the Lord." (Everyone felt great delight.)

Ramakrishna: There is only one God, but He has many names. Some call a knower of God a wise man. Some call him a yogi, and some call him a devotee. One who knows Brahma as the Infinite Beyond Conception, we call a jnani, a wise being. A yogi who achieves union merges with the inner self. Devotees contain God within their hearts. There is one Supreme Divinity, and many ways to know Him.

When you worship, you are called a pujari. When you cook food, you are called a cook. A jnani follows the yoga of wisdom. He continually discriminates that "It is not this and not that." Brahma is not this life force. Brahma is not this world. Thinking in this way, gradually all becomes still, and then it dissolves. He then merges in samadhi and attains oneness with the Supreme.

The contemplation of a Brahma jnani, a knower of the Supreme, is that the Supreme is Truth and all of manifested existence is transient. All names and forms are like a dream.

What is Brahma? You cannot speak about it. You can't say that Brahma is any one thing. The jnanis, like the Vedantins, become dissolved in the object of their devotion, but devotees of God believe that even this relative world is true. They don't think that this manifested existence is a dream. They never say it is. The devotees will say that this entire universe is the perceivable form of God. The heavens, stars, moon, sun, mountains, ocean, animals, and all the manifestations of God have been created by Him. This is His eternal form. He resides in the hearts of everyone, and yet He is outside as well.

The greatest devotee says, "He, Himself, has created these 24 cosmic principles and through these 24 principles --

Swamiji: This is Sankhya philosophy.

-- He has made the individual souls manifest." Devotees take great joy in eating sugar; they don't wish to become sugar. (They all began to laugh.)

Ramakrishna: Do you know what the devotion of a devotee of God is like? He says "Hey, Bhagavan, you are the Lord and I am your servant. You are the mother and I am your child. You are both my mother and my father. You are the whole and perfect and I am a part." Devotees don't like to say "I am God." They like to experience the Divine Presence and have the vision of the Supreme Soul. Their main objective is the union of the individual soul with the Supreme Soul.

The yogis try to remove their minds from the objects of perception. They try to make their minds still in the contemplation of the Supreme Soul. That's why in the beginning you must sit still in one asana in a quiet place in solitude, and look deeply inside. It's all one God, only the name changes or is different. That which is Brahma, the

Supreme, is also Atman, the Soul, and that also is the
Supreme Lord. To the jnani, the follower of wisdom, it is
called the Supreme Divinity. To the yogis, it is called the
Supreme Soul. To the devotees, it is called the Image of
Divinity.

Fourth Discussion

Swamiji: Ramakrishna discusses the Vedas
and Tantras, how they relate, and the relationship
between the primary energy of the universe and
the Infinite Beyond Conception.

It was a very warm day in Dakshineswar. All those
assembled in Ramakrishna's room came to hear his talks
filled with the nectar of delight and to get his darshan, a
vision of him. Everyone listening to Ramakrishna's wisdom
was mesmerized. When a bee sits on a flower and begins to
extract the nectar, does it have any desire to roam the forest?
In this way, all the devotees were filled with this kind of love
for Ramakrishna. They were listening to him so intently that
there was pin-drop silence in the room. Everyone hung on
his every word. What a beautiful picture of the residence of
the Gods! The waves of the Ganga were so loud that they
were the only audible sound in the room other than
Ramakrishna's voice. Everyone was filled with love and
sweetness. Ramakrishna wore a thousand faces and seemed
to be the very embodiment of bliss. His eyes were filled with
love. He was a yogi whose darshan was incomparable.
Everyone was looking at him totally transfixed. He was the
lover of all and yet a total renunciant, dispassionate of every
object. Other than God, he knew nothing. In this scene
Ramakrishna's words began to flow.

Ramakrishna: Those who have the wisdom of Brahma
and speak the words of Vedanta state that creation,
preservation, and transformation are the embodiment of all

life. They say that this is all a play of energy, and if you use your reasoning power, you can see that everything is illusory like a dream. Brahma, the Supreme Divinity, is the true existence, and everything else is transient. Shakti, the energy, is also dream-like because it is always moving, changing. It is not still. However, you can reason about it a thousand times, but until you are established in the highest samadhi, you are still living within Shakti's realm, and you have no capacity to move beyond it at all. As long as you haven't attained samadhi, you don't have the Divine Experience. When you move into samadhi, your energy becomes completely potential. It is no longer kinetic. "I am meditating upon this. I am thinking of this." All energy becomes totally potential energy. It merges completely with the eternal. It is no longer transient.

That is why the Supreme Divinity and its energy are inseparable. If you believe in one, you must believe in the other. Just like fire and its capacity to burn. If you believe in fire, it is inconceivable not to believe in its capacity to burn. If you omit fire, how can you have the capacity to burn? If you eliminate the sun, how can you accept the rays? It's inconceivable.

The color of the milk is white. You can't separate the color from it. When you think of the whiteness of milk, you automatically think of the milk. Without energy it is impossible to contemplate the existence of Supreme Consciousness. Without the play of existence, it is impossible to conceive of the eternal. The primary energy is the embodiment of the play of existence. "It" is what is creating, preserving, and transforming. Kali is the Supreme Divinity and the Supreme Divinity is Kali. They are one and the same. When "It" is without action, there is no creation, preservation, or transformation. When you look closely at this principle, "That" is what is known as Brahman, the Supreme Divinity beyond activity.

When that Supreme Divinity performs actions, then we call it Kali, energy. It is one Divinity with many forms. Water, for example, we call "jal," "pani," or "water." There are four sets of stairs leading down to a pond. At one set of stairs, the Hindus drink water and they call it "jal." At another set of stairs, the Muslims take the same water and they call it "pani." At still another set of stairs, the English-speaking people drink and they call it "water." It is all one, only the names are different. Some call "It" Allah, some God, and some Brahma, Kali, Rama, Hari, Jesus, Durga, etc.

Keshab (beginning to laugh): In what ways does Kali like to play with us? Won't you please explain all this to us at least once?

Ramakrishna (listening to Keshab's words also laughed): That Supreme Existence has Her drama and play in many different ways. She is Mahakali. She is Eternal Kali. She is Kali who remains in the cremation grounds. She is the Kali who is one with the Supreme Divinity. She is the Kali who is the protector of all. She is the Dark One. Mahakali and the Eternal Kali emanate from the Tantras. Before the creation evolved, the moon, the sun, the stars, and the planets did not exist. There was only complete darkness. Then Maa was in the form of the formless beyond form as Mahakali. Mahakali united with Mahakala, the Great Time or He who is Beyond Time. Dark Kali has a very sympathetic demeanor. She gives the boon of freedom from fear. In the home of house-holders, She is the one who is mostly worshiped. Whenever there is a great calamity, when there are great obstacles to overcome (an earthquake, dearth of rain or drought, big flood, etc.), we have to worship Her as the form of Kali Who Protects. The Kali who remains in the cremation grounds is the Kali Who Takes Away, She Who Dissolves All Creation. She is the one who remains with the corpses while they make their final transformation. And She stays with them until they merge with God.

On her neck She wears a garland of skulls. She wears an apron around Her waist made with the severed limbs of all the asuras She has cut down.

Ramakrishna (continuing to describe the various forms of Kali): At the cessation of the universe when there is total dissolution, She sows the seeds of the next creation. There is an old custom in many households. Whenever they offer something that is being cooked for food or offered for food, they take a piece of it and put it in a container and save it for the future. For example, if you're cooking a big pot of rice, you take a handful of rice before cooking it and stick it in a container. (Keshab and the others began to laugh.)

Ramakrishna: Beloved children, householders have this nature, always saving something for the future. Mahakali shows this same nature when she dissolves the perceivable universe. At that time She takes some of the seeds and puts them in a pot to save them for the next creation. Inside the pot is some of the foam from the ocean.

She takes some cucumber seeds and some pumpkin seeds and some laukey seeds and she puts them all in her pot. Whenever there's a need, She can take them out and sow them for the next creation. This is like what householders do. Mother is the embodiment of the universe, and after the dissolution of the entire universe, She takes all these seeds and protects them. After the new creation has begun, this Primary Energy resides within the creation. She gives birth to the entire creation, and then She resides within it. She is in various forms and distinctions. She is the container as well as the contained.

Swamiji: Now we are going to discuss the various distinctions within the creation. Just as a spider takes its web from inside itself and spins it outside and then resides within the web, God

takes the whole of creation out of Herself. So
Ramakrishna is now comparing how the Mother
brings the creation out of Her own being and then
sows the seeds for the next creation to how the
spider spins the web out of itself and then resides
within the web itself.

She gives birth to the creation and resides within it and
above it. Kali is the Supreme Divinity. Kali is with and without qualities. What? You think Kali is black? Yes, from a
distance She appears so, but when you really know who She
is, then She no longer appears to be black. From afar the sky
appears to be blue, but close up you see it really has no color
at all. When you look at the ocean from afar, it appears to be
blue, but when you scoop up a handful, you see it has no
color whatsoever.

Speaking in this way, he was united in love and began to
sing, "Is my Mother Kali really black? The darkness really
means that She's clothed in space. In the lotus of your heart,
look and see the light."

Fifth Discussion

Ramakrishna (looking at Keshab): Why do we have this
world of objects and relationships? What is the difference
between being bound and being liberated? Both of them are
conceived by Her. All this maya, all this illusion, binds us to
this world of objects and relationships by our desires and
attachments. By means of Her compassion, we become
liberated. She is the one who binds all to worldliness, and
She is the one who liberates.

Ramakrishna (speaking in this way, began to sing): The
Dark Mother is rising like a kite in the bazaar of worldliness.
With the winds of our hopes, the kite flies higher, but it's
bound by the string of Maya. The crows and the birds up in

the air, our five senses, are binding this kite that wants to fly, and then we come back to the perception of that with form. As you pull on the string of the kite and bounce it up and down, it rises higher and higher. If you don't keep pulling it back in, the kite won't rise any higher. Every now and then, when you're flying the kite, one or two strings will break. Then Mother laughs and claps her hands with joy! Ramprasad is saying, "That kite will fly off with the southern winds, never to return." In this ocean of worldliness, if you stay on the shores of the ocean, you go there and stay there very quickly. She is the author of all the dramas. This whole world of objects and relationships is Her play. She is the embodiment of all desires and bliss. If there are 100,000 people, maybe one or two will strive for liberation.

Keshab: Oh, Great Sir (Mahashay), if She desired, couldn't She give everyone liberation? Why does She bind us to this world?"

Ramakrishna: It's all Her desire. She is playing according to Her desires. When you get old, you won't be able to run very fast. If She touches everyone in the same way, how will the drama continue? When you play tag and one of the players is an old man, he can't run after all the youngsters. If he were able to grab all the youngsters, then the game would be over in a hurry. In the same way, if She liberated everyone, then the game would be over. While the old man is playing with the kids, he's really very happy because the game continues. If he tagged everyone and they were out, then the game would be over. And that is why, out of a lakh, out of 100,000, She allows one or two to be liberated. Then She claps Her hands and laughs. (Everyone else began to laugh.)

Maa says to us, "Ok, kids, go out and play in this world." What is the fault of the mind? If She is compassionate to us,

then She'll bring our minds back to Her. Then we find
liberation from all these worldly thoughts, and we keep our
minds at the Lotus Feet of the Divine.

Ramakrishna (with great affection began to sing to Maa):

> If You are the Mother,
> why are You stealing from my house?
> I am singing Your name and
> describing Your good qualities.
> I know and understand completely well.
> This is all Your cleverness.
> You gave to me and I didn't get it.
> You took away from me and I didn't play.
> It's not my fault.
> You give, You take, You feed, and You eat.
> This is all Your action.
> And this fame and welfare
> and lack of fame and lack of welfare,
> this delightful nectar and foul taste,
> these are all Yours.
> Oh, Beloved, You're throwing us in the nectar
> and You're making us dance.
> You give us the bhava and
> You take away the bhava.
> Why are You doing this?
> This isn't our fault, it's Yours!
> You gave us our minds and
> then You make them wander.
> Oh, Mother, You've given us the creation
> and you've given us this perception.
> All the sweet has been burned.
> We've forgotten Her maya
> and in this way we become worldly.
> Ramprasad says, "You've given us this mind.
> Where else are you taking it?"

And this is the song that Ramakrishna sang. Om.

Karma Yoga and the Teaching of All

Swamiji: Let us now talk about samsara, working within the world and within relationships without personal or selfish desire.

A devotee from the Brahma Samaj: Oh, Great Sir (Mahashay), is it impossible to realize God if you haven't renounced everything?

Ramakrishna (began to laugh): No, it's not. Why do you have to leave everything? You're floating in this ocean of worldliness, with all its sweetness and stickiness, with all your minds. (Everyone began to laugh.)

You are very worldly. Do you know how to play a game with a map on a board? I have already scored high enough to be out of the competition, but you guys are very naughty. Some of you are scoring tens and some sixes and some fives. Many of you have not moved very far at all. Your bonds of worldliness haven't dissolved as mine have. Your play or drama is continuing a lot. (They all began to laugh.)

I'm telling you the truth. It's no fault of yours to be worldly, but you should keep your mind focused on God. If you don't do that, you won't be able to achieve your spiritual goals. Do your work with one hand and with the other hand grab onto God. When the karma is complete, then you'll be able to hold onto God with both hands. The mind is both the source of your liberation as well as the source of your bondage. Whatever color you dip your mind in, that's the color your mind will reflect. Just like in a washerman's house you find white cloth. If you dye the cloth red, it will become red. If you dye the cloth blue, it will become blue. If you dye it green, it will become green. Whatever color dye you choose, that's the color the cloth will reflect. When you study English, it will be natural to use English expressions in your speech like 'foot and fut, and meet and mat'.

> Swamiji: Ramakrishna began to mimic the 'sounds' of English. And then they all began to laugh at the funny way that English sounds.

If you wear fancy shoes on your feet, then you will sing or whistle like an Englishman. In whatever way you apply your mind, that way the mind will reflect. If a pundit studies Sanskrit, then from his mouth the shlokas will pour out very quickly. If you keep your mind with bad influences, you'll begin to think about bad influences. That is the way you'll begin to think; that is the way you'll begin to speak. If you keep your mind with devotees, then your mind will think about God. You'll speak about God. This is the natural way. Mind is all. There is a family nearby with children. Everyone will love their children in a different way, but the mind is one.

After you have attained the perfection of discrimination and renunciation, only then should you enter the world. In the ocean of worldliness, there are a bunch of crocodiles with names like "desires," "attachments," and "anger." If you rub turmeric on your body and submerge yourself in the waters, you have no fear of crocodiles. If you rub the turmeric of discrimination and renunciation over your body, you can submerge yourself in the ocean of worldliness without any fear at all. God is Truth. That is the eternal phenomenon. Everything else is transient. It is impermanent. It's only here for two days or so. This knowledge is the love of God. If you are attracted by Godliness, that is called love. The gopis had so much attraction for Krishna. Listen to a song.

> Radha says, "Krishna is playing His flute.
> It just can't be that I don't go.
> He's standing in the path.

Hey, are you guys going to go or not?
You talk about Krishna just from your mouths.
The Krishna that resides within me
creates so much pain in my heart
that I remember Him all the time.
He's playing the flute only in your ears,
but I'm listening to that flute in my heart."

She says to all the gopis, to all her friends,
"You're listening to Krishna's flute only with your ears!

He's playing the flute inside my heart.
You girls make a fence around Krishna
and His radiance will grow and grow."

Ramakrishna started to shed tears as he was singing this song.

Ramakrishna (to Keshab): Whether you accept Radha and Krishna or not, whether you believe in Them, let Their pure love and attraction for each other settle in your heart. You must express sincerity in your love for God. If you have sincerity, then you can get Godliness.

Seventh Discussion

Ramakrishna was going by boat along with Keshab Sen. The waves were slapping against the boat as they were crossing the Ganga. The captain of the boat was ordered to steer past the factory on the north side of the Dakshineshwar temple. All the devotees in the boat had no idea how far the boat had traveled. They had all been mesmerized by the words of Ramakrishna. They had no conception of how fast time had been passing. Then they were served muri, a snack made of puffed rice and shredded coconut. Ramakrishna loved this puffed rice. Keshab brought out a large bowl of the puffed rice and distributed it to the devotees. Everyone was munching on it, and all were really filled with bliss. Ramakrishna looked over and noticed that Keshab and Vijay were keeping somewhat apart from each other and not participating in the feast. Then Ramakrishna got the idea of how to establish friendship between them, since he is the "Distributor of the Welfare of all Existence."

Vijay Krishna Goswami

Ramakrishna (to Keshab): Hey there, beloved child, Vijay has come. Do you have an argument between the two of you? It's rather like the fight between Shiva and Rama. Rama's guru is still Shiva even if there is a fight. They fight and then they come back into the bonds of friendship. Shiva is accompanied by ghosts and goblins, and Rama is accompanied by a band of monkeys. The monkeys and the ghosts and goblins never get along and come together! (Everyone began to laugh.) You have your people and beliefs, and Vijay has his, and that's why all life continues in this way. Did you know Lav and Kush, the sons of Rama, fought with Rama?

The mother and the daughter both observed the Tuesday fast as if the welfare of the daughter is different from the welfare of the mother. But the welfare of the daughter is actually the welfare of the mother, and the welfare of the mother is actually the welfare of the daughter. In the same way, you each have your own separate societies, and in this way, you appear to be different.

If you say that God Herself is performing Her own drama, where is the necessity for distinction and separation in the drama? (They all began to laugh.) If you don't have any distinctions and there is no separation, then there is no room for conflict or altercation. It is impossible to understand the lila. Ramanuj was a great propounder of the system of duality. His guru was a great propounder of non-duality. Ultimately they went their own separate ways. The guru and the disciple had different ideas. The forms of belief come and go, but they are all still your people!

Eighth Discussion

> Keshab is about to receive a teaching -- the guru is sat-chit-ananda. Everyone is having a wonderful time.

Ramakrishna (to Keshab): You are giving initiation and accepting just about anyone as a disciple. That is why your association or congregation is splintering off into so many directions. If you look at all of humanity, they look like they are all the same, but each one has a different nature.

In some sattva guna is predominant. Some have mostly raja guna, and some have mostly tama guna. These are all qualities of nature. Each of us has a predominance or preponderance of one quality over the others. Do you know what characteristics you have? "I eat" and "I digest" and "I remember." The rest Mother knows. Those three things, sattva, raja, and tama (the energy of purity and clarity, the energy of activity, and the energy of desire), all make my body shake. The guru is the performer and the guru is the performance. And the guru is truth-consciousness-bliss. He is the teacher, and I am a child of God.

There are hundreds of thousands of "gurus." Everyone wants to be a guru, but how many want to be disciples? It's very hard to teach people. If He is perceivable, if He is actual, if He is the reality and He has given you the authority to teach, only then will you be an effective teacher. Narada and Shukdeva were instructed to teach. Shankaracharya was authorized to teach. If you're not authorized to teach, who's going to listen to what you have to say?

The world is full of miscellaneous and sundry gurus. When the wood is burning, then the milk on top of the stove will start to boil. When you take the wood out of the stove, then the milk doesn't boil anymore. If someone doesn't attract you, then you won't go anywhere. In this way, the people of Calcutta are pursuing miscellaneous and sundry gurus.

Each individual is digging many wells saying that they are looking for water. As soon as they hit a stone, then they leave that hole and start digging in another place. There they find some sand, and so they abandon that hole. They start digging somewhere else, and on it goes. If you conceive these instructions in your own mind, this is not sufficient. God is the Truth of the Truth and the actual Reality. He also speaks, and then you get instruction, authorization. You don't know the power of Her words. They can raise mountains! How long will people listen to lectures and then forget about it all? In that way, you can't perform efficient work.

> Swamiji: Ramakrishna is remembering his olden days at the Haldarpukur, the pond behind his native village Kamapukur.

Ramakrishna: Every morning near the pond all the villagers go to empty their bowels. All the people that go there scream at the others not to make a mess in the path, and the next day it's the same thing. They can't stop their bowels. (Everyone began to laugh.)

Then the villagers complained to the owners of the pond. They put a caretaker at the edge of the pond. The caretaker posted a sign that said "Commit no nuisance." The caretaker's job is to give the proper instruction, and if the proper instruction is not given, people will do as they please.

All the blind people gather together and walk down the path, the blind leading the blind. When you reach to Godliness, you can go inside. You understand who has what illness, and you can give instruction appropriately. If you don't have the proper authority and you're giving instruction, then it's only ego and ignorance. It's only the understanding of ignorance. It's the feeling that "I am the doer." God is the doer. God has performed all. I do nothing. This understanding is called liberation. The misunderstanding that "I am the doer" provides you with nothing but pain and a lack of peace.

Ninth Discussion

Ramakrishna is discussing the subject of karma yoga with Keshab and the others.

Ramakrishna (to Keshab's devotees): You tell me, who has the capacity to offer a benefit to the world? Is this world so small that you can benefit it? Who are you who can actually do some benefit to the world? In order to really benefit the world, one must realize God through sadhana. Then you can gain Godliness. If She gives you the energy, then you can perform welfare for others. In the absence of divine inspiration it's impossible."

One devotee: As long as we have not as yet attained Godliness, should we refrain from all action?

Ramakrishna: No. Why will you renounce all action? Remember God, think about God, contemplate, and meditate upon God. This you will continue to do.

Devotee: You mean we can do the work of the world and also contemplate God?

Ramakrishna: Yes, you will do them both. You have to perform the work of the world, but from time to time go into solitude and pray that you can perform those activities without personal desire. Then you will say, "Hey, God, reduce my worldly desires because when I see that there is so much work in front of me, I forget you. I think that I am acting selflessly, but I actually have lots of desires." So much as you become a philanthropist, that much outward respect you receive, and from this you cannot remain without desire. If you are pursuing name, gain, and fame, you cannot be free from desire.

Listen to a story about Shambu Mallik and donating and performing works. Shambu Mallik was talking about building a school, a hospital, a road, and a well to benefit the poor people. I said to him, "To do as much as is necessary, is your responsibility. That part you can do without desire. If you have desire, and you get involved in many activities, then you may forget God. There used to be a man who used to give alms to everyone at Kalighat. He was so busy outside the Temple, that he didn't get to go inside to get the Darshan of Kali." (They all began to laugh.)

You have to go to Kalighat to understand. First you have to elbow your way to the front of the line, so you can have darshan. Then after you've had darshan, you can give as much as you want. If you desire, give a lot.

Perform the activities to gain Godliness. That's why I said to Shambu, "If God is actually your reality, when God comes to you, will you ask Him to create hospitals and schools?" (They all began to laugh.)

Shambu Mallik

That's not what is called a devotee. The devotee will say, "Oh, God, please give me a place at Your Lotus Feet. Keep me with You always. Please give me true devotion to Your Lotus Feet. This world of activity is very difficult. All the injunctions in the scriptures that call me to perform actions in the world, they are all very difficult to perform. In this Age of Darkness, it is very difficult to maintain freedom from desires and attachments. All this activity, all this worldliness, does not bring me to You."

The doctor, when she goes to treat her patients, also becomes infected with disease. She can't stay with the patient for too long, or she'll come down with the same disease. When you have a great fever, you can't just take herbs and such. You need real medicine. In this Age of

Darkness, we have to unite with devotion. We have to continuously recite the names of God and the qualities of God in order to have devotion to God. Devotion is the highest ideal of perfection in this age of time. Devotion is the real medicine.

Ramakrishna (looked at all the devotees): You all are united in devotion. You all have been blessed because you sing the names of Hari and the qualities of Divine Mother. Your attitude is complete, not like those Vedantins that say this world is a dream. That is a lie. You're not like that. You're not Brahma jnanis. You are devotees. You think that God is a real phenomenon. You are devotees. Call with sincerity and without doubt, and you will surely find Him!

Tenth Discussion

It was Kojagiri Purnima, Lakshmi Purnima, in October. Ramakrishna went to Surendra's house with Narendra. The boat came back. Everyone lined up to disembark. They brought a carriage to carry Ramakrishna to the front of the house. After a while Master and two or three devotees climbed into the carriage. His nephew, Nanda Lal, got into the carriage as well, thinking that he would go with Ramakrishna for a short distance. They all sat down and asked, "Who is he? And where is Keshab?" And then they saw that Keshab was coming up by himself and had a very happy face. He asked Ramakrishna, "Who will go with you?" After all were in the carriage, Keshab bowed down in pranam to Ramakrishna. With great love and affection Ramakrishna took his leave, and the carriage began to move down a beautiful kingly avenue called English thola. (This is in Britishtown, a suburb of Calcutta.) There was an artistic beauty on both sides of the road with the full moon high in the sky. It appeared that all the houses were taking rest in its peaceful glow. From house to house there were lights burning. In various houses the sound of pianos and harmoniums could be heard, and ladies' voices singing in English could be heard as well.

Ramakrishna was laughing with delight.

Ramakrishna (suddenly): I'm thirsty. I would like to drink some water. What will happen? Who will provide it for me?

Nanda Lal stopped the carriage in front of the Indian club and went in to get some water. In a glass he got some water for Ramakrishna.

Ramakrishna (smiling): It's a clean glass, right?

Nanda: Yes.

Ramakrishna drank from the glass, and he was very pleased. As the carriage proceeded down the avenue, Ramakrishna was hanging out the window looking at all the people. Ramakrishna was greatly enjoying looking at everything. Nanda Lal stopped at Kolu thola. Then they turned onto Shimulia Street to go to Suresh's house.

Ramakrishna called Suresh as Surendra, the king of the Gods. He was a great devotee of Ramakrishna's. He was not at home, as he had gone to his new garden home. The people in the house opened up the lower rooms. Then they thought, "How will we pay for the carriage? Who will pay the taxi fare? If Surendra was home, he would surely pay for it."

Ramakrishna (to one devotee): Ask the ladies of the house and see if they have the taxi fare. Don't they know the taxi must be paid? They come and go. Somebody must have enough money to pay the taxi.

Narendra lived nearby in that section of the city. Ramakrishna sent for him. The people of the house took Ramakrishna upstairs. They took two cots and put a fresh sheet over them. Keshab was showing Ramakrishna all the pictures that were on the walls of the room. All the different religions were represented. All the various divisions of Hinduism were present. Ramakrishna was sitting, and they all began to gossip.

Then Narendra came into the room, and Ramakrishna perked up with delight and said, "You should have seen how we were gossiping with Keshab today! Vijay was there and so was everyone else."

Ramakrishna: You ask them. See Keshab and Vijay were traveling with me today, and now we are all sitting together here.

Then evening came and still Surendra did not come back. Ramakrishna was going to Dakshineshwar, and there was no need to be late. It was already 10:30 in the evening. The carriage came, and Ramakrishna got in. Narendra made pranam to Ramakrishna, and they left Calcutta for Dakshineshwar.

Chapter 3

With the Brahmo Devotees

October 1882 Calcutta

First Discussion

It was Saturday the second day of the dark fortnight in the month of Ashwin, and a religious festival was in progress at the garden estate of Benimadhav Pal, situated on the bank of the Ganga about three miles north of Calcutta.

There was a monk who lived in this garden. Twice a year he would hold a festival, once in the autumn and once again in the spring. Every year he used to invite many people from the nearby villages surrounding Calcutta as well as from greater Calcutta. On this day the Brahmo leader Shivanath and a number of his followers from Calcutta were to attend the festival.

The Brahmo Samaj used to congregate regularly in this garden, and all of its members loved Sri Ramakrishna very much. It was strange that the devotees of the Samaj, who had vowed to worship only the transcendental, formless aspect of God, had such faith and devotion to Sri Ramakrishna, the worshiper of Kali. On the previous Friday the Brahmo members had experienced great bliss in his company, and Keshab Sen, a prominent leader of the Samaj, had been there as well. On this day Shivanath and the Brahmo members had come up the river to the beautiful garden by steamer.

Manomohan, both a Brahmo member and a devotee of Ramakrishna, had told the Brahmos that this garden was a wonderful place for meditation and devotional practice. They began their devotions in the morning and continued throughout much of the day. Again as evening fell, they joyfully conducted their worship in anticipation of the arrival of the great soul, Sri Ramakrishna Paramahamsa, who had been invited to the festival. All awaited the opportunity to view the blissful countenance of the Master. That afternoon at about three or four o'clock, Ramakrishna sat in a carriage at Dakshineswar with several devotees and began the three mile trip to the festival.

Throughout the day a great many people from the surrounding villages had been congregating in the garden. Some were seated under the vines and creepers to shade themselves from the hot sun. Near the entry to the garden was a shop that sold refreshments. Underneath the vines and creepers, everyone was speaking with great joy and delight. All the four quarters were filled with bliss. The blue skies of autumn were radiating their beauty, as all awaited Ramakrishna's arrival. The birds sitting in the trees under the clear skies joined in the songs. There was an atmosphere of divinity, and all were thirsty for a sight of the man of God. Many devotees were thinking that soon they would hear the delightful conversations of Sri Ramakrishna. They would have the opportunity to listen to his enlightened discourse and his melodious songs, to witness his ecstatic union with God, and to view his divine dancing enraptured with the love of God.

Then came the moment when the carriage arrived at the gate of the garden entrance. Ramakrishna's heart was filled with great delight to see the pure devotion of so many devotees of God. Everyone stood up with gestures of greeting and shouted, "He has come!" From all sides people were straining to catch a glimpse of the Paramahamsa as he entered the garden. A seat on a raised platform under the tree in the center of the garden had been prepared for the Master. In this place there was a forest of people. All four sides were crowded with people. In the houses of the neighborhood, surrounding the garden, in every veranda, on every balcony, and even on the roof tops, people were standing and looking down into the garden trying to catch a glimpse of Sri Ramakrishna.

Ramakrishna was full of joy and was laughing as he took his seat on the raised platform beneath the garden tree. All hearts were filled with bliss on having this opportunity to view the blissful countenance of Ramakrishna. It was just like the audience in a dance theater staring at the stage anxiously waiting for the dancer to appear. Just previously some had been laughing, some thinking about their personal affairs, and some conversing with their friends. Some had been eating refreshments and others chewing tobacco. But as soon as the Master arrived, it became pin-drop silence. All were filled with bliss, and they had one-pointed focus as they gazed at the blissful form of Sri Ramakrishna.

Second Discussion

Ramakrishna's sweet face was lit up with a smile as he lovingly directed his gaze toward Shivanath and the other devotees.

Ramakrishna: Oh, my beloved Shivanath, look at your devotees. They're sitting with you in such great bliss. Ramakrishna was filled with bliss himself. (In fact, they all looked like they had just taken marijuana.) When a pot smoker meets another pot smoker, they are both very, very happy, and they embrace each other with great delight. (Shivanath and the other devotees began to laugh.)

> Swamiji: Ramakrishna now describes the nature of worldly people.

Ramakrishna: Whoever won't take the name of God and has no devotion to God, please go sit over there. (He gave another option.) Please stroll about a little and spend your time some place else. You can have a look at the scenery and the buildings in the neighborhood. (They all began to laugh.)

Any of the devotees who have come here with many desires in their mind won't listen to the word of God. Those who have many worldly thoughts in their minds won't be able to sit very long to listen to me. Their minds will be wandering, and they'll have to get up. Again and again they hear voices whispering in their ears, "When will you go? When will we leave? Come on, it's time to go." The true devotees will say, "Wait a while, wait a while. We'll go in a little bit." Then with great dissatisfaction, the others will say, "You listen to the words of this man. We'll go wait by the boat."

If I were to tell worldly people to renounce all their attachments, they wouldn't listen to a word I say. Chaitanya would invite the worldly people by saying, "Come. Drink fish soup, enjoy the embrace of a young woman, and chant the name of God!" In greed out of desire to enjoy the fish soup and the embrace, everyone would begin to sing the name of God. Then once they tasted the nectar of God's name, they would understand. The delicious taste of the fish soup is God's name. And when you sing the name of God until tears begin to flow from your eyes and you enter into ecstasy falling on the ground, rolling in the dust and embracing the earth, that is the embrace of the young woman. Then everything else seems unreal.

In this way, Chaitanya used to inspire people to sing the name of God. Chaitanya would say, "The name of God has such power you may not find the fruit quickly, but it will come without a doubt."

There was a man who planted seeds in a window box. Afterward there was an earthquake, and all of the seeds fell out of the box onto the ground. Eventually the trees grew up, and soon they blossomed and gave forth fruit. In the same way, if you sing the name of God, even in order to have "fish soup and the embrace of your beloved," the seeds will sprout, blossom, and unfailingly produce fruit.

Swamiji: Ramakrishna now talks about the nature of human beings and the three gunas.

Ramakrishna: Devotion is of three kinds: sattwa, rajas, and tamas. In this entire world of objects and relationships, these three qualities or gunas predominate. Therefore, devotion is also of these three qualities.

Do you know how sattwa exists in worldly people? Imagine a broken down house. Nobody makes repairs. Pigeons are making a mess in the courtyard, and no one cleans up the dirt. The whole place is neglected. The fixtures and the furnishings have become old. Whatever clothing the family may have is sufficient. But the people are very peaceful. They are compassionate and have no attachment. They have no ill feeling toward anyone. That is the house of sattva.

Do you know how rajas expresses itself? Such people have a gold watch and chain. They have two or three rings on each hand. Their home is very expensive. They have a picture of Queen Anne on the wall and pictures of the Princess and other important people. Their house is immaculately clean. There is not a spot anywhere. They always have plenty of fine food and wear fine, expensive clothing. The servants of the house are always dressed impeccably. This is the quality of rajas.

Do you know the expressions of the quality of tamas in worldly people? They sleep a lot and express many unsavory desires. They are easily angered and are very selfish.

When people have sattwic devotion, they meditate in private. They meditate even underneath the mosquito net, while everyone else thinks they are asleep. Actually in the night they're awake, and that's why they sleep late in the morning. They don't care too much for their bodies. If they get a little food, it is sufficient. They have no desire for delicacies. They have no desire for expensive clothing. They have simple furnishings and no wish for fine decor. Yet they feel no want.

When devotion is rajasic, the devotee has a big tilak, a rudraksha mala with a little gold in between each of the beads. When he performs his worship, he wears a very fancy silk cloth.

Third Discussion

Ramakrishna: Tamasic devotion is like a burning fire. These devotees make demands of God, just like a thief who steals all of the goods. They are like thieves who demand blessings from God.

With great love and his beautiful, melodic voice, Ramakrishna began to sing.

> Why should I go to Gaya and the Ganga River,
> Allahabad, and Kashi (Benares).
> If you say the name Kali, Kali, Kali without
> count, the recitation of mantras comes back
> What need is there of puja
> if a man repeats the name of Kali
> at the three times of prayer?
> They never find a time
> that is not the time of prayer.
> Compassionate behavior, giving alms,
> and philanthropy,
> doesn't enter into Madan's mind.

In union with this beautiful mind, you feel the
presence of the manifestation of the Supreme.
The name of Kali has many qualities
and contains so many divine moods
that no one can understand them all.
Even the Lord of all Lords, Shiva,
with all His five faces cannot express
all the qualities.

Ramakrishna went into an ecstatic bhava just as if he
were singing the song of the initiation of the Divine Fire. In
great ecstasy in the attitude of complete communion with
God, he began to sing again.

If I die while singing the name
"Durga, Durga, Durga,"
how can You keep me from becoming liberated,
even though I may be unworthy?

Ramakrishna (suddenly): What? I have sung Her name.
What sin can touch me? I am Her son. Her immortal
qualities are mine by right to receive, and I have the right to
be stubborn. When you give a spiritual turn to tamas, you can
have the vision of God. Be forceful in your demands to God!
She is not a stranger. She is your very own.

The quality of tamas can be used for the welfare of
others, also. There are three kinds of doctors: a great doctor,
a mediocre doctor, and the lowest kind of doctor.

The doctor that comes, takes the pulse, and says, "Please
take this medicine," and then leaves is the lowest kind of
doctor. He doesn't even check to see if the patient took the
medicine or not.

The doctor who comes and explains to the patient in
appropriate ways that he must take this medicine and says,
"How will you be cured if you don't take your medicine?

You should take it without fail. I made it myself so you please take it." That is the mediocre type of doctor.

The doctor who, seeing that the patient did not take the medicine, even opens the mouth of the patient, if necessary, and forces the medicine down his throat. He is called a great doctor! This is the doctor who employs the guna of tamas. This quality actually helps the patient. It does not injure the patient.

In the same way, there are three kinds of teachers. One kind of teacher gives instructions about dharma and doesn't check up on the disciples. That is the lowest kind of teacher.

An average teacher repeatedly explains the subject for the welfare of the students so that they will understand his instructions and utilize them in their lives. He explains with many examples and with much love.

But if a great teacher finds that his disciples are still not listening at all, he will even use force to compel them to follow the proper instructions.

Fourth Discussion

The Formless Infinite is Beyond Words

A devotee of the Brahmo Samaj: Is God with form or without form?

Ramakrishna: There is no end to the Infinite. She is both without form and with form. For the gratification of devotees, She takes form. For jnanis or those who consider this entire perceivable universe as a dream, She is without form. But devotees feel that their "I" is real and that the perceivable universe is also real. Therefore, for devotees God is a personal God. The followers of non-dualistic

Vedanta repeat "not this, not that." They meditate in this way. According to their understanding, the "I" is unreal. The world is false. It is all a dream. Such people believe only in the Supreme Divinity beyond relationship.

But the essence of truth cannot be taught in words. How can I say, "She is like this, She is like that?" The Ocean of Truth, Bliss, and Consciousness is an ocean in which there are no waves and no ripples. If you immerse yourself in devotion, the coldness of your devotion, as it were, solidifies the water in places. In this way, the water takes on a form. When devotees come near to God, the formless becomes relative. Occasionally She takes a personal form and remains embodied in that personal form.

When the Sun of Wisdom rises, all the ice melts, and then you don't perceive God in a personal form at all. She melts back into the Ocean of Infinity. You can't have the vision of the "form of the formless." You can't define that Infinite Ocean in words. Whatever you say, whatever words you use, it is not Her. At that time I can't find "the Her" no matter how much I search!

If you keep contemplating in this way, then you will find that the "I" is a concept with no reality. When you skin an onion from the outside, the first peeling is red. Then after that there are many white layers. If you continue to skin the onion layer by layer, ultimately you come to nothing at all in the center. When you are searching for your own "Self," you search and search until you finally realize that you are nothing at all.

Although we understand that the Supreme Divinity is the Highest Intelligence, who can speak of what form that Highest Intelligence takes? A doll made out of salt went to measure the depths of the ocean. When the doll immersed itself in the water, it completely dissolved. No one could find the doll because it had become one with the ocean. Now who's left to give the answer?

When we attain to wisdom that is full, complete, and perfect, the human mind becomes silent. Then one's "I" is like the salt doll that went into the ocean. It dissolved and merged with the oneness of the ocean and never came back to give a report. In that state no knowledge of distinction remains. Until all of your worldly tendencies have become complete, people make a bubbling dialogue with their egos. Ultimately all becomes quiet.

When you immerse a water pot in a pond, the bubbles of air go out, making a gurgling sound as water fills the pot. Then when the pot is full, it doesn't make any more noise. As long as the pot is not full, it continues to gurgle as it discharges air bubbles. In olden times people used to say, "When a ship goes into the unknown seas, it may never come back. It may even fall off the edge." But I don't go there. I must relieve myself of the bubbles first. (All began to laugh.)

You may discriminate a thousand times, yet the "I" who is the thinker does not leave. For devotees to regard me with devotion is a very good thing. To the devotees I am the Supreme Divinity embodied in a human form, meaning that the Supreme Divinity Beyond Form has taken on qualities. When individuals take a form, they express through that form, and God listens to the prayers of a pure individual. Those who worship with form offer prayers to God with form. They are not Vedanta philosophers. They are not jnanis. They are devotees.

Whether you accept the Divine with form or not, if you have the understanding that God is real, then your prayers will be heard. If you don't believe that God is real, then you're wasting your time. God is an individual who hears the prayers of all, and He creates, preserves, and transforms this entire perceivable universe. He is the embodiment of Infinite Power. By means of devotion it is easy to attain to God.

Fifth Discussion

God Reveals Herself Either With or Without Form

One of the Brahmo Samaj devotees: Please explain, Sir, is it possible to see God? And, if it is possible, why can't I see God?

Ramakrishna: Yes, certainly you can see God. You can see God with form. And you can see God beyond form. How can I explain it to you? You are a devotee of the Brahmo Samaj and so believe in the formless.

Brahmo Devotee: Can you tell me the means of having the vision of the Infinite?

Ramakrishna: It will happen if you have complete sincerity and if you can cry for God. How many people cry for their children? They cry for their wives and for their money. For those things they cry a whole pot full of tears, but who cries for God? As long as a child is sucking on a pacifier or eating, the mother of the house continues to cook and do all the work of the house. But when the child throws the pacifier away and begins to cry loudly for its mother, then the mother puts down the pot of rice and runs to the child and puts the child on her lap.

Brahmo Devotee: Great Sir (Mahashay), why are there so many different opinions about God? Some say He is with form; some say He is without form. And if He has form, everyone has a different opinion of what that form is. Why is there so much confusion?

Ramakrishna: When a devotee has a belief in a particular form of God and further develops a living relationship with that form, then there is no more confusion whatsoever. If you have a vision of God in any form, then He Himself explains it all to you. How will you learn your way around the city if you do not wander around the neighborhood? Listen to a story.

A man was sitting at the foot of a tree, when he happened to look up and saw a remarkable animal sitting on a limb above. Later he told his friend, "There is a beautiful red animal sitting on a limb in that tree." His friend replied, "Oh, yes, I know that tree, and I have also seen the animal, but why do you call it red? It is green." Soon others were also consulted. One person said it was purple. Another said it was yellow, another said blue, and so on. So they all went to investigate, and as they drew near, they saw a man sitting at the foot of the tree. They approached and asked the man about the color of the animal. He said, "I live under this tree, and I know that animal very well. Whatever you say about it is perfectly true. Sometimes it's red and sometimes it's green; sometimes yellow and sometimes blue. It assumes many different colors. It is a chameleon. And sometimes it doesn't have any color at all."

So I say that God is sometimes with form and sometimes without form. Those who continually contemplate the Supreme Divinity are able to know the true intrinsic nature of that Divinity. Such a person knows that the Divine expresses itself through various forms and attitudes. He is with form. He is beyond form. He who remains always at the foot of the tree knows that a chameleon has many colors and sometimes no color at all. Other people only debate and argue and occasionally fight, and they experience many difficulties.

A poet said, "The formless is my Father. The one with form is my Mother." So whatever form the devotee desires, in that very form He will reveal Himself. He is the one who satisfies all devotees. In the Puranas it's written that Hanuman was such a strong devotee that for his benefit God assumed the form of Rama.

> Swamiji: Now we're going to discuss the definition of the form of Kali and the form of Krishna.

Ramakrishna: You can't know the Infinite. Placed before Vedanta, all forms fly away. The ultimate philosophical proposition of Vedanta is that Brahman, the Supreme Divinity is Satya (Truth), and that all the perceivable universe, composed of names and forms is transient and, therefore false.

As long as I remain a devotee and this apprehension of "I" remains, this ego, the I-consciousness, my identification as a devotee, remains. At that time I have the belief that God is a perceivable entity and that I can have a relationship with Her. But if you allow worldly ideas to intrude, then this attitude that "I am a devotee" disappears. Then you believe "I am the actor" instead of "I am a devotee."

What form does Kali have? When the sun is very far away, it appears to be small. When you go close to the sun, it looks so huge that you can't begin to conceive how enormous it is. In the same way, Kali's form is Infinite like the Infinity of the sky, so then it is impossible to determine where Her limits are. When you look at the water of the pond from afar, it appears to be green or blue or even black. If you go close and take a handful of water from the pond, it has no color whatsoever. If you look at the sky from afar, it appears blue. If you go close, it has no color at all. Hence, the idea of Vedanta is that Brahman is beyond qualities, beyond form.

What is His intrinsic form? You cannot explain it in words. As long as you consider your "I" real, then the entire perceivable universe is also real, and the form of God as an individual in relationship to us is also real.

Is it ever possible to know the Infinite Supreme Divinity? What is the necessity of knowing "It?" We have, with great difficulty, attained a human birth. I only need devotion to Her Lotus Feet. If my thirst is quenched with one small pot of water, why should I measure how much water is in the pond? If I am intoxicated with one bottle of wine, why should I count how many bottles are in the store? Why should I concern myself about how big Infinity is?

Sixth Discussion

The Way You Can Have the Darshan of God

The Seven Levels and the

Knowledge of the Supreme Divinity

Ramakrishna: There are many different types of knowers of the Supreme Divinity described in the Vedas. The path of jnana is very difficult. If the slightest bit of attachment and worldly desire remain, wisdom cannot be attained. In the Kali Yuga, the age of darkness, this is the more difficult path taken to attain the Supreme Wisdom.

The Vedas have elucidated seven levels of consciousness. The awareness resides in these seven levels of consciousness. When awareness remains in the world of objects and relationships, it is residing in the three lower chakras -- the anus, the genitals, and the navel. Then the contemplations don't move towards the upper chakras. All the mental faculties are devoted to desires and attachments.

The fourth residence of awareness is in the chakra of the heart. There you get your first glimpse of True Consciousness where on all sides you find the Vision of Light. The individual at that time is mesmerized or astounded by the wonder of this Eternal Light, and he says, "What is this?" Then his mind no longer has any tendency to move towards the lower levels of worldly attachments. The fifth residence of awareness is in the throat. When the contemplations rise to the throat, the Vishuddha chakra, all the ignorance and all the foolishness are renounced in favor of listening to the Eternal Truth of God and Words of Wisdom. If anyone indulges in worldly gossip, such an individual leaves that place at once. The sixth residence is the Ajna chakra in the forehead. If awareness goes there, you have the Eternal Vision of the Supreme Divinity. Still a little bit of "I" remains.

Individuals who have the Vision of That Which is Beyond Form quickly become united with the Divine. They want to touch that form of the formless and embrace it. They want to embrace that form of the formless, but they are unable to. It's just like when there is a light within a lantern. The light is seen within the lantern, and you think that you can touch it, but there's a glass surrounding it making it impossible to touch the flame.

The seventh region is in the Sahasrara at the top of the head. If your contemplation goes there, then you go into samadhi. All the knowers of the Supreme Divinity have the actual vision of divine communion with God. In that condition the body does not remain for long. All of a sudden it will become limp and without energy. You won't be able to eat. If you put food into the mouth of such an individual, the food falls out. He won't be able to eat. If he stays in such condition for twenty-one days, he will leave the body. This is the condition of a Knower of Supreme Divinity.

For you I prescribe the path of devotion. It is very good, and it is very simple. It is a straight path. In samadhi you cannot perform any activity.

Once a friend asked me, "Great Sir (Mahashay), would you please teach me how to go into samadhi?" (Everyone laughed.)

I replied, "If you go into samadhi, how will you fulfill all your responsibilities? You cannot even perform puja, japa, and all of your various spiritual exercises."

At first in sadhana everything is mixed up and confused. But as you go towards God, your burden of activities will be reduced. The time will come when even repeating the names and reciting the qualities of the deities will drop off.

Ramakrishna (to Shivanath): You give lectures. When you were going to many conferences and giving lots of lectures and speeches, you had great fame, and you were widely known. Whenever you entered a place, everyone became silent. Just as soon as you arrived, all the talking in the audience ceased. Just looking at you, everyone felt delight. When the people said, "Shivanath has come," all worldly gossip and chatter in everyone's minds was immediately stopped.

Seventh Discussion

Swamiji: This is a discussion about the
system of prayer in the Brahmo Samaj and about
a description of the eternal qualities of God.

Ramakrishna (to Shivanath): My dear sir, why do you talk so much about the eternal qualities and character of God? I once said to Keshab Sen on a day when they had all come to the Kali temple, "I would like to hear what kind of lectures you give." We sat under the moon on the bank of the Ganga, and Keshab began to speak. He spoke a lot. Then I fell into a special mood, and I said to Keshab, "Why do you talk so much about God's descriptions? Oh, God, how beautiful You are! What lovely flowers You have made! You have created the heavens and the stars. You have made the seas, etc." Who loves God for Himself? They love to describe the eternal qualities and the creations of God.

A few years ago the golden ornaments were stolen from the deity in the Radhakrishna temple. When he heard that they had been stolen, Rani Rasmuni's son, Mathur Babu, ran to the temple and complained bitterly to God, "Oh, my goodness! You couldn't even protect Your own ornaments." I said to the young man, "What kind of intelligence do you have? Has He who has Lakshmi, the Goddess of Wealth, as His own servant any lack or need? These ornaments are very important to you, but for God they are just like pieces of mud or earth. Eh? What a foolish and ignorant thing to say to God. What eternal qualities can you give to God?"

Mathur Babu

That is why I say what is desirable is to attain Divine Bliss. When you meet your friend, do you ask how many houses he owns, how many gardens, how many servants? Does it matter to you how much money he has or how many good works he has performed? When I see Narendra, I forget everything else -- his history, his house, his father, how many brothers he has. I forget to ask. When I look at Narendra, I sink into the Ocean of the Nectar of God. So as to God's Infinite creation, His imperishable qualities, all the news about His power and possessions, why should I care about all that?

Ramakrishna begins to sing:

> My mind sinks deeper and deeper
> into the ocean of the formless.
> I searched into the lower regions of hell,
> but in the middle of my heart is
> the Forest of Delight.
> I sink, sink, sink into the Light of Wisdom.
> The Light of Wisdom is shining in my heart,
> shining, shining, shining in my heart.
> Splash, splash, splash go the oars
> as I am rowed across the river.
> But who is it that is actually taking me across?
> The poet, Kabir, is singing.
> Listen, listen, listen.
> My mind is at the feet of my revered guru.

After the vision of God, devotees retain that flavor. They enjoy seeing the drama of the Divine Play. After slaying Ravana, Rama entered Ravana's evil city. One elderly lady saw Rama coming and began to run away as fast as she was able. Rama's brother, Lakshmana, asked Rama, "What is that old lady doing? Everyone knows that You are an Avatar of God come to liberate this city, and she is fleeing away! Why is this?" Rama called to her compassionately, promised not to injure her in any way, and asked her why she was fleeing. She answered, "Rama, I've lived for so many years and I've seen so much of your Divine Play. Now I have a desire to live even longer, so I can see what new dramas You are going to create here!" (All began to laugh.)

Ramakrishna (to Shivanath): I had a desire to see you. If I don't see pure souls, who shall I converse with?

One of the members of the Brahmo Samaj: Great Sir (Mahashay), do you believe in life after death?

Ramakrishna: Yes, I have heard that there is life after death. With our little intelligence how can we understand the greatness of God? Many have said there is life after death, so we can't ignore their words.

Bhishma was going to leave his body, and he was lying on a his death-bed of arrows. All the Pandavas were standing around his body along with Sri Krishna. They all saw that Bhishma's eyes had tears falling from them. Arjuna said to Krishna, "Oh, my brother, this is fantastic, what a wonder! The great Grandfather Bhishma is always truthful and controls his senses. He's so wise, and he is even one of the Ashtha Vashus.[7] Look at him shedding tears. He, too, at the time of leaving his body has fallen into the Maya of attachment!" Sri Krishna asked Bhishma about this, and Bhishma replied, "Krishna! You know very well, I'm not crying because of attachment to my own body! What I was thinking was that for the Pandavas, Sri Krishna Himself, God Himself, is their guide and charioteer. Still their pains and afflictions have no end. I started to think of this and began to cry because I still can't understand anything of God's ways."

Later Ramakrishna was in bliss singing kirtans along with the devotees. In the assembly hall everyone was practicing meditation. It was about 8:30 in the evening. Sometime after the sun set, the moon rose in the sky.

7 A manifestation of one of the eight forms of wealth.

Everyone was smiling with delight and looking at the face of the Master. They all began to sing kirtan. Ramakrishna became so intoxicated with God's love that he got up and began to dance. All the devotees joyfully formed a circle around Sri Ramakrishna. What a glorious sight! There was Ramakrishna dancing in ecstasy surrounded by devotees playing musical instruments. They began playing faster and faster and louder and louder. Ramakrishna continued to dance in complete ecstasy. Everyone was intoxicated with the wine of God's love. "God Himself is dancing in our midst," this divine feeling echoed within the hearts of all. The name of God that flowed from the sweet lips of the devotees created an Ocean of Bliss.

In all the villages in all directions, one could hear the name of God being sung with great devotion. At the end of the kirtan, Ramakrishna went completely into sashtanga pranam. He lay down on the ground and bowed down to Mata Jagadamba.

Ramakrishna (as he was bowing): To the Holy Scriptures, to the devotees, to the Supreme Beyond Form, and to all the wise beings, I bow down. Again and again I bow down. I bow down to those who worship with form. I bow down to the lotus feet of those who worship without form. I bow down to all those wise beings who know the Supreme Divinity.

He bowed again and again to all those wise beings who know the Supreme Divinity. Everyone shared in his bhava of ecstasy and then joyfully partook of prasad. Om.

Chapter 4

December 1882

It does not take birth nor does It experience death, nor does It become only after manifestation. It is unborn, eternal, everlasting since ancient times, and It is not slain when the body is thought to die. *Bhagavad Gita* II, 20.

First Discussion

If a liberated person leaves his

body is it called suicide?

Vijay Krishna Goswami came to the Dakshineshwar Kali Temple to visit Sri Ramakrishna. With him were three or four devotees of the Brahmo Samaj. It was the fourth day of the bright fortnight of the month of Agrahayana, Thursday, 14th December, 1882.

They came from Calcutta by boat along with Balaram who was a great devotee of the paramahamsa. Sri Ramakrishna had just completed his afternoon rest. On Sundays a big crowd would gather. Those devotees who wanted to have a private conversation with him usually came on other days.

Sri Ramakrishna was seated on his wooden cot. Vijay, Balaram, M. and other devotees were sitting on mats or on the floor, facing west looking at him. Through the open door on the west side, they could see

Balaram Basu

the River Ganga ambling by. Because it was winter, Ganga
was very calm. Just beyond the western door was the semi-
circular veranda, after which was a flower garden, and then
the river bank. West of the river bank, the flow of the puri-
fying Ganga washed the feet of God's temple with great
delight.

Because it was winter, everyone was dressed in warm
clothes. Vijay was suffering greatly from colic pain, and had
brought a bottle of medicine with him, so he could take it at
the appropriate time. Now Vijay earned his livelihood as a
teacher at the Sadharan Brahmo Samaj. He spoke from the
dias at their assemblies, and gave instructions and inspiration,
but now he had many philosophical differences of opinion
with the group. Having accepted the job, what could he do?
As an employee, he could not speak or work freely.

Vijay was born in a very pure family of the lineage of
Advaita Goswami. Advaita Goswami was a jnani who used
to contemplate the formless Supreme Divinity, and yet still
manifested the highest devotion! He was one of the
followers of Lord Chaitanya, who would dance in ecstacy
with the love of God. He would forget himself to such an
extent that his clothes would fall off while he was dancing.
Vijay had joined the Brahmo Samaj and also meditated on the
formless Supreme Divinity, but the blood of the great
devotee, Sri Advaita, flowed in his veins. The seed of the
love of God was within him and now was ready to sprout. It
was just waiting for the appropriate time! That is why he was
so fascinated by the incredible state of Ramakrishna's divine
madness, which was difficult even for the Gods to attain. Just
as a cobra with upraised hood is under the control of the flute
of the snake charmer, so also Vijay was sitting in complete
attention charmed by the divine words flowing from the lips
of Ramakrishna. Again when Ramakrishna danced with love
for God like a child, Vijay also danced with him.

Vishnu, a boy who lived in Enderya, had left his body by cutting his throat. Today the first discussion began with this subject.

Sri Ramakrishna (to Vijay, M. and the devotees): Look, I heard that the boy had left his body and my mind is beset with pain. He would come here after school and say that he did not like worldly life. He had gone to the west to live with a relative for some days. There he would meditate in the fields, forests or hills. He told me about his visions of so many divine forms.

Perhaps it was his last birth. He had done much work in his previous births. I understand that only a little remained to be done, and that is why he left so soon.

One has to admit the tendencies inherited from previous births. I heard about a man performing a spiritual practice with a corpse (shava sadhana), worshiping the Divine Mother in a lonely place in the deep forest. But he began to see many frightening events. Ultimately a tiger carried him off. Another man, being terrified from the tiger, had climbed a nearby tree. Seeing all the articles ready for worship, he climbed down from the tree, washed his hands and mouth, and sat down on the corpse. He recited the mantra a few times, and the Divine Mother gave Her darshan and said, "I am pleased with you. Ask for a boon." Bowing to the lotus feet of the Divine Mother he said, "Mother, may I ask you a question? Seeing your actions I am astounded! That other man had given so much effort, had gathered so many materials for your worship, had been performing disciplined worship for you for such a long time, but you didn't show your compassion to him. And for me who doesn't know any-thing, who doesn't listen, who doesn't worship, who has no discipline, who has no wisdom, who has no devotion, you are showering so much grace upon me!" Laughing the Divine

Mother replied, "Child! You have no memory of your previous births in which you practiced severe austerities for Me. Because of that spiritual discipline, you received my darshan so quickly. Now tell me what boon you want?"

One devotee: I feel fear listening to talk about suicide.

Sri Ramakrishna: Suicide is a great sin. He who takes his own life must return to the world of objects and relationships again and again and experience its pains.

"But if someone leaves his body after having the darshan of God, it is not called suicide. There is no fault in giving up the body that way. After attaining wisdom, some do leave their bodies. When a golden image has been cast in a clay mold, the mold can be either broken or saved for another casting.

"Many years ago a boy of about twenty years of age used to come here from Baranagore. His name was Gopal Sen. When he came here, he used to have such intense attitudes that Hriday had to hold on to him so he wouldn't fall and break his arm or leg. Suddenly one day the boy touched my feet and said, "I won't be able to come here any more. I want to take your leave." A few days later I heard that he had left his body.

Second Discussion

Ramakrishna: Human beings are of four kinds: those who are bound to the world of desires and attachments, those who renounce the world, those who become liberated, and those rare souls who are eternally free.

Human beings are like fish swimming in the ocean of existence, and God is like a fisherman. When a fisherman casts his net into the sea, many fish are caught in the net.

Some, realizing that they are trapped, struggle to escape. These fish are like those humans who, through renunciation, seek freedom from the net of maya. However, of these fish only one or two, perhaps, are actually able to leap out of the net. When this happens, people say, "Oh, a big one got away!" These fish are like the human beings who become liberated in life. However, there are some fish who are so careful that they never become caught in the first place. These are the eternally free souls such as Narada. Most of the fish remain trapped in the net. They don't even try to escape, or they may dive down into the mud at the bottom of the pond in the belief that they are safely hidden. These are like the great majority of mankind who think, "I am in this world, and death comes to all. What can be done?" Some think, "I am really all right. I have found security and a safe place."

Men and women who are liberated are not infatuated with this world of objects and relationships. That is why, after becoming free, some just leave their bodies. This type of leaving the body is a very difficult attainment. Bound souls living in the world have no independence. They have no wisdom. They experience pain and suffer much injury. They get into one difficulty after another, yet they have no awakening of spiritual consciousness.

The camel loves to eat thorny vegetation. As he eats, the thorns cut his mouth, but still he goes on eating. Worldly people suffer so much pain, but they go back to the same pleasures that brought the pain in the first place. Even when a wife or husband dies, before long the spouse begins planning to marry again. A child dies and the grief is unbearable, yet after a few days the parents forget all about their pain. The mother of that child was so beset with grief, yet soon she is thinking, "Oh, I'm going to tie up my hair and put on new ornaments and a new sari." In this way, after each painful event the world of attachment and desire continues.

Every now and then, bound individuals think to themselves, "There must be some other way." However, they don't search for another way. They just can't leave their old habits. Their minds don't turn to God. Keshab Sen had an elderly relative, 50 years of age, who used to pass the time playing cards, but he could never find time to repeat the name of God.

There is another characteristic of a bound soul. If you were to take that individual out of the world he is used to and put him into a holy environment, he would probably die from boredom. Worms that live in dung have a lot of fun. They enjoy their lives very much. All their companions and relatives are there. But if you take a worm out of the filth and place it in a bowl of rice, that worm will die.

Third Discussion

Swamiji: This is about extreme renunciation as contrasted with that of individuals who are bound.

Vijay: By what means can those who are bound by worldliness attain to liberation?

Ramakrishna: With God's grace, you can achieve such a sense of extreme renunciation that you can remain oblivious to the onslaught of attachments and desires. What is considered to be extreme renunciation? The lower form of renunciation and detachment comes when you sing the name of God in every circumstance.

Who has extreme renunciation? Those whose life force is totally dedicated to God with the sincere dedication a mother has for the child in her womb. He who has extreme renunciation desires nothing other than God. He sees this ocean of worldliness as a mere mud puddle. In his mind he always contemplates God. He submerges himself in complete devotion to God. He looks on his relatives as he would a deadly black snake, and he desires to flee from their presence, and he does indeed flee. Others think they will first make arrangements for their livelihood and home, and then they will contemplate God. Real devotees never think this way. Within them burns a great fire. What is considered to be extreme renunciation? Please listen to a story.

There was a drought in one district, and farmers had to bring water from a great distance in order to save their crops. There was one farmer who was very determined. He vowed that until the water came and the river was connected to his crops, he would continue to dig. The time came for his bath in the evening. His wife sent some oil with their daughter for him to rub on his body. His daughter said, "Father, the time has come. Rub oil on your body so you can take your bath." He replied, "Go away! I have more work yet to do." She came again, but the farmer was still digging. He didn't take a break even to bathe. Next, his wife came to the field and said, "You haven't bathed even yet? Your dinner has become cold. You're doing too much. You can finish tomorrow. Eat something, and then you can finish." Giving her a good scolding, he picked up his shovel and chased her away. He sent her back and said, "You have no understanding. The rain hasn't come. With no water the crops will die. If I stop now, how can I save the crops? How will the children eat? If we have nothing to eat, we will all starve. I have vowed that I will dig the earth until I bring water. Only then will I eat." When his wife saw his firm resolve, his sankalpa, she returned alone. That entire day he worked digging for water. Then late in the night, he finally succeeded, and the waters of the river flowed into his canal with a gurgling sound. Only then did he sit down. He peacefully sat and gazed at the water from the river. He watched it filling his field with great contentment. His mind was peaceful, and he was filled with bliss. He went to his home and saw his wife, and he said, "Now give me the oil, and give me some tobacco." Then he sat down without any other thought and ate a delicious meal. Afterwards he fell asleep completely at peace. This is what is called extreme renunciation.

There was another cultivator. He was just bringing water to his field when his wife came up to him and said, "It's time to come home. You don't have to work so hard." He made no objection or protest whatsoever. He simply put down his shovel and turned to his wife and said, "Since you have come, then let us go." That cultivator was not able to bring water to his field. This is called very slow and easy renunciation. If you don't have extreme, sincere determination, it's not possible to bring water to your field. In the same way, without extreme renunciation it will be impossible to realize God.

Fourth Discussion

Why Become a Servant to Desires and Attachments?

Ramakrishna (to Vijay): Previously you used to come here quite frequently, but now you don't come so often.

Vijay: I have a great desire to come here, but I'm not free. I have accepted some of the work of the Brahmo Samaj.

Ramakrishna (to Vijay): Desires and attachments bind people's lives, and because of this their independence flees. In order to fulfill desires, resources are necessary. For that reason we become servants to others, and our freedom is lost. In Jaipur, there was a temple of Govinda and the pujaris of that temple in the initial stages were all bachelors. None of them were married.

At that time they were all filled with fire. One day the king called them, but they didn't go. They said, "Tell the king to come to the temple if he wants a puja done." Then the king, on the advice of his ministers, arranged marriages for all of the pujaris. As a result of their marriages, the king never had to call them again. They began to go to the king of their own accord. "Oh, Great King, I have come to give you a blessing. I have brought prasad for you. Will you please wear this kavach (amulet often worn for protection)? It will come in handy for any work that you want to do. Today my son is having his first solid food. Today my child is beginning his studies. I have many sons and daughters, and I have to give ornaments and cloth to them all." And on and on and on it went.

You see? Their attachments had made them beggars, where before they would answer to no one. What was once a huge raging fire within them had become a small flickering flame.

There is another story. Nityananda Goswami's son was amongst the thirteen hundred disciples of Birbhadra. When they all became siddhas, Birbhadra, the guru, became concerned. He began to think, "They've all attained perfection. Whatever they tell to people, that's what's going to happen. Wherever they go, there will be fear. If people unknowingly offend any of these disciples, they will come to great harm." With this in mind Birbhadra said to his disciples, "You all go down to the Ganga, take a bath, say your evening prayers, and then return here." The disciples went down to the Ganga. They took their bath, offered their prayers, and then began to meditate. They soon became immersed in samadhi. They had attained such power that when the waves of the Ganga sometimes went over their heads, they were quite oblivious to it. The winds blew the spray of the water against them, but their meditation was not disrupted in any way.

Amongst the thirteen hundred, one hundred understood what the guru was about to say. They did not wish to disobey the words of their guru, so they went away and did not return. The rest of the twelve hundred went back to see the guru. Birbhadra, the guru, said, "These thirteen hundred women are going to serve you. You must all get married." They said, "Just as the guru has ordered, but one hundred of us are missing." So twelve hundred of the ladies were given in matrimony to the twelve hundred men. As a result, they lost their fire, and their austerities had no more power. After marriage they didn't have the strength of their tapasya. Why not? Their freedom had been compromised.

Ramakrishna (to Vijay): Look at your own circumstances. Why are you looking to others? You have taken on the karma of the Brahmo Samaj, and what have you gotten? How many young men have received an English education? They go out and they search for employment among the businesses of the Englishmen. When you seek employment from these people, you have to bow to their feet, shine their shoes, and take all kinds of insults. This all occurs because of desires. Once you are married, your responsibilities expand. Then there is no more energy to flee. That's why we Indians have to accept so many insults and why we have to surrender ourselves and become servants. Once you attain to realization of God, you will regard all desires as the expression of God. Once you have the vision of God by sincere and intense devotion, you won't then fall prey to desires for women. Even if you remain in the presence of women, they will be unable to bind you. You will be fearless.

If you have a very large magnet and a very small magnet, which one will attract the iron filings to itself? The big magnet will attract the little pieces of metal. God is a very great magnet. Before God all of our greatest desires are like little pieces of metal. What can such desires do? What can desires do to the magnet?

Devotee: Oh, Great Sir (Mahashay), shall I hate all women then?

Ramakrishna: He who has attained to God doesn't look at women with any selfish desire, so no fear accrues. He correctly sees that all women are the expressions and manifestations of the Supreme Divinity. Calling them "Mother of the Universe," he bows to them all.

Ramakrishna (to Vijay): You should come here more often. I like to see you.

Fifth Discussion

The Master with Vijay Goswami

December 1882

Swamiji: This is the fifth discussion. When one is instructed by God to do so, one may become a teacher.

Vijay (to Ramakrishna): I am so busy with the work of the Brahmo Samaj that it is very difficult for me to visit you regularly. Whenever I have time, I come.

Ramakrishna: It is very difficult to take on the responsibilities of a teacher. Without being given the authority from God, it is very difficult to teach. If you begin to give instructions without authority from God, people will not listen to you. Such teachings have no power. First you must do sadhana. In some way you have to attain to God. When you get the authority from God, then you may lecture.

There is a pond in Kamarpukur. It's called the Haldar pond. Every day people used to go there to answer the calls of nature. All the other people, who later came down the stairs to the water to bathe, would be greatly offended and would scold those people bitterly and loudly. It had no effect. The next day they would do the same thing. Finally the owners of the pond came and hung a sign that said "Commit

Haldar Pond, Kamarpukur

no nuisance. If you do, you will be punished." After the notice was posted, not one person came again to defile the pond.

So if you receive the "notice," you can lecture. Without it no one will listen. After getting authority from God, you can give lectures. When people understand that behind this person is someone with great authority, they treat that individual with greater respect. We are all ordinary mortals. If one has not had the vision of God, then one cannot work effectively as a spiritual teacher.

Vijay: Great Sir (Mahashay), do not the lectures that are given by the Brahmo Samaj assist people in their spiritual journey?

Ramakrishna: Satchidananda, Pure Existence - Consciousness - Bliss is the guru. He alone gives liberation. Is it easy to liberate people from bondage to this world? Those who have so many desires and attachments to this world and who are spiritually ignorant can only be liberated by God. Other than Satchidananda there is nowhere to take refuge. Those who have not attained realization of God, those who have not received instruction and authority from God, and those who have not been given their power by God, do they themselves have even the desire to be liberated from the bonds of this world?

One day I was going to answer the calls of nature near the Panchavati when I heard the loud cries of a frog in distress. I could understand that it had been caught by a snake. After quite a while, when I was returning, I was surprised to hear the same frog still croaking very loudly. I went to investigate, and there I found that a small venomless snake had caught the frog and was trying desperately to swallow it. It could neither swallow the frog, nor could it let it go. This was causing untold suffering for both of them. I then thought within my heart, "Hari, if a big poisonous snake like a cobra had grabbed him, after only three croaks he would have been silent. But a little snake has caught him. That's why the frog is suffering so much, and the snake also is in pain.

If you find a true guru, then your ego and attachments will be removed within three croaks, as it were. If the guru is not perfect, then the disciple will have pain, and the guru will have pain as well. The egoism of the disciple will not be removed nor the bonds of worldly relationships. If the guru is not perfect, then the disciple will not be liberated.

Sixth Discussion

Ramakrishna: So long as you persist in inviting the deluding power of maya into your life, how can you expect to become free of the bondage of "I"- consciousness? Only if you stop inviting maya, will it be possible."

Vijay: Great Sir (Mahashay), why are we bound in this way? Why can't we see God?

Ramakrishna: This egoism, this sense of "I" that exists in all beings, has been bound by the deluding power of maya. This ego is continually inviting maya. Maya covers and deludes the ego of every individual.

Ramakrishna (humorously): Oh, only when I die will all this maya go. When one fully understands that God alone is the doer, such a one becomes liberated even while in the body. Such liberated beings have no fear. Because of the deluding power of maya, our "I" is like a small cloud which obstructs the sun. Because of the cloud, you can't see the sun. When the cloud of egoism is removed, you may see the light of God.   If even once you can fully leave your identification with "I and mine" (egoism) at the feet of the guru, then you will have the Vision of God.

Ramachandra was, in fact, an incarnation of God. Because of Rama's attachment to Sita, Lakshman couldn't believe that Rama was an avatar. He couldn't see that Rama was God Himself. Look here. If I hold this towel in front of my face, you can no longer see me, and yet I'm so close. In the same way, God is so close to every one of us, but because of the covering of maya we don't see God.

Every single individual life form is intrinsically of the nature of Unqualified Truth, Consciousness, and Bliss. Because of the covering of egoism caused by maya, we forget the true nature of each individual. We see only the manifestation of the various external attributes. One after another quality and characteristic comes forth, and the intrinsic nature of the person is hidden.

A status-conscious gentleman wearing a cloth with a black border will have a tendency to wander about and play cards and gamble. A person who has been given a pen will have the tendency to look around for some paper and then begin to write about anything he sees. In the same way, egoism and attachment are enhanced by the possession of wealth. When one acquires some money, the nature of a person often changes. There was a member of the priestly cast who used to come here to visit. To all appearances he was a very humble man. One day Hriday and I went to Konnagar village on a visit. As we were getting down from the boat, we noticed that same brahmin sitting on the bank of the Ganga having a breath of fresh air. When he saw us, he called out, "Hey, hello, Thakur! How are you?" When I heard his words, I chuckled, and I said privately to Hriday, "Oh, Hriday, certainly this man has come into some money. That's why he is calling to us with such familiarity." (Hriday began to laugh.)

Once there was a frog who found a rupee, and he put it in his hole. Sometime later an elephant came walking and stepped over the hole. At once the angry frog burst out of his hole shaking a stick in fury and cried out, "You have so much nerve. You dare to walk over my hole!" Such is the power of money. It gave birth to the self-importance of the frog!

Only if one has the direct experience of the Supreme Divinity can the ego be transcended. Then one is said to have attained to the wisdom of God Realization. This is a very difficult achievement.

It is said in the Vedas, "Only when the mind has risen through the seven levels of consciousness, does it enter samadhi." When you achieve samadhi, your ego dissolves. I say once again—this is a very difficult thing to accomplish.

Where does the mind usually reside? It resides in the lowest three levels of consciousness: in the Muladhara, the Swadishtana, and the Manipura chakras. These three levels, interacting, bind the mind to the objects, attachments, and relationships of the everyday world. When your awareness reaches the heart level, the Anahata chakra, you perceive the Divine Light of God. Then one exclaims, "What is this? What is this?" When your consciousness reaches the Vishuddha chakra, at the level of the throat, you will only want to listen to and speak about God. When your consciousness moves to the Ajna chakra between the brows, you will experience God, Satchidananda. You will have the vision of Divinity with Form, and you will have a great desire to embrace that form, but it is not possible. It is like a light shining inside of a glass lantern. It will seem that you are almost able to touch it, but you can't touch the light within the lantern. When your consciousness rises to the Sahasrara chakra, the ego can no longer remain and you enter samadhi.

Vijay: When you rise to the highest level, to the Sahasrara, do you achieve the realization of the Supreme Divinity? What does one perceive in that state?

Ramakrishna: Yes. What you will experience then cannot be expressed in words. Once a ship has sunk in the vast ocean, it can never return. Even if you organize a search, you will gain no information about what has happened to that ship.

Once a doll made of salt went to measure the depth of the ocean. As soon as the salt doll dove into the ocean and was submerged in the water, it dissolved and could never return.

How deep is the ocean? Who can tell us? Whoever enters the deep waters of God consciousness will dissolve and mix with the oneness of the ocean. They are not able to return and give a report.

At the seventh level your mind and your egoism are destroyed. You enter samadhi. What you will understand from that experience, no one can ever say.

Ramakrishna: The ego doesn't say there's an evil "I," and there's an "I" who is a servant. The "I" that does this whole worldly business and runs behind desires and attachments is the ego. It makes a distinction between the life force and the soul of humanity.

If you throw a stick on top of the water, then you'll see two parts of the water, one on this side and one on that side. There is only one body of water, but because of the presence of the stick, you see two parts. Egoism is that kind of stick. If you take the stick out of the water, then you see only one body of water. Actually who am "I," this little ego "I"? Who says "I"? The ego is always present. "I have so much wealth. I have become such an important person."

If they catch a thief, the first thing they do is grab the money. Then they beat the thief. They don't let him go. All the guards of the area call the police, and they give him great pains. The little ego is saying, "Doesn't he know that he stole money from me! He had such nerve. He took my money!"

Vijay: If the ego does go, is it possible to live in the world? Can you have samadhi and have the ego at the same time? Is following the path of jnana (knowledge) enough until you reach samadhi? If in the path of devotion a little egoism remains, then is not the path of wisdom superior?

Ramakrishna: Only a few people who reach samadhi vanquish the ego entirely. Usually it doesn't go completely. Discriminate a thousand times and yet the ego returns in devious ways. If you cut down a banyan tree and you come back tomorrow, you'll find that it has sprung a new shoot. If you meditate in a lonely, solitary place, and the ego doesn't go, then make that so and so a servant of God. "Oh, God, You are the Supreme Lord, and I am your servant." Stay in this attitude. "I am the servant. I am a devotee." With this attitude the ego will be harmless. If you eat too many sweets, you'll get a stomachache, but not if you eat rock candy.

The path of wisdom is extremely difficult. If the attachment to the body doesn't go, then you cannot achieve jnana. In this age of darkness, there are many responsibilities and duties in life. This understanding is knowledge of the body, but knowledge of the ego doesn't go. That's why in this age of darkness the path of devotion is best. Devotion is the easier path. If you have great sincerity of heart, repeat God's name, and pray to God. Then you will attain to God realization. There is no doubt of this. You can draw a line on water with your finger, and there appear to be two sides of the water. But the line drawn on the water doesn't last for long. The ego that is a servant of God, the "I" who is a devotee, the ego who is a child of God, what is that? These forms of ego are harmless like the lines formed on the water.

Seventh Discussion

Ramakrishna: The highest ideal of perfection in this age is union with God through devotion. Union through the path of knowledge is extremely difficult. It is best to keep the "I" of a servant, a devotee, or of a child of God.

Vijay: Oh, Great Sir (Mahashay), you are instructing me to leave and renounce all inferior works, all evil karma. Is there no fault in retaining the "I" who is a servant?

Ramakrishna: No, the servant "I" means "I am a servant of God, I am a devotee of God." There is no fault in having such an ego. Through that, ultimately, one will attain God.

Vijay: In one who has the ego of a servant, what will his anger and desire be like?

Ramakrishna: If you have the right attitude, then you have no attachment to your anger or to your desires. After attaining the highest realization of God, even if this "I" who is a servant or this "I" who is a devotee remains, that individual can do no evil work nor cause harm to others. After touching the philosopher's stone, iron becomes gold. If you touch a sword to the stone, the iron sword becomes a golden sword. It remains in the form of a weapon, but it can't harm anyone.

Even after attaining God, if the ego remains as a servant or as a devotee, one is free from personal or selfish desires and anger. One can do harm to none. As the coconut tree grows, it sends out its branches which afterward shrivel up as the tree grows bigger. Only a line remains where the branches were. By seeing the marks on the tree, you can see how much the tree has grown. In the same way, the ego of those who have attained to the realization of God remains only as a mark, an indication that the ego was once there. They have no attachment to any desires or anger. They become like little children. Even as little children are endowed with the qualities, or gunas, of sattwa, rajas, and tamas, yet they are not attached or bound by these qualities. A child will remain attached to its toys and happily play with them and then suddenly leave those toys and move on to something else without a second thought or look backwards. You can place a cloth worth a lot of money and a doll worth very little before a child, who will pay no attention to the cloth, but be very much attracted to the doll. With great force the child will say, "I won't give it to you. My father has bought it for me."

A child has no awareness of who is important and who is unimportant. He has no concept of cast or pride of birth. If his mother says, "That is your big brother," a child will believe it, even if it is not true. A child has neither self-consciousness nor hatred. He has no sense of purity or impurity.

Even after attaining samadhi, a devotee remains as a servant of God. He thinks only, "I am the servant and You are my Lord. I am Your devotee and You are the Supreme Divinity." This is the attitude of a devotee. Even after attaining to realization of God, this attitude remains. All of the ego does not go. By practicing this attitude, we attain God. This is called union through the path of devotion.

If you take hold of this path of devotion, you can attain to the goal of the path of wisdom, jnana, as well. The Supreme Lord is all-powerful. If He wills it, He can even bestow jnana upon us. The devotee doesn't long for the Supreme Wisdom. He says, "I want to remain a servant and You are my Lord. I am a child and You are my Mother." This is the attitude he wants to maintain.

Vijay: Do those who practice non-dualistic Vedanta also attain to the Supreme Wisdom?

Ramakrishna: Yes, you can reach Him through the practice of non-dualism. This is what is called the path of wisdom. This path is extremely difficult. I have already explained to you about the seven levels of consciousness.

When your consciousness arrives at the seventh level, you go into samadhi. Brahman, the Supreme Divinity, is the One True Reality. This entire perceivable universe is false, transitory. When you discriminate in this manner, your mind dissolves and you go into samadhi. In this age of darkness, the Kali Yuga, people have a different attitude. Only Brahman, the Supreme Reality is true. All this perceivable universe is false. How can one living in Kali Yuga understand that? As long as you have attachment to your body, this understanding cannot come. I am not the body. I am not the mind. I am not the twenty-four principles of Sankhya philosophy. I am beyond pleasure and pain. What are disease and grief and old age? What do these mean to me? This understanding in this age of darkness is very difficult.

You may reason in this way, yet this body-consciousness returns to you again and again. It is like when you cut down a banyan tree. A new shoot comes up again in no time. The awareness of the body does not go. That is why in this age the path of devotion is very good. I enjoy eating sugar -- I don't want to become sugar. This is the attitude.

I don't have any desires for myself. Some people like to walk around saying, "I am Brahman, the Supreme Divinity." I myself prefer to keep the attitude, "You are God, and I am your servant." It is more fun to play between the fifth and sixth levels of consciousness. I don't like to stay at the seventh level very long. It doesn't have the rasa, the taste. I want to sing the names and recite the glories of God. That has great flavor, so very sweet! It is great fun and a privilege to do selfless service for the Lord.

Look at the waves on the Ganga. They don't call a wave the Ganga. "I am That." This attitude is not appropriate for Kali Yuga. As long as awareness of the body and the belief that "I am this body" last, one cannot attain union with God. One can't go forward and soon falls from the path. By such an inappropriate attitude, you cheat others and you cheat yourself. You don't even understand your own situation.

There are two kinds of devotion. Only those who successfully follow the supreme type of devotion find the way to attain the vision of God. If you just practice the ordinary kind of devotion in order to impress others, you will not find God. Until you have real loving devotion, it is impossible to reach God. There is another name for loving devotion. It's called raga bhakti. Until you have that real, intense love, you can't attain God. If you just like God a little bit, you can't achieve the Highest Divinity.

There is another kind of devotion called vaidhi bhakti. Such a devotee says, "I have to do this much japa. I have to fast. I have to go on pilgrimage. I have to offer this many articles in my worship." This is called vaidhi bhakti, the love which binds. If you practice in this way for a long time, you may develop love for God, but so long as you don't have the real, loving devotion, you can't hope to have the vision of God. He wants your sincere love. When you have that kind of love, your worldly tendencies just vanish. When you give one hundred per cent of your mind, you will find God.

Occasionally some people develop true longing and sincere love just on their own accord. They are among the eternally realized souls. They are perfect from their youth and grow up as attained souls. From their childhood they cry to God just like Prahlada, who had such great devotion.

If you want a cool breeze, you must wave the fan back and forth. In order to get the air, you need the fan. You can't just say that love for God will come with no effort. All this japa and austerity and fasting are very necessary. They are the fan. When you develop real sincere love for God, when your love comes of itself, all the japa and other forms of tapasya will fall off naturally. Then you can just bask in the cool breeze. The fan is no longer required.

If you become intoxicated with the love of God, who will study the Vedas? What need have you then to study the Vedas? Until you attain to such love of God, your devotion is unripe devotion. When you attain to such love, it becomes ripe devotion. Who has unripe devotion? Those who are not interested in hearing the teachings about God have unripe devotion. When you have ripe devotion, you always want to contemplate God's words. If you put a dark cloth over a photograph, you can't see the picture. When the cloth is removed, you can see the picture clearly. If you don't have pure love for God, then you can't understand the instructions about God.

Vijay: Oh, Great Sir (Mahashay), in order to attain to God, must one then have ripe devotion?

Ramakrishna: Yes, only through devotion can you have the vision of God. You have to have ripe devotion. You have to have loving devotion. You have to have extreme love with your devotion. That kind of devotion brings God to you. Just as a child loves its mother, and the mother loves the child. Just as a wife loves her husband, when that pure love comes, there is no more illusion of this world, and no attraction to the illusion. Only compassion remains. Then this world of objects and relationships seems like a foreign country.

Then you understand that this is only the "field where I do my work," my karma. Just as when a rural village person comes for employment to Calcutta, Calcutta is where he does his work. We have to remain in Calcutta, as it were, in order to do our karma. When you attain pure love for God, then all your attachments to this karma dissolve. You may do your work in the city, but your whole mind is back at your home in the village. When you truly love God, then you will only think of God. All these worldly thoughts completely dissolve.

Swamiji: This discussion is about the Vision of
God.   Without God's grace one cannot have the
vision of God.

Vijay: How does one attain the vision of God?

Ramakrishna: Without purification of the mind, it is
impossible. As long as desires and attachments reside in the
mind, the mind will remain impure. If a sewing needle is
embedded in mud, a magnet will not be able to attract the
needle. If you wash the mud from the needle, the magnet will
attract it at once. In a similar way, one can wash away the dirt
of the mind with tears of devotion. "Oh, God, I will never do
that again!" If you can pray sincerely with tears in your eyes,
all the impurities will be washed away. Then just as a sewing
needle is drawn to a magnet, your mind will be drawn into
samadhi. Then you will have the vision of God.

You may try a thousand times, but without God's grace
you cannot hope to have the vision of God. Without grace no
one can have the direct intimate perception of the Divine. Is
it easy to earn Divine grace? One must renounce every trace
of "I" - consciousness, the thought that "I am the doer."

By relying on one's intellectual understanding alone, one
can never realize God. Imagine a room full of valuables and
outside a guard standing at the door of that room. If the
owner of the house were to say to someone, "Sir, please go to
that room and bring all the valuables that are in the room to
me," the person would reply, "Wait a minute. There is a
guard protecting that room. If I go there, what will happen to
me?" In a similar way, there are those who have protected
their hearts so well with the thought "I am the doer" that God
cannot easily enter those hearts.

When one has received God's grace, one can then
perceive Divinity. This is called the Light of Wisdom. Just

one ray of God's Infinite Light has illumined the whole universe. That's why we can see and perceive all that we know. We learn so much from the various experiences of life. If God were to shine His Light even once on His own Self, we would then know God.

There was a gentleman who went out into the night with a lantern. He was an Englishman, a foreigner. No one knew this because no one could see his face. He held up the lantern so he could see all the other faces, but no one could see his face. If anyone wanted to see who that gentleman was, he would have to request him, "Please, sir, take your light and shine it on your own face." In the same way, if you want to see God, you will have to pray to God, "Please, God, just once shine your Divine Light on Your own Self so that I can see You." Then only will you have the vision of God.

If there is no light burning within a house at night, it is very difficult to move around inside that house. That's why one must illumine the space within the heart. If the heart is illumined by the Light of Divine Wisdom, then one will perceive the Face of Supreme Divinity.

Vijay then brought medicine for Sri Ramakrishna and gave it to him. Ramakrishna took the medicine with a little water. Ramakrishna is the Ocean of Compassion. Vijay was not wealthy and could not even afford the carriage or boat fare to visit the Master. Every now and then Ramakrishna sent devotees to invite him to come. Once he sent Balaram, and Balaram then paid the carriage fare for both. Another time Balaram brought Vijay and nine other devotees to Dakshineswar to visit the Master. After an evening with Ramakrishna, Balaram took all the devotees to his home in Bhagbazar. They landed at Annapurna Ghat and walked to Balaram's home. M. was also present. It was the fourth day of the bright fortnight and it was winter. As the moon rose into the sky, all were remembering the inspiring words of the

Master and contemplating his beautiful form. In this way, they made their way each to his own home. Om.

Kalpataru, the Wish-fullfilling tree

Chapter 5

March 1883 Calcutta

First Discussion

It was the dark fortnight, the sixteenth day of Chaitra, Thursday the thirty-first of March, 1883.

The previous night Sri Ramakrishna had participated in an all night singing of songs, feasting, and prayer. Today after his midday meal he was taking rest. His room was located to the east of the Kali temple. To the west the Ganga River was flowing.

It was two o'clock in the afternoon, and there was a strong wind and lots of waves on the Ganga. A few devotees had assembled in the Master's room. Trailokya was present. He was a great singer who sang for the gatherings of the Brahmo Samaj. His singing would invariably captivate the minds of his listeners and create a mood of harmony and spiritual depth in their hearts.

Rakhal was not feeling well. The Master was discussing his illness with the other devotees. "Look at him taking his medicine. If he just took plain soda water, wouldn't that help? What will happen to Rakhal? He has fallen ill. Rakhal, you should eat some Jaganath prasadam." Speaking in this way, the Master went into a deeply spiritual mood that was wonderful to witness. Everyone present felt that the actual form of Narayana had manifested right before them. On one side was Rakhal, a pure souled devotee who had renounced all worldly attachments and desires and who was feeling ill. On the other side was the divine countenance of the revered Ramakrishna, the manifestation of the Highest Divinity, with tears of love in his eyes. Ramakrishna gazed at Rakhal as if he were his own child treating him with unbounded love and affection. He began to call with the greatest love, "Govinda, Govinda." It was just like the Mother Yashoda calling to her child Krishna.

After reciting the name Govinda, Sri Ramakrishna went into samadhi. His whole body was perfectly still. All of his senses and his organs of knowledge and action were totally inactive. There was neither movement of his nostrils nor fluttering of his eyelids. No one could tell if he was breathing or not. He was still just like a statue. It seemed as though his soul had taken wings like a bird and flown high up into the sky. Until just previously he had been calling on God to protect his child, and now where had he gone? It was a wonderful sight to see someone so engrossed in the name of God and then in the next moment deep in samadhi.

At this time an unknown sannyasin wearing the gerrua cloth came into the room and took a seat. One gentleman named Mani Mallick was a great devotee of Sri Ramakrishna. He was about 60 or 65 years old, and some days before he had gone to the temple of Vishwanath in Kashi (Benares) to pay homage to the Deity. Today he had come with the same kind of reverence to visit Sri Ramakrishna. He began to speak about his experiences in Benares. He said, "I met a sadhu who told me that until you have controlled your senses, you can't have spiritual experiences. He said that by only calling on God nothing will happen."

Ramakrishna: So you know their opinion? First you need sadhana, peacefulness, compassion and going beyond the mind. You see, these are seekers of nirvana. They are followers of non-dualist Vedanta. They believe that Brahman, the Supreme Reality, is real and that the perceivable world is false. This is a very difficult path. If you say that the world is false, then you too are false. The very words you are speaking are false like a dream. After you burn camphor, nothing remains. If you burn wood, at least there are some ashes. Ultimately your contemplation takes you into samadhi. Then this concept of "I and you" and the entire perceivable world disappears.

Ishwara Chandra Vidyasagar

Ramakrishna: Pundit Padmalochan was a very wise and renowned scholar. Yet even though I call on the Divine Mother, he had great trust and faith in me. Padmalochan was the chief pundit of the Maharaja of Burdwan. He had come to Calcutta to have a discussion with Vidyasagar and was staying in a garden house. I sent Hriday to call on him and ask him to come here. I had heard that he had no ego, and I wanted to see if he had ego or not. He came to see me. He was so wise and a very renowned pundit, yet when he heard the songs of Ramprasad, he began to cry. After our discussion, he said that he had not found that kind of comfort and pleasure anywhere else. He said, "I enjoy sat sangha (the company of devotees). If one abandons the company of devotees of God, then one surely falls from the spiritual path." He was the guru of Vaishnavacharan. He was a very pure soul.

Ramakrishna: Once Padmalochan was asked by the brahmin pundits, "Who is the greater, Shiva or Brahma?" He was such a simple and humble soul. He replied to them, "No one in twenty-four generations of my family has ever seen Shiva, and none has seen Brahma either!" When he heard that I had renounced all desires and attachments to this world, he said to me, "Why are you abandoning all that? The distinction that this is gold and this is mud comes from ignorance." I said, "I don't know why, Father. I just don't like to be in association with money."

Ramakrishna: There was one pundit who had great egoism. He didn't even believe in the forms of God. Who can understand God's ways? Then God showed him the primal Shakti. The pundit was completely overwhelmed for a long time. When he finally regained some consciousness, he began to call out Kali's name.

A devotee: Revered Sir, have you met Vidyasagar? What did you think of him?

Ramakrishna: Vidyasagar is a greatly learned man, and he has great compassion, but he does not have inner perception. There is gold in his heart, but it is hidden. If he once found the gold that is within him, his outer works would diminish, and ultimately he would renounce it all. Within his inner heart, within the essence of his being, God resides. If one can understand and realize this, then contemplation of God becomes the number one preoccupation of one's mind. If one performs action without desire and attachment for a long time, ultimately that renunciation purifies the mind.

Then the mind is drawn to God. The works that Vidyasagar is performing on behalf of God are very noble. He has great compassion. But there is a distinction between compassion and delusion. Compassion is good, but not delusion. Maya likes to bind one with relationships. "This is my wife, my child, my niece, my son, and so on. I love only my relatives." With compassion all are equally loved.

Second Discussion

M: Is compassion also a source of bondage?

Ramakrishna: Compassion arises from sattwa, the quality of truth, and it is protected by the quality of truth. The quality of action gives it birth, rajas. Tamas is the quality of illusion. Brahman, the Supreme Divinity, is beyond the qualities; it is beyond nature. You can't reach the Supreme Divinity as long as the qualities of sattwa, rajas, and tamas remain. They are like thieves who can't enter wherever they please because they might be caught. The three qualities, or gunas, are all thieves. I will tell a story. Please listen.

There was a man who was walking on a path through a forest. At some point in his journey, three thieves captured him and stole all his goods. One of the thieves said, "What good is this person to us now? We've stolen all of his things." The thief then pulled out his sword and was about to slay the man, when the second thief said, "Why should we kill him? Let's just bind his hands and his feet and throw him in a ditch." They all decided that was a good idea, so they bound his hands and feet. They tied him up and threw him in the ditch. Then they left with all his goods. After some time the third thief began to think. He came back to where the victim was lying and said, "You've been injured very badly. I'm going to untie the bonds that bind you."

He cut open the bonds and said to the victim, "Come with me and I'll put you on a safe path." After a long time they reached the main road. The thief said to the victim, "Travel along this path. If you proceed in this direction, you will soon see your house." Then the victim said to the thief, "My friend, you have been so kind to me. Please come with me and stay at my house." The thief said, "No, I am not free to go to your house. The police will surely capture me there. They will know that I am a thief."

Ramakrishna: The forest in the story is this world of objects and relationships. As we proceed through the forest, the three qualities of sattwa, tamas, and rajas are the thieves. They destroy our understanding and bind us. Tamas wants to slay the living being, the jiva, life. Rajas binds us to objects and relationships. Sattwa saves the individual from the bondage of tamas and rajas. Sattwa is also a thief though, because it cannot give us the knowledge of truth. It shows us the straight path to our true home. Sattwa says to you, "Hey, look over there. You can see your house. Just proceed that way toward the wisdom of Supreme Divinity." Sattwa is far, far away from the ultimate wisdom of Supreme Divinity. What Brahman is, what that Supreme Divinity is, we cannot explain in words. Whoever has known it has never been capable of expressing it in words.

Ramakrishna: It is said that if a boat ventures into the dark waters of the ocean, it never returns. Listen to a story. Four friends were traveling about. They came to a great wall during their travels, a very high wall, indeed. Everybody asked, "What's on the other side of the wall?" Finally one friend climbed up the wall. He climbed to the top and looked at what was beyond. He exclaimed "Hah! Hah!" and leapt in. So who would give the news of what they experienced? Whoever is on the other side of the wall. Sukadeva, Janaka, and Bharat all had Brahma jnana. They all had the realization of the Supreme Divinity, but they could not communicate what they knew. When you have the wisdom of Supreme Divinity, when you move into Samadhi, "I" does not remain. That's why Ramprasad said:

> If you can't change my mind into absolute
> purity, then don't take me.
> I want the total disolution of my mind,
> and I want the disolution
> of all this principle of ego.
> Then I can have the
> Wisdom of Supreme Divinity.

Ramakrishna: Some people say that Sukadeva only touched the Ocean of Supreme Wisdom, but didn't submerge himself. That's why he was able to come back and give so many instructions.   Others say that he did attain to the Highest Wisdom, but then came back in order to teach people through his discourse to Parikshit on the Wisdom of the Bhagavat.

> Swamiji: Remember, Parikshit was the king
> who listened to the Bhagavat when he was cursed
> to die within seven days by a snake bite. In order
> to teach Parikshit the Wisdom of the Bhagavat,
> Suka didn't dissolve his ego completely, but main-
> tained a little bit so that he could come back and
> teach the world through his discourse to Parikshit.
> He saved and preserved just a little bit of the ego
> for the disemmanation of knowledge and wisdom.

Chapter 6

July 1883

Calcutta

First Discussion

It was the third day of the Bengali month of Ashar, Sunday, the twenty-second of July, 1883. It was Krishna Paksha. All the devotees had come to have darshan of the revered Paramahamsa Ramakrishna. Many devotees were not able to come during the week, so this was a special occasion. On Sundays many more were free to come and see the Master. After lunch Sri Ramakrishna had taken some rest.

About two o'clock in the afternoon, Adhar, Rakhal, and M. arrived by horse carriage from Calcutta. Mani Mallick and some of the other devotees were sitting in the Master's room. To the east side of Rani Rasmani's Kali Mandir was the Temple of Radha-Krishna. On the west side of the compound were twelve Shiva Lingams. To the north of these twelve Jyoti Lingams was Sri Ramakrishna's room. Just outside the western entrance of his room was a beautiful veranda overlooking the Ganga, where the Master often stood gazing at the sacred river.

Between the river and Ramakrishna's room was a beautiful little garden filled with fragrant flowers. The fragrance from this garden traveled far -- all the way to the southern border of the south garden and to the north all the way to the Panchavati, the five trees where he performed so many austerities, and all the way to the eastern gate where one entered the Dakineshwar temple compound.

Just outside the door to Sri Ramakrishna's room stood two Krishna Chura trees, and near to them was a gardenia bush. Beautiful nightingales sang in the trees, and a lovely shrub with red flowers grew just below where the birds were singing. Often when people walked along the path beside Sri Ramakrishna's room and they looked inside, they saw him seated in meditation. Even the sacred Ganga was blessed by seeing the Master absorbed in meditation.

Within the room on one wall a photograph of Ramakrishna was hung. There was also a picture of Saint Peter, who had lost his faith and fallen into the water. Jesus was holding him by the hand and lifting him up. There was also a small image of Buddha on a shelf.

Ramakrishna was sitting on the wooden cot facing the west. Many devotees had assembled in the room. One was seated on a small stool, and a couple more were sitting on cushions. They were all gazing with great delight and with one-pointed concentration at the Master, the embodiment of bliss. Through the open door one could see the river Ganga flowing by. It was the rainy season, and the flow was rather heavy. It seemed as though the river was trying to quickly unite with its goal, the ocean.

Second Discussion

Swamiji: About the gerrua color and sannyas.

"Pretending is not good," Sri Ramakrishna said as he came out from samadhi. He was filled with the Divine Presence as he began to speak. The words were coming as if of their own accord. He asked the question rhetorically, "Why should one wear the gerrua? If you wear a white cloth, that is all right. It is enough. Why the gerrua cloth?" (Everyone in the room began to laugh.)

Someone quoted from a story: Once he chanted the Chandi, but now he is playing a drum. (Everyone laughed.)

Ramakrishna: There are various types of renunciation. Some individuals wear the gerrua cloth even in the midst of worldly interaction and worldly attachment. This type of renunciation does not last very long. Others, as if they had no karma left, put on the gerrua cloth and depart for Benares. But after three or four months, a letter arrives at his home, "I have found a good job here, and I'll come home for a visit after a few days." There is another type of renunciation. In his home he has everything he needs, but he is not attached to any of it. In secret he always cries for God. This type of renunciation is the true one. It is real without any duplicity.

Falsehood is not good, and acting falsely is also not good. If you wear the gerrua, you are showing your renunciation to many people. It is better to wear the white cloth and inwardly be a renunciant than to walk around showing your renunciation to all. You are wearing the gerrua cloth, the symbol of renunciation, and yet within you are full of anger, passion, greed, jealousy, and all the other qualities which you profess to have transcended. What is the benefit of wearing the gerrua cloth? Better is the white cloth.

Ramakrishna went to see a drama in Keshab Sen's house called *The New Vrindavan*. There he saw an actor who was dancing in a crazy way. He was sprinkling water all over everyone saying, "This is the water of peace." Another actor appeared to be quite intoxicated as though in a stupor.

Ramakrishna: It is not appropriate for people to demonstrate their devotion by acting in a crazy way. By acting as though one is intoxicated, after a while one actually acquires those undesirable traits. The mind is like a white cloth just back from the laundryman. Whatever color dye you dip that cloth into, that is the color the cloth will absorb and become. If you fill your mind with untruthfulness again and again, then your mind will reflect untruth.

One day Sri Ramakrishna went to see a play about Chaitanya at Keshab's house. Those who were playing the parts were not professionals and acted very poorly. One gentleman commented, "In this Kali Yuga, in this age of darkness, even Chaitanya is not convincing." Keshab began to laugh and said, "Why? Did something happen to Chaitanya?"

Ramakrishna (complaining to Keshab): You invited all these people here to see a religious drama, but you didn't inquire as to what sort of people were to perform the drama. You didn't inquire into the quality of the actors.

Keshab was only thinking of his own name and fame.

Another day several devotees were present. Ramakrishna began to speak to Narendra who would later become Swami Vivekananda.

Ramakrishna: These young men, Narendra and Rakhal, are among the eternally perfect beings. Such people are born life after life as devotees of God. Many people do a little bit of sadhana and maybe gain a little bit of devotion, but these two are born in every life with full devotion to God. It is just like a natural Shiva Lingam that is rooted deep in the earth. It is not the same as a Shiva Lingam that has been constructed by man. These eternally attained beings always keep a little separate from the world. There is an old Bengali saying, "The beaks of all birds are not bent." They never develop attachment to the world just like Prahlada.

Normal people do normal things, and they may have a little devotion to God, but they also have attachment to this world. In fact, they become hypnotized by their attachments and desires. A fly sits sometimes on a flower and sometimes on delicious sweets. Sometimes it also sits on a pile of filth. (Everyone in the room became very quiet.) Those who are Eternally Perfect Beings are like the bees who will only sit on a flower and sip the nectar. They only drink the nectar of God-consciousness.

The devotion that sadhus derive from their sadhana is not the same as the devotion of worldly people. Worldly devotion always calculates, "I have to do this much japa. I have to sit for so many hours of meditation. I have to do that much worship." They keep an account of how much they do.

When they harvest the rice and spread it out on the pathway to dry, you have to walk around it to pass. When you come upon a cow that is nursing its calf, you don't go right up to it. You step around it. If you go by boat to a far-off village, you must follow all the bends and curves of the river. In order to have real loving devotion to God, you must have a living relationship with God. When you have pure loving devotion to God, you love God as your own nearest and dearest relation. When you realize God's Holy Presence and your relationship to Him, there is no more discipline that you must practice. Then you can cross, as it were, directly over the rice field after the harvest. You don't have to walk around the border of the field. You just walk straight across. When a flood comes, you don't have to follow a twisted, winding river. You can row your boat in a straight course right across the land. If you don't have this kind of loving, sincere devotion, it is impossible to have the vision of God.

Swamiji: The discussion turns to the subject of samadhi.

Amrita: Great Sir (Mahashay), please tell us about your experiences in samadhi. What do you experience?

Ramakrishna: Listen. It is as if you had a fish in a small pot, and you suddenly released it into the Ganga.

Amrita: Does any ego consciousness remain when you go into samadhi?

Ramakrishna: Yes. Usually I have a little bit of ego that stays with me. I have one little piece of gold. However much you may rub a piece of gold against a brick, a small piece will always remain. In the same way, a little bit of external consciousness remains even in samadhi because of old desires. A little bit of duality remains in order to enjoy a relationship with God. But sometimes He takes even that "I" and makes it disappear. This is called deep samadhi without form or idea. Then what remains? You cannot describe it in words.

Just like a salt doll that went to measure the ocean, as soon as he touched the water, he dissolved. Then who will come back and give the news? How could he return and explain the vastness of the ocean?

What we call Supreme Divinity is also the Supreme Energy. As long as you have consciousness of your body, you have to understand that both are present. When you speak, someone must be there to listen. Keshab believed in the Supreme Divinity in the form of Kali. One day Keshab came with his disciples to see us. I said to him, "I'm going to listen to your lecture." We sat underneath the moon, and he gave a lecture. Then we went down to the ghat and sat on the stairs and talked for a long time. That which we call the Supreme Divinity is also the form of a devotee. He is also the form of the scripture. Keshab said that the scripture, devotee, and God are one. When I said, "You also have to say Guru, Krishna, and Vaishnava Dharma are one," Keshab answered, "I haven't reached that far. Then people will call me fair."

When Ramakrishna saw Keshab's unconsciousness and the play of the Divine Mother, he realized how difficult it was to move beyond the three gunas before God Realization.

If you don't attain to Godliness, it can't be accomplished. The individual soul remains bound by maya. This maya, illusion, does not allow us to know what is God. This maya has made mankind unconscious and ignorant.

Hriday brought a newborn calf. I saw that he tied the calf up in the garden so he could eat the grass. I asked him, "Hriday, why do you tie up the calf every day in the garden?"

Hriday: Uncle, one day I'm going to send him home to our village. When he gets big, he'll pull our plow.

When he said that, I became unconscious. I thought to myself, "What kind of play of illusion is this. How far away is Kamarpukur, our village, from where we are in Calcutta? Will this calf be able to go the distance? Will he grow up over there, and then some days later he will pull the plow? This is called samsara, illusion." After some time I regained consciousness.

Samadhi in the Temple

Ramakrishna used to go into samadhi in the darkest part of night. In the day or night, he could go at any time. He would only come to waking consciousness from time to time to sing kirtan with his devotees or talk about God. M. saw him about three or four times. Ramakrishna was sitting on the small cot that stood in front of the larger bed, and he was full of bhava.

After a while he began talking with the Divine Mother. "Mother, why did you give a banana to M.?" He remained silent for some time, and then he said, "Maa, I understand.

One banana is more than sufficient. With one banana all your work will be complete. He will become a source of great teaching to many God-hungry souls."

Ramakrishna could perceive their inner capacities and, therefore, awaken the energy within each devotee.

Along with M., Rakhal was also sitting in the room. Ramakrishna was full of bhava.

Ramakrishna (to Rakhal): Did you get angry with me? Why did I make you angry? There is meaning to this. In order to get the proper dosage of medicine, one must restrict the flow of the medicine out of the bottle.

Rakhal, Swami Brahmananda

Ramakrishna (after some time): I saw Hazra, and he is a very slender, dried-up being, dry as wood. Why does he stay here? There's meaning here. When one is very clever, he makes a big drama adding nourishment to the play.

Ramakrishna (to M.): You have to believe in the imperishable qualities of God. Do you know the meaning of the form of Jagadhatri, the goddess who supports the perceivable universe? If She who is supporting the entire perceivable universe didn't hold aloft and protect the universe, the universe would fall down and be destroyed. When you want your mind to sit still, you must go into the heart of Jagadhatri.

Rakhal: Mind is the measurement of all.

Ramakrishna: Singha Bahini is She who sits upon a lion. The lion is the one who scared away the elephant.

Who is that wild elephant that Her Lion of Dharma scared away? The uncontrolled mind.

At evening prayers there was arati in Ramakrishna's room, after which he visited the temple arati. After arati in the temple, Ramakrishna returned to his room. They lit some frankincense, and the fragrant smoke poured forth. Ramakrishna listened to the songs of praise while sitting on the small cot and started immersing himself in thoughts of the Divine. Govinda Mukherji from Balghoria came with several friends and bowed down to Ramakrishna. M. and Rakhal were sitting there too. Outside the moon had risen, and the world was laughing silently. Everyone was sitting silently inside the room and looking at the peaceful countenance of Ramakrishna. He was filled with bhava. After some time he began speaking, still in bhava, about the form of the Dark One, Kali.

Ramakrishna: She is Purusha and Prakriti. She is the illusion created from their union. She is Shiva and Kali, and She is the form of Radha and Krishna. What is a great devotee, and what is the path of contemplation?

Ramakrishna (speaking full of bhava): Whatever doubts you have, I am going to clarify them right now.

Govinda and the other devotees began thinking.

Govinda: Why does Kali have this form? Why does She look like that?

Ramakrishna: Because She's very far away. If you get really close, She has no form at all, no color. Deep water looks very dark from afar, but has no color of its own. If you scoop a handful of water from the pond, you see it has no color. The closer you get to God, the greater the feeling that He has no form or name. If you go farther away, He becomes Kali. It's like the color of the flowers or grass. She is neither Purusha nor Prakriti, neither male nor female, neither consciousness nor nature.

One devotee performed puja (worship). Another came and had darshan and saw that the murti was wearing a sacred thread traditionally reserved for male brahmins. He asked the pujari, "Why did you put a sacred thread around Divine Mother?" The priest answered, "Brother, you must have understood who is Mother. I can't understand who She is. Is She male or female? I don't know. That's why I gave her a sacred thread."

The Dark One, Kali, is also Brahma, the Supreme Divinity Beyond Form. She has form and then again no form. She has qualities, and She is also beyond qualities. The Supreme Divinity is Energy and Energy is the Supreme Divinity. They are indistinguishable. They are the manifestations of Truth, Consciousness, Bliss, and they are beyond the manifestations of Truth, Consciousness, and Bliss.

Govinda: Why do they call her Yoga Maya, the illusion that comes from union?

Ramakrishna: Yoga Maya means the union between
Purusha and Prakriti, Consciousness and Nature. Whatever
form you see is only and always the union of Purusha and
Prakriti. In the images of Shiva and Kali, Kali is dancing on
the chest of Shiva, and Shiva looks like a corpse. Kali only
has eyes for Shiva. All this is the union of Purusha and
Prakriti. Purusha is without action, and that is why Shiva
looks like a corpse. In union with Purusha, it is Prakriti who
is performing all the action, Mother Nature dancing upon the
stage of Consciousness. She creates, protects, and transforms
all that comes into being. The meaning of the image of
Radha and Krishna is the same. Because of their union, they
have an inseparable attitude. This union is made apparent by
the pearl nose ring Sri Krishna wears, while Radha wears a
blue stone in Her nose. Radha's body is radiant like a
golden pearl.   Sri Krishna has a dark bluish-black
complexion. That's why Radha likes to wear a blue stone.
Sri Krishna wears a yellow cloth, and Radha wears blue.

Who is an excellent devotee? Whoever after seeing this
wisdom of Supreme Divinity understands that God is this life
and this perceivable universe.   God is the twenty-four
principles that take us to the realization.   First by
discriminating "not this, not that," you reach the roof. Once
you reach the roof, you are able to see that the materials that
comprise it are bricks, mortar, and a frame. Then you see that
the stairs are made of the same material that the roof is made
of. Next you will see that the Supreme Divinity comprises
the entire universe as well as all the individual phenomena
within it.

One needs only to contemplate. These calculating ideas
bring no fruit.   They are only the dry thoughts of a
calculating mind. (Ramakrishna spits as if to say waste of
time.) Why will you sit there idly lost in very dry thoughts?
As long as you and I are here, let's have pure devotion. Let

us enjoy being in this Garden of Delight, and stop endlessly counting the trees and flowers.

Ramakrishna (to Govinda): Sometimes I say to Mother, "You are me and I am You." Then sometimes, "You are only You." Then sometimes, "I search for myself, but I can't find my 'I.' My 'I' has dissolved in You!"

This energy is the Incarnated Spirit. On one hand is Rama and on the other Krishna. In the ocean of bliss and consciousness, these are waves. After you have achieved the wisdom of non-duality, you gain full consciousness. Then you see that all manifested existence is nothing but a form of Consciousness. God is present in everything and is everywhere. After you have achieved the Divine Consciousness, there's a lot of bliss. Why? Because the Consciousness Beyond Duality is Eternal Bliss!

Shree Maa: God has form.

Ramakrishna: When you have desires for enjoyment, you have sincerity with a certain compulsion.

Ramakrishna (to M.): I'm telling you, don't search for this Eternal Form. You must try not to distinguish between form and Eternal Form. Have faith that Divinity with Form exists. Whatever form you prefer, meditate upon it.

Ramakrishna (to Govinda): You know, so long as you have worldly desires, it is impossible for you to know God. As soon as you start playing with your children, you forget all about Divinity. It is like a child who, when he receives sweets from his mother, forgets all about his difficulties or pain. In this same way, when he doesn't like the game anymore or the sweets, he cries, "Maa, I don't want any more sweets!" Whoever doesn't understand or isn't able to see

says, "Take me to my Mother." The child will go with whoever volunteers to take him to his mother, whoever will carry
him there. When you get tired of the enjoyments of this
world, then you get a sense of compulsion and sincerity in
your longing for God. "How will I find Him?" becomes your
only contemplation and the number one preoccupation of
your mind. You then look sincerely for the one who can
instruct you, a true guru."

M. (softly to himself): When your worldly desires
and all your desires for the pleasures of the world go away,
then you get the sincerity in your search for God. Om.

Keshab Sen

Chapter 7

Sunday, August 19, 1883

Calcutta

First Discussion

Swamiji: This is the seventh chapter, and the subject of the discussion is the Vedanta philosophy of non-dualism, which holds that the individual soul is, in reality, identical with the Universal Soul.

It was the first day of the dark fortnight of the month of Shravan, the nineteenth of August, 1883. It was Sunday. The offering had been made in the Kali temple, and Ramakrishna's room was closed. After taking a little of the prasad from the worship in the temple, the Master returned to his room to rest. It was about midday. After his rest, Master moved from his sleeping bed to the small cot.

Just then M. entered the room and bowed down respectfully. After a short period of silence, he began to speak with the Master on the subject of Vedanta Philosophy.

Ramakrishna: Look, in the Ashtavakra Gita much has been written about the knowledge of the Atman, the True Self of man. Those who have attained to Atma jnana, Self-Realization, proclaim, "Tat Tvam Asi, I Am That," meaning, "I am the Supreme Soul." Such proclamations of the followers of Vedanta Philosophy properly belong to the path of those who have taken sannyasa, the renunciation of all worldly identifications and attachments. Such aspirants never allow their minds to be attracted by samsara, the world of objects and relationships. Such an attitude as "I am That" is appropriate for the Sannyasis who renounce all. It is not appropriate for householders who must perform many worldly activities.

When one says "I am That," it means "I am the Supreme Self, the Paramatman." How is this possible? The followers of Vedanta claim that the True Self of man is indivisible and beyond duality. Pleasure and pain, and sin and merit can never touch the Atman, the True Self. They have no harmful effect upon the Atman. But for those who are identified with the body and are attached to the body, such an attitude only causes confusion.

Smoke will make the walls dirty, but it can never taint the heavens or the sky. Krishna used to describe the attitude of the followers of the path of knowledge of the Self by saying "I am like the infinite sky." This is also the attitude of a supreme devotee. This conviction is natural to one who has self-knowledge, but not everyone is qualified to speak in such a way.

Swamiji: This is a discussion about sin and merit and about maya and compassion.

Ramakrishna: The assertion that "I am already liberated" is very good. Repeating "I am liberated" again and again, one actually becomes free. Whereas asserting "I am bound, I am bound" only takes one deeper into bondage. One who constantly says "I am sinful, I am a sinner" will eventually fall from Grace. One should have such faith that one can say "I have uttered the Name of God. What sin can attach itself to me? What bondage can touch me? How can I be bound?"

Ramakrishna (to M.): Look, my mind is very disturbed. Hriday wrote me a letter saying that he is very ill. Is this maya (the illusion of attachment), or is it compassion?

M. did not know how to answer, so he remained silent.

Ramakrishna: Do you know what maya is? "I love my brother and my cousin. I love my wife, my children, and all my other relations." This is maya. But compassion feels "I love all of existence equally." So what has happened to me? Is this maya, or is it compassion?

Hriday has done so much for me. He has served me for a long time. With his own hands he even cleaned up after me when I was very ill. Yet even with all that, I still scolded him and punished him. But he also caused me great distress. He gave me so much pain that I went down to the Ganga to drown myself in its waters. But he did many good things for me as well. Nowadays he has become very attached to money. But what can be done? Who is there that can inspire his generosity?

Second Discussion

> Swamiji: The image of the Divine Mother is also the image of Infinite Consciousness. When one sees the image of Vishnu, one is seeing the image of the Mother as well.

It was about two or three in the afternoon. Two devotees Adhar Sen and Balaram Bose had just arrived to visit Sri Ramakrishna. After bowing down respectfully and seating themselves, they began to inquire about the Master's health.

Ramakrishna: My body is fine, but my mind is feeling a bit uneasy. You see, I haven't been able to get any news about Hriday's illness from the Mallick family. I went to their home to see the image of the Divine Mother as Singhavahini (the Goddess Who's Vehicle is the Lion).

On the way to the Mallick's, a poor farmer wanted to see me. He lived in an old dilapidated house. It was filthy with bird droppings everywhere. It was very littered and dirty. Then I proceeded to the Mallick's. Their home was very beautiful, spotlessly clean, respectable, and elegant.

Ramakrishna (to M.): What does this mean? Can you explain it to me?

Ramakrishna (answering the question himself): Whoever has a certain type of karma to experience will experience it, like it or not. One has to believe in prarabdha karma (the actions which we performed in the past and whose results are coming to fruition in the present).

Ramakrishna (to M.): I saw that old dilapidated house, but even in such an impoverished setting, the face of the Goddess Singavahini was radiant. One must believe that the Goddess does manifest Her Presence in the image.

One time I went to Vishnupur, where the King had built a most beautiful temple. There was an image of the Goddess there. Her name was Mrinmayi, the Goddess of Delight. There was a large pond next to the temple, and the grounds were very beautiful. I thought that some lady had washed her hair in the pond, because I could smell the perfume that women use in their hair. I didn't know that it was the custom for women who come there to first wash their hair in that pond before entering the temple to worship the Goddess. Standing beside the pond, I went into bhava samadhi. With my inner vision, I hadn't as yet seen the image in the temple, but right there beside the pond I saw the Presence of the Divine Mother!

Swamiji: Even devotees experience pleasure and pain.

A group of devotees arrived at Dakshineshwar and began discussing the political upheaval and civil war that had been raging in Kabul. One devotee asked Sri Ramakrishna, "Great Sir (Mahashay), the Amir of Afghanistan, Yakub Khan, is a great devotee of God, yet he has now lost his kingdom. How can this be?"

Ramakrishna: You know that pleasure and pain are inevitable for all embodied souls. Everyone who wears a body will experience pleasure as well as pain. There was a great devotee named Kaluvir. He had taken birth as a direct result of the Divine Mother's blessing. Even he was put in prison, and a heavy stone was placed on his chest. Imagine. Such a great devotee, and they put a heavy stone on his chest. So, you see, sometimes even the greatest devotee experiences pain; every "body" experiences pleasure and pain.

Shri Manta was a great devotee, and his mother, Kulat, was also devoted to the Divine Mother, yet he had many troubles. He was sold as a sacrifice and almost killed. Kathur was another great devotee. The Divine Mother appeared to him, and he sang many songs to Her. He was a woodcutter and received bounteous Grace from the Divine Mother, yet he remained a poor woodcutter all of his life. While in jail Devaki, the mother of the avatara Krishna, had the vision of the four-armed Lord Vishnu, but she still remained imprisoned.

Swamiji: This is about the pains and pleasures of being a devotee.

M: This body composed of the five elements is a stupid horse that gives us as much pain as it can. It is more appropriate to leave this body as soon as possible rather than to merely get out of jail!

Ramakrishna: These are all the fruits of prarabdha karma (the results of our own actions that we performed in the past). For some time we must experience those fruits, and in order to do that we must wear a body. There was a blind man who went to bathe in the Holy Ganga, and as a result he was exonerated of all his sins. But that still did not cure his blindness. (All laugh.) He had some karma remaining from a previous life. That's why he had to have that experience in this one.

M: Once you have shot an arrow from your bow, you have no further control over the arrow.

Ramakrishna: Whatever may be the pleasures and pains of the body, a true devotee never abandons his devotion. His pure love for God will not diminish in the least. The Pandavas experienced so many hardships, but even in the midst of all their difficulties, they never once lost their love for God. Where do you find devotees like these? Where do you find wise people like them?

Third Discussion

Captain and Narendra entered Sri Ramakrishna's room. They bowed down respectfully and seated themselves. Vishwanath Upadhyaya was an officer and an attorney representing the king of Nepal. Sri Ramakrishna used to call him "Captain." Narendra was at that time 22 years old and was in college studying for the BA degree. Occasionally he came on Sundays to visit the Master.

Sri Ramakrishna asked Narendra to sing a song. There was a tanpura hanging beside the western door of the room. The devotees watched as Narendra began tuning the tablas.

Narendra: These drums don't have a full sound.

Captain: They are like a sadhu who sits silently like a water pot filled to the brim full of divine bliss! (Everyone began to laugh.)

Ramakrishna: But Narada and Sukadeva, after achieving samadhi, came down for the benefit of others to explain what they had experienced. In order to remove the pains of the world, they taught how to enter samadhi.

Now Narendra began to sing:

> Truth, God-Consciousness, and Divine Bliss
> dwell deep within the temple of my heart.
> When will that day come,
> when they will reveal themselves to me?
> Slowly, slowly, I sink into that Sea of Joy.
> How can this Ocean of Wisdom reside
> within my small heart.
> My mind is filled with wonder
> as I fall at the Feet of the Beloved.
> In this abode of Peace and Bliss
> there can be no duality.
> As I surrender and take refuge in my Lord of
> Lords, my life is filled with meaning.
> I always recite the Name.
> No evil can dare approach me.
> Just as darkness departs
> with the dawning of the day,
> all sin flees from me forever,
> as I dwell in My Heart's Light.
> Drunk with the sweetness of the Nectar within,
> my Heart rises up
> to the Realm of Immortal Bliss.

As Narendra sang of the "Nectar of Immortality," Sri Ramakrishna dove deeper and deeper into that Sea of Nectar until he was completely immersed in the deepest samadhi.

He was totally absorbed within his own Self. His body was completely still like a wooden statue. He was completely intoxicated by the Wine of the Bliss of the Divine Mother, She Who gives Immeasurable Delight. He had no more consciousness of the external world. There was not the slightest movement or sign of breathing. It appeared that he had left this world and fled to another realm.

Fourth Discussion

Swamiji: This is about the way to attain the realization of Sat Chit Ananda and the distinction between those on the path of wisdom and those on the path of devotion.

As the Master was returning from samadhi, Narendra got up and left the room. He went to the eastern veranda where he found Hazra sitting on a mat, mala in hand as was his habit.

In the room Sri Ramakrishna opened his eyes to find the room filled with people. He looked at all the devotees and saw that Narendra had left. All the devotees were gazing at his countenance with great anticipation. They saw that he had noticed that Narendra was no longer present.

Ramakrishna: He has lit the fire. Now it doesn't matter whether he remains here or goes outside.

Ramakrishna (to Captain): Enjoy the bliss of consciousness. It will give you great delight. That bliss is always present, even if somewhat covered. As much as you are able to reduce your worldly thoughts, that much you will be able to increase your devotion to God. There is a great distance between your house in Calcutta and your house in Benares. The more you proceed toward your house in Benares, the more you leave your house in Calcutta behind.

As Radha approached toward Krishna, she could increasingly detect the perfumed fragrance of His Body. As you approach closer to God, the intensity of your devotion increases. As the river draws near to the ocean, it increasingly feels the great waves of the sea.

In the hearts of the wise, there is an inner Ganga ever flowing toward the Sea of Divinity. To them everything else is like a dream. They always remain immersed in their own self-knowledge.

But for devotees there is no fear of storm or of great waves. In the hearts of devotees are the great waves of devotion. They laugh and dance and sing. All the devotees have a grand time. Sometimes they go swimming in the Ganga. Sometimes they submerge themselves, and sometimes they rise up to the surface again. Just as when you put a piece of ice in the water, it bounces and floats. Devotees are like that. They bounce and float. (Everyone laughs.)

Swamiji: This is about Brahman, the Supreme Divinity, and the primal energy, the Adya Shakti.

Ramakrishna: The jnanis, who are on the path of wisdom, strive to realize Nirguna Brahman, the Supreme Divinity, the Infinite Beyond Conception. But the devotees desire to love the personal God. For the devotee, there is nothing higher than God with qualities, Saguna Brahman. But in fact Nirguna Brahman and Saguna Brahman are one and the same. It is just like a gem and its light. You see the light that comes from a gem, and you call it a gem. Without its light you can't think of the gem. Without the gem you can't think of its light.

Sat Chit Ananda is One. But various distinctions and qualities arise, as the One "apparently" evolves and manifests as creation, preservation, and transformation. On the one side we have Para Brahman, the Supreme Divinity beyond manifestation, and on the other we have the Divine Mother, the Supreme Energy, Who becomes embodied as the Avatara and also manifests as the universe and all its beings and transformations.

A still body of water is water. Nevertheless, when it is flowing rapidly downhill, it is also water. When Captain sits still and does no work, he is still Captain. And if Captain is doing the worship or going off to work, he is also Captain. Only the qualities and characteristics are different.

Captain: Yes, I agree.

Ramakrishna: I gave this understanding to Keshab Sen as well.

Captain (a strong upholder of orthodox conventions): Keshab Sen is neither a sadhu nor an orthodox Hindu. He is merely a great orator, a man of the world who gives big talks.

Ramakrishna (to the devotees): Captain does not like me to go to Keshab's house.

Captain: Oh, Sir, you'll go there anyway no doubt. What can I do about it?

Ramakrishna looks quite disgusted with this comment.

Ramakrishna (quite pointedly to Captain): I see. So you can go to a wealthy man's house in order to get money from him, but I can't visit Keshab? Keshab always thinks about God and sings the Name of God. Is it not you who says "God resides within all beings? It is God alone who has created all these lives, as well as this entire perceivable universe."

Fifth Discussion

Sunday, August 19, 1883

Calcutta

Swamiji: Sri Ramakrishna is discussing with Narendra the distinctions between Bhakti and Jnana yogas.

After his reply to Captain, Sri Ramakrishna left the room and went to the northeastern veranda. Captain and most of the devotees remained sitting in the room, but M. followed the Master to the veranda where Narendra and Hazra were conversing. Ramakrishna knew that Hazra was given to dry academic discussions about the truths of the scriptures, but with no realization of his own to back up his words. He always maintained that this world is a dream and that worship and making offerings to God are merely confusions of the mind. The only true spiritual path, according to Hazra, is to contemplate one's own Self. He would always repeat, "Tat Tvam Asi, I am That."

Ramakrishna (entering the veranda and laughing): What are you talking about? What is the subject of your discussion?

Narendra (laughing): We are discussing very deep things, too subtle for most people to follow.

Ramakrishna: Pure devotion and pure wisdom are one and the same. The goal of pure love is also the goal of pure knowledge, but the path of pure love is much easier.

Narendra (quoting a song of Ramprasad): Oh, Mother, relieve me of this mind which reasons. May I lose my mind forever in your pure love.

Narendra (to M.):   I've been reading a book by the philosopher Hamilton. He said that a wise ignorance is the end of philosophy and the beginning of religion.

Ramakrishna: What does that mean?

Narendra: If you study philosophy and carry it to the highest extent, you will become a fool. Then only begins the practice of spiritual perfection.

Ramakrishna (laughing, from his handful of English words): Thank you. (All laughed.)

Sixth Discussion

As evening approached, many of the devotees departed, including Narendra. As darkness settled over the compound, lamps were lit, and the fragrance of frankincense wafted across the temple grounds accompanied by the sound of the singing of God's Holy Name. The two priests of the Kali and Vishnu temples had been bathing in the Ganga. They now made their way to their respective temples to prepare the deities for the evening worship.

A young man from the nearby village of Dakshineswar as well as a few others were quietly walking on the garden paths of the temple grounds. Some of them carried walking sticks in their hands. As the darkness deepened, lamps were lit along the road. A lady servant entered Sri Ramakrishna's room to light the lamps. In the twelve Shiva temples along the bank of the Ganga, the worship had already begun. In the Kali and Vishnu temples, the pujaris were playing the cymbals and drums and ringing the large brass bell. The sweet sound of the temple music carried far across the Ganga which flowed steadily along its banks with a murmuring sound.

It was the month of August, the dark fortnight of the moon. Soon the moon began to rise in the sky lighting up the entire scene as it rose and shedding its rays of light on the waves of the Ganga and the temple grounds below. It was a blissful sight to behold.

In his room Sri Ramakrishna bowed down reverently before a picture of the goddess Kali and began clapping his hands and singing bhajans, hymns, to the Mother. There were pictures of other gods and saints in the room as well. There was one of Druva and one of Prahlada, two great devotees. There was a picture of Rama being crowned King of Ayodhya and pictures of Mahakali and Radha and Krishna.

Sri Ramakrishna bowed to them all knowing them as various forms of Divinity, and he sang to them in his very sweet voice. Then he said, "Brahman is Truth. Brahman is the Cosmic Energy, and the Cosmic Energy is Brahman. I bow to the Vedas and the Puranas. I bow to the Tantras and the Gita and to the Gayatri Mantra. I take refuge in your Lotus Feet, O Mother! Not I, not I, but You, You! I am the tool. You are the craftsman." After chanting the names of many gods and goddesses, he fell into a very deep contemplation of the Presence of the Divine Mother.

A few devotees remained in the garden or walked along the bank of the Ganga. After witnessing the worship in several of the temples, they returned to Sri Ramakrishna's room. He was sitting on the small cot. M., Adhar, Kishari, and a few others were seated on mats on the floor.

Ramakrishna (to the devotees): Narendra, Bhavanath, Rakhal, and a few other young people who come here have Pure Devotion. They are nityasiddhas, eternally perfect souls. Look how Narendra doesn't pay heed to anyone. He has no attachments. I was riding with Captain in his carriage when Captain suggested that Narendra take a more comfortable seat. Narendra paid no attention. He didn't even respond. He is not dependent even on me. He doesn't reveal how much he knows. It is for me to speak of his good qualities. He will never speak about them himself. He is very intelligent. Within him there is no maya, no ignorance, and no bondage. He has a wonderful nature and many talents. He can sing well and plays several instruments. He reads and writes and has mastered his senses. He says he has no desire to marry. Narendra and Bhavanath have a great unity. They are just like man and wife. (Ramakrishna meant that Narendra has a masculine nature, while Bhavanath has a more feminine nature.) Narendra doesn't come here frequently. That's good because if he came too often, I would always be in samadhi! Om.

Chapter 8

November 26, 1883

Calcutta

First Discussion

It was the twenty-sixth of November, 1883, the eleventh day of the dark fortnight. It was the yearly festival of the Brahmo Samaj, which was being held this year at the house of Manilal Mallick. Sri Ramakrishna had been invited, and many devotees of the Brahmo Samaj came to have the company of the Master. Vijay Krishna Goswami was among them.

The Mallick estate was on Chitpur Road. There were a number of shops down at the crossroad. They sold apples, dried fruits, and pistachio nuts. A worship hall where the members of the Brahmo Samaj were to meet was on the second floor. A great worship and festival was about to be held in the hall, and great joy was being felt by all. The house had been lovingly decorated with flowers and garlands, which hung from the ceilings and walls both inside and outside the house.

Inside the house many devotees had seated themselves on asans and were waiting for the worship to commence. There was not enough room within the building for all the people who had come, but even so the enthusiastic devotees tried the best they could to squeeze in and still have a view.

As evening began to fall, the leadership of the Brahmo Samaj began to arrive. They were greatly inspired this day, because something very special was about to happen. Sri Ramakrishna was coming. The leaders of the Samaj, which included Keshab Sen, Vijay Krishna, and Shivanath, all loved and respected the Master greatly. Actually, Master was loved by all the Brahmo devotees. There were countless reasons why he was so loved and admired. He was full of faith and devotion and always shedding tears of bliss and joy, completely intoxicated with the love of God. He was very humble and sincere. He talked to God just like a small child would talk to his mother. In fact, he worshiped all women as the very emblem of divinity. In addition, Sri Ramakrishna respected all religions and spiritual paths. He never criticized another person's faith. All of these qualities had endeared him to the hearts of the Brahmo devotees, who were waiting with one-pointed attention for the Master to arrive. That is why so many people had come from so far away just to see and to have darshan of Sri Ramakrishna.

Swamiji: Shivanath speaks words of truth.

Shivanath Shashtri

Ramakrishna arrived a little before the commencement of the worship. Several devotees including Vijay Krishna began to converse with him.

Ramakrishna: Hasn't Shivanath come?

A devotee of the Brahmo group: He has a lot of work today, so he was not able to come.

Ramakrishna: Every time I see Shivanath, I feel great joy because he is always submerged, as it were, in the nectar of devotion. Whoever is so much loved and respected has divine power within him, but Shivanath has one great fault. His words are not always truthful. He told me once that he would come to the Kali temple in Dakshineshwar on a certain day, but he didn't come, nor did he even send a message. That was not proper. You see, in this Kaliyuga truthfulness is the tapasya. If one can hold onto truth and never let it go, one can achieve everything. But if you are not truthful, no matter what spiritual practice you may follow, its power will all dissipate. One time I said that I would go to the bathroom. However, a little later even though I no longer felt the urge, I went there anyway. I didn't want my words to be untrue. I have a fear that if I don't do what I say I will do, I may be guilty of telling a lie.

After I first experienced this present state of mind, I took some flowers in my hands and said to the Divine Mother, "Oh, Mother, take your wisdom, and take your ignorance. Just give me pure devotion to You. Mother, take your purity and take your impurity, and give me only pure devotion to You. Take your dharma and take your adharma, and give me only pure devotion to you. Mother, take your virtue and take your sin, and give me only pure devotion." I couldn't bring myself to say, "Take your truth, and take your untruth." I gave Her everything else, but I couldn't give up truth.

The worship was now beginning in the temple hall. It followed the customary form of the Brahmo Samaj. The minister sat on a raised platform and began to recite mantras from the Vedas. Then the entire congregation recited together. They chanted, "Truth, wisdom, infinitude. The Supreme Divinity is the nectar of immortal bliss. Peace, divinity, purity, and knowledge untouched by sin." Then all recited the mantra "Om." All impure desires fled from the hearts of the devotees. Their minds became still, and everyone began to meditate with closed eyes. Sri Ramakrishna went into a divine mood. He became perfectly motionless, his vision fixed. He presented the most wonderful picture of stillness and holiness. Where had the bird of his soul flown? His body had become an empty temple.

As he returned from samadhi, his eyelids began to flutter. Then he gradually opened his eyes and looked in all directions. He saw that the devotees were still sitting with closed eyes. Then saying "Brahma, Brahma," he began to slowly stand up.

Their meditation over, the Brahmo devotees took their cymbals and drums and began to sing. Intoxicated with divine love, Ramakrishna began to dance. The minds of all the devotees were captivated watching his sweet dance. Then Vijay Krishna and others also got up and began dancing around him. Everyone gazed at this wonderful sight, and all were enthralled with the bliss of the heavenly music. For the time being all forgot their worldly concerns and attachments. They were drinking the intoxicating nectar of devotion, forgetting everything but the bliss of the present moment. Now any worldly thought would taste very bitter to them. After the kirtan came to an end, all sat down around Sri Ramakrishna.

Second Discussion

Swamiji: This discussion is instruction to householders.

Ramakrishna (to the Brahmo devotees):   It is very difficult to do your work in the world of objects and relationships without attachment. Pratap once said, "Sir, our ideal is King Janaka. Janaka worked in the world unattached. We should do the same." I replied, "Is it possible for you to be like Janaka? He performed unthinkable austerities. He even stood on his head for years while reciting mantras, and he did a lot of other tapasya as well. Only then did he return to the world." Then Pratap asked, "Is it not possible while in the world to attain that kind of freedom from attachment?" I replied to him, "Certainly there is a way.   As often as possible retreat to a quiet place for some days and do spiritual practice. By doing that, you will become inspired with devotion for God. Once you have attained to divine wisdom, you may do your work in the world. Then you won't take a false step."

Ramakrishna: When you do regular sadhana in a secluded place, you will find that your worldliness and attachments will diminish. At that time do not think of your wife, husband, or children. Don't think about your brothers or sisters, not even your father or mother. Do not think of any of your relations. Forget them all. You should feel that you have nothing but God, God alone. Cry to God. Pray for wisdom and devotion. You ask how many days you should remain away from your relations. I would answer, even if you could do it for one day, it would be very good. If you could do it for at least three days, of course, that would be better. If you can stay away for twelve days to a month or more, perhaps even as long as a year, that would be better still.

Once you attain both wisdom and devotion, you will have little fear of working in the world. If you rub oil on your hands before cutting the jackfruit, the fruit does not stick to your hands. In playing hide and seek, once you have come home, there is no more fear of being tagged. If iron is touched by the philosopher's stone, it becomes gold. Once you have become gold, you can be kept anywhere and never lose your spiritual shine.

The mind is like milk. If you put milk in the container of the world, it will mix with water and become diluted. But if you set the milk aside in a quiet place for some time, it becomes curdled. Then if you churn the curdled milk into butter, it is possible to put that golden butter into the water without it ever becoming mixed or diluted. Rather, it will float lightly upon the water of the world.

Third Discussion

Swamiji: Vijay Goswami is describing his
sadhana in a remote place of pilgrimage.

Vijay Goswami had just returned from Gaya, where he had been practicing spiritual disciplines in a quiet and solitary place. While there he also spent some time visiting nearby sadhus and having spiritual discussions with them. He has returned wearing the gerrua cloth of renunciation. His appearance was radiant. His eyes had the indrawn look of those who spend much time in deep meditation. He approached Paramahamsa Ramakrishna with his head bowed in reverence. He seemed to be in such a state of intoxication that one wondered what his inner experience could have been.

Ramakrishna (seeing Vijay in this condition): Vijay, did you find a place to stay? Once there were two traveling sadhus. They had wandered to many places when one day they came to a large city. Entering the city, they went their separate ways. One of the sadhus was very much impressed by the size of the city, the great number of houses, and the marketplace. He was gazing in wonder at all the sights in the bazaar, when he met his friend, the other sadhu, who asked him, "Where are all your belongings?" The first sadhu answered, "The first thing I did was to find a place to stay. There I locked my things in my room, and now I am carrying the key in my pocket. I am worry-free and can enjoy the sights of the city." That is why I asked you, Vijay, "Have you found a place to stay?"

Ramakrishna (to M. and the other devotees): For a long time Vijay's spiritual heart was covered up and hidden within, but now that he is wearing the gerrua cloth, it has really begun to blossom.

> Swamiji: Sri Ramakrishna now explains to Vijay about performing action without attachment and what it means to wear the gerrua cloth of the all-renouncing sannyasin.

Ramakrishna (to Vijay): Look, Shivanath has a lot of difficulties. He has to write a newspaper, and he has many worldly activities which give him no peace. In the Srimad Bhagavatam, it says that among the twenty-four gurus that the Avadhuta had, one of them was a hawk. Once a man was fishing, and a hawk swooped down and caught a fish. As it flew back up into the air, a thousand crows, which had been waiting nearby, all flew after the fish. The hawk flew as fast as it could, but the crows were relentless in their pursuit, cawing and pecking at him continuously all along the way. The hawk flew to the east, the north, the south, and the west. Then he began to circle around in the sky, but the crows followed close behind. Finally, the fish dropped from the exhausted hawk's beak, and at once the crows left the hawk and flew after the fish. Afterward the hawk sat on the branch of a tree and thought, "That fish was the cause of my problems. Now that the fish is gone, I have no worries at all."

The Avadhuta learned from the hawk that as long as you keep the fish with you (meaning that so long as you have unfulfilled desires), your karma will remain, and karma can have a fearsome nature bringing with it lots of worries and a lack of peace. If you can renounce those desires, then your unpleasant karma will dissipate, and you will finally find peace. It is very difficult to perform action without desire. We think that we are acting without attachment, but even so desire still creeps in, from where no one can say.

If one has performed a lot of spiritual discipline before beginning to work in the world, it may be possible to act without attachment. Only after the vision of God is it possible to be completely free from desire. In such a case, all action generally drops away. Nevertheless, in some special cases like that of Narada, one continues to work in the world in order to teach others.

> Swamiji: Sannyasins don't store up objects of attachment. If you have love of God in your heart, your activities will automatically diminish.

Ramakrishna: The Avadhuta had another guru, a honey-bee. He observed that with great difficulty over many days, the honeybee stored up a lot of honey in its honeycomb. The bee did not have a chance to enjoy the honey, because before long someone came and broke the honeycomb and took it all away. Thus, from the humble honeybee the Avadhuta learned that one should not store up objects of attachment. A true sadhu will never store up for the future. He will rely one hundred percent on God.

This is not possible for people still attached to the world. To live in the world, one must store for the future and protect one's possessions and relations. Neither birds nor sadhus store for the future, but when they have young ones, even the birds will store food for their chicks. In order to put food in the mouths of their children, birds will carry food home.

Vijay, if you see a monk carrying several bags of possessions with him, his cloth tied in ten or fifteen places where more things are being carried, don't trust that sadhu! I saw monks of that kind at the foot of the banyan tree in the Panchavati. There were two or three of them sitting there. One was removing stones from the lentils they were about to cook, and another was sewing his cloth. They were all talking about the feast that was recently given for the sadhus at a rich man's house. They said, "Oh, that wealthy man spent a hundred thousand rupees on the feast. He fed so many sadhus. We had puris and jilipis and many different kinds of sweets. And the little cakes! Oh, my, there were so many fine dishes!" (All began to laugh.)

Vijay: Yes, I saw monks of that kind at Gaya. They are called the sadhus who carry a water pot.

Ramakrishna (to Vijay): When you love God purely for God's sake, your karma flies away. Let those who are doing religious work in the world continue to do so. For you, Vijay, it is time for you to renounce all that. It is time for you to say to your mind, "Oh, mind, let us now gaze at the Beloved Mother alone, and please, dear Mother, let no one else enter there."

Saying this, Ramakrishna began to sing in his melodious voice:

> Strive, oh mind, to always keep your beloved
> Mother Shyama within your heart.
> You and I will see
> that no one else may enter there.

Then cravings and desires will flee from us,
and we will taste
the nectar of eternal bliss within
as we call upon our Mother Divine.
Bring no low desires nor worldly thoughts
with you, oh mind.
Keep far away from the bondages of the soul.
Light the eye of wisdom.
Let that be your trusted guard.
Ever vigilant and alert,
bid your guard protect you always.

Fourth Discussion

Ramakrishna (to Vijay): When you take refuge in God, you must give up all feelings of shame and fear. If I dance with the name of God, what will people say about me? This is simply egoism. Shame, fear, and false modesty -- you must renounce these ideas completely. These are bonds which bind one to the world of desires and attachments. When they depart, the individual soul is free, liberated. There are two types of souls: the bound soul, jiva, and the free soul, Shiva.

To attain to *prema*, the highest degree of devotion to God, is very difficult. One must begin with bhakti. When one can feel the same devotional attitude toward God that a loving and faithful wife feels toward her husband, it is called bhakti.

Bhava is a higher, more intense degree of divine love which is felt when one has surrendered one's all to God (one's life, mind, everything) and when one is completely filled with God's divine presence. In bhava one becomes entranced with the wonderment of God. One's breath becomes still of its own accord in natural kumbhaka. It is like when one takes aim with a rifle, and the breath stops. This is called bhava.

Then comes *prema*, and it is very rare. Those who attain to prema have ecstatic love of God. Chaintanya Mahaprabhu had prema. When you have prema, you forget the external world completely. You forget the whole perceivable universe. You even forget your own body.

Sri Ramakrishna began to sing again:

> When will that day come
> when I sing the name of God
> and can't stand up,
> when I fall down in ecstasy,
> and all the desires of the mind will fade away?
> When will that day come
> when all attachments of this world will depart,
> when all my limbs will shake
> with joy and delight, and my body dissolve
> in flames of love?
> When will that day come?

Fifth Discussion

> Swamiji: On bhava, communion with God, and kumbhaka, when the breath is totally still and contained within.

As the discussion continued, a number of Brahmin pundits entered and presented themselves to Sri Ramakrishna. There were some among them who held high positions in the government. Ramakrishna had been saying, "When you have bhava, the prana becomes still of its own accord."

Ramakrishna: At the Svayambara wedding of Draupadi, a fish was fixed to the ceiling in such a way that it was spinning around. The objective was to shoot an arrow through the eye of the revolving fish while looking at its reflection in a bowl of water. The suitor who could accomplish this remarkable feat would win Draupadi's hand in marriage. Of the many contenders only the hero Arjuna's concentration was perfect. As he took aim, his breath became still, and he entered kumbhaka. In that state he saw only the eye of the fish, not the assembly, not even the fish itself, but only the eye of the fish. When he shot, he hit the mark and won Draupadi's hand in marriage. When thinking of God with such intensity that the breath becomes still in kumbhaka, that is called bhava.

To attain to the infinite, imperishable qualities of God, just being a pundit of the scriptures is not enough, for that is a false understanding. Those who are merely pundits have no sincere devotion to God. One such pundit said, "God has no sweetness." Can you imagine? The very source of all sweetness has no sweetness. That same pundit went on to say, "We must make God sweet through our love and devotion." The Vedas say that God is of the very nature of sweetness and bliss. The shallow understanding of such pundits without realization of God is unsubstantial and worthless. It is like a child saying, "Look at those horses in the cow shed over there." (All laugh.)

Your position, your respect, your authority, and your regal nature, all these qualities which people of the world try so hard to attain, only give rise to greater egoism and attachment. They only last for a day or two. They will not remain with you. Listen to a song.

> Don't forget the Goddess Kali.
> It is She who binds us with the net of maya.
> We are killing ourselves
> for the benefit of others,
> but can we take them with us
> when we leave this world?
> Only for two days does this attachment last.
> Remember, Oh Mind, God alone is the Doer.

Only for a few days do we think
that we are acting.
Only when we renounce
all attachments and desires
do we discover that God alone is the Doer,
Maha-Kala, the Great Time, Shiva.

Sixth Discussion

Swamiji: The great medicine for egoism.

Ramakrishna: Please don't be proud, and don't be attached to money.   If you say that you are wealthy, remember that being very wealthy brings a great responsibility with it.

The fireflies that blink and glow in the darkness at evening time think to themselves, "We are illuminating the universe." When the stars come out, the egoism of the fire-flies dissolve. Then the stars begin to think, "We give the light to the universe." After some time the moon rises, and the stars are shamed by their dimness. Then the moon begins to think, "The whole world is joyful because of my light. It is I who gives light to the world." Soon, as the dawn begins to break, the sun rises, and the moon all but disappears. Before long, you can hardly see the moon at all.

If wealthy people will consider this, then they won't feel so proud and attached to their money.

A devotee named Manilal had arranged a feast for Ramakrishna and all the devotees. So at this time everyone went to his house. It was very late at night when the devotees departed and made their way to their respective homes. Om.

Chapter 9

November 28, 1883

Calcutta

First Discussion

It was the twenty-eighth of November, 1883. This afternoon at about four or five o'clock, Sri Ramakrishna was due
to arrive at Keshab Chandra Sen's garden house. Keshab was
very ill, and it was expected that he will soon leave this world
of mortals. Having arrived a couple of hours early, M. was
pacing back and forth outside Keshab's house as he awaited
Sri Ramakrishna's arrival. As he waited and paced, he
contemplated the Master's incomparable nature.

M. (thinking): He has so much spiritual bhava. Day and
night he is simply submerged in the love of God. He is a
married man, but he doesn't act like a householder. He looks
upon his own wife as the Divine Mother and always treats her
as such. He only speaks of God with her.

He performs worship and is always in meditation on the
divine. He has no worldly desires or attachments whatsoever. He believes that God alone is the one truth and that all
else is false. He has no regard for money or wealth in any
form. In his room he has no valuable belongings or utensils,
and he won't even touch such things, nor does he ever touch
women. If he were to inadvertently brush against a woman,
he would begin to shake uncontrollably, and the experience
would be very painful to him.

If one were to put money or gold into his hand, the hand
would become contorted and numb, and it would cause him
great pain. His breath would stop, and until you removed the
money from his hand, he would be unable to breathe.

M. (continuing his train of thought): Is it really necessary to renounce the world to realize God? Why should we study in school then? Why did we bother to get university degrees? If we don't marry, then we don't need to work. We don't need a job. Do we have to renounce our parents as well? I am already married. I even have children. I have the responsibility of protecting and supporting a family. What will happen to them if I renounce everything?

I also have the desire that day and night I might remain in the love of God. I see Sri Ramakrishna, and I feel "What have I done?" He is absorbed in the love and presence of God night and day, while I on the other hand am day and night thinking about my worldly affairs and attachments. Only by having met the Master, have I found a light in what is otherwise a dark and cloudy night. How can I find my way here, among all the difficulties of this life?

He himself has shown us the way, but even so we still doubt. Why can't I restrain my own temptations and desires? As I age, my energy will become less. I will no longer have the capacity to do spiritual practice. I must cultivate the love of God now by any means possible.

Ramakrishna: When one is in love with God, no account with this world remains. Then you give without calculating. When the river comes flowing down from the mountaintop, who can stop it? Who can impede that current? Who can prohibit that river from rushing to its source? Gauranga took the ochre cloth of renunciation, so enamored of God was he. So filled with devotion and love was he that he threw off all his attachments to this world and took to the path of renunciation. Lord Buddha was filled with so much love and renunciation that he left his family and kingdom to pursue his love of God. If you have even one drop of that kind of love, this world of attachments departs from us and just flies away.

The problem remains. If someone's devotion is very weak and lukewarm, then that kind of renunciation does not arise. Such individuals are bound by samsara. They have the bonds of maya tied around their waists, as it were. What is their way to salvation? Intoxicated with desires and attachments, bound by maya, they perform their work in this world with attachment. Maya wields such force that it makes mankind so infatuated and ignorant that even if a path to freedom is clearly shown, few take up the opportunity. There is a song:

> My Mother crafted Her maya so cleverly
> that even Brahma, Vishnu,
> and Chaitanya Mahaprabhu
> are incapable of fully knowing Her.
> When fish are caught in a whirlpool,
> the force is so great
> that they cannot free themselves.
> There is an insect that bores into a tree.
> Maya is so strong that it bores its own grave
> and dies in the very hole it has made.
> You see in your own life
> how strong is this samsara.
> Do you see this house?
> Look! How many people have been born here?
> How many have been taken by Death?
> This world is passing.
> Those who continually say "mine, mine, mine"
> cannot find time even to close their eyes.
> When they close their eyes in death,
> they fear that there will be nothing,
> no one there.
> And still they are killing themselves
> in pursuit of desires and attachments.
> This world is transient, and it is false.

After the visit with Keshab, Sri Ramakrishna stopped at Jai Gopal Sen's house, where he and his relatives and neighbors had been awaiting the Master's arrival. The discussion began with the subject of the householder's life in the world. Sri Ramakrishna said that the householder must hold on to God with one hand and attend to his work in the world with the other.

A neighbor: But Sir, why should I hold to the world with one hand? If the world is transitory, why should one hold on to it at all?

Ramakrishna: If you first realize God and then do your work in the world, the world will not be transitory. Listen to a song.

> Oh, my mind, you don't know how to cultivate.
> Human beings are a fertile field
> in which to grow a good crop.
> If you put the fence of the name of Kali
> around your field,
> then your crops will not be attacked
> from the outside.
> The Goddess with flowing hair
> makes a very strong defense.
> Not even the Lord of Death can approach Her.
> Now I'm playing the music
> of my mind on a single string.
> Now I can gather the crops for the harvest.
> Remember to carefully plant the seeds
> your guru has given you,
> and you will harvest the fruits of devotion.
> If you are not able to do this,
> then call on Ramprasad to come and help you.

Second Discussion

Swamiji: The means to attain God while living
the life of a householder.

Ramakrishna: Did you listen to the song? If you fence
your field with the name of Kali, your harvest will be
protected. It will not be destroyed. By taking refuge in God,
you will achieve everything. The Goddess with the flowing
hair is your true protection. The Lord of Death cannot go
near Her. If you can attain to Her, you will no longer
experience this ocean of the world as a burden. Whoever
knows Her sees that She has become all beings as well as the
whole universe. She feeds all of Her children just as Yashoda
fed Gopal.

If you can look on your parents as forms of God, She will
care for you as Her own children. Those who first know Her
and then perform their work in the world don't think of
married life as a life of desire and attachment. They become
devotees. They spend their time worshiping the Goddess and
serving the devotees. She exists in every atom of existence
throughout all of creation, so they serve all creation as God.

A neighbor named Prativeshi: Sir, one can't find such
men and women anywhere.

Ramakrishna: Oh, yes, they exist, though they are very
rare. Worldly people aren't able to recognize them. But if
you want to worship the Goddess like this, both husband and
wife must participate. If you both find that bliss of God, then
it is possible to manifest divinity through your relationship.

On the other hand, if both are not devotees, then it's very
difficult to maintain harmony, and the relationship can
become a great burden. If the wife, for instance, is not a
devotee, she will say in the day and in the night, "Oh, my

father, why did you give me in marriage to this man? We don't have good things to eat. I can't feed my children, nor educate them properly. They will never grow and prosper here. And he will never give me any golden ornaments either. What kind of comfort, Father, did you get from giving me in marriage to this jerk?" All the while the husband just sits with closed eyes, saying, Oh, God, oh God, oh God." The wife screams at him, "You just give up this craziness right now, and go out and get a decent job!"

This is the kind of bondage that exists in ordinary relationships. The children become unruly and don't listen to their parents. There are many other difficulties as well.

A devotee: Then, Sir, what is the way to success?

Ramakrishna: It is very difficult to do spiritual practice while living in the world. I don't have to explain it to you, nor count how many obstacles there are -- disease, grief, various forms of mental anguish. The children don't mind the parents, and you don't get along with your wife. Still there is a means of spiritual attainment. From time to time go to a quiet and secluded place and pray. Make an effort to attain God.

Pratibeshi: Do you mean, Sir, that we will have to leave our home?

Ramakrishna: Not completely. When you get the opportunity, go to some place that is conducive to meditation and prayer, and stay for a few days. During that time forget all your worries and relationships. Don't associate in any way with anyone who has worldly attachments and worldly gossip to share with you. If you can't stay completely alone, then seek the association of saints and sadhus.

Pratibeshi: How can one recognize a true sadhu?

Ramakrishna: Those who have dedicated their mind, their vital force, and their life to the attainment of God are the true sadhus. He who has renounced all desire except the desire to realize God in this life is a true sadhu. He is a genuine sadhu who looks on all women without attachment or desire. His attention is always indrawn. If he has any contact with a woman, he looks on her as his mother and venerates her as divine. Real sadhus always contemplate God and never indulge in worldly gossip. A true sadhu knows that God resides in every atom of existence and therefore serves all creation. These are the indications of a true sadhu.

Pratibeshi: Does one have to remain for a long time in solitude?

Ramakrishna: Have you seen small trees planted next to the footpath? For many days you have to place a fence around the little tree to protect it from being eaten by cows or goats. When it grows large with deep roots and a thick trunk, the fence is no longer necessary. Then you can even tie an elephant to that tree, and it will not break. Therefore, if you sink your roots deep, you will have no fear of the world. First try to acquire viveka, discrimination, then worldliness will not cling to you. When a person cuts open a jackfruit, he first puts oil on his hands, then the sticky juice of the jackfruit will not stick to his hands.

Pratibeshi: What do you mean by discrimination?

Ramakrishna: To always remember that God alone is true and everything else is untrue. That is discrimination. True means that it is eternal. Untrue means that it is transient, changing. One who has discrimination knows that God is the One True Unchanging Reality and that all else is transitory. With the rise of discrimination, the desire to know God begins to grow in us. If you love the transient, the world, then your concern will be for your body and for your wealth.

beings to be transient, unreal. At that time one thinks that the meat of the fruit, the divine, is the one reality. Only the meat of the fruit is nourishing and can be eaten. But the time comes when one wants to know the truth of the whole fruit. The truth is that the whole fruit consists of the shell, the seeds, and the meat. Only one who knows the whole fruit knows the belfruit in truth.

One must churn cream to get butter. Sadhana is like churning the cream. Once the butter has been churned from the cream, it becomes obvious that it was in the cream all the time. In the same way, the eternal has a transitory drama, and the transitory drama is also the eternal. One who knows God, knows that He has become all -- mother, father, son, children, friends, the animals, the good, the bad, the pure, and the impure, all.

Fourth Discussion

Swamiji: The understanding of sin.

Pratibeshi: Then is there no such thing as virtue or sin?

Ramakrishna: Yes, there is. And then again, there is not. God keeps the principle of ego in mankind. If God removes the principle of ego in a man, that man will no longer discriminate between sin and virtue, between purity and impurity. This is very rare. As long as one has not had the vision of God, the distinction between good and evil, purity and impurity will remain. You may say the words, "For me sin and virtue are equal. It is God alone who is causing me to act." But in your own mind, you know those are only words. When you do something that you know is not right, your heart goes thump, thump, thump!

After having the vision of God, some may have the desire to retain the ego in the attitude of a servant of God. In that case a devotee will say, "I am the servant, and You are the Master." A devotee with this attitude performs God's work with love in his heart. He doesn't like to associate with worldly people. It is God who makes the devotee distinguish between devotees and worldly people.

Pratibeshi: Sir, you advise us to first know God and then to do our work in the world. Is it really possible to know God?

Ramakrishna: It is not possible to know God through the senses or to think your way to God through the mind. It is possible for those with a pure heart, those who have no ulterior motives and who are free from selfishness, to know Him.

Pratibeshi: Who is there who is capable of knowing God?

Ramakrishna: True. Who is there who can know Him fully and completely? But it is enough if we get what is necessary for us, if we get that much, it is enough. When I am thirsty, I have no need for a whole pond of water. If I get one cup, it will be enough for me.

Once an ant came upon a whole mountain of sugar. Was it necessary for the ant to carry off the whole mountain? He removed only a few grains of the sugar. That was more than enough for him.

Pratibeshi: But we are so greedy! Is it possible to be satisfied with only one small cup of water? I want to know Him completely!

Fifth Discussion

Swamiji: On this world and the remedy for worldliness.

Ramakrishna: True, but there is a medicine that will cure your greed.

Pratibeshi: What is that medicine, Sir?

Ramakrishna: Aha! Stay with the sadhus, sing God's name, and praise Her divine qualities. Always pray to Her. I would pray, "Mother, I don't want Wisdom. Take Your wisdom, and take Your ignorance. Give me only pure devotion to Your lotus feet. I want nothing else."

The cure is appropriate to the disease.' In the *Gita*, Krishna says, "Oh, Arjuna, take refuge in Me. I will deliver you from all sin." He will give you divine understanding. He will take all the responsibility, and then the disease of the world will be far away.

Can you understand such things with your intellect? Is it possible to pour four quarts of milk into a one quart container? If She doesn't reveal Herself, then who is going to explain Her to you? That is why I am saying to you, take refuge in Her. Let Her desire guide you. She is the Mother of all desires. How much power does a mere man have? Om.

Chapter 10

June 15, 1884

Calcutta

First Discussion

At Surendra Mitra's garden house, a religious festival was in progress during which Sri Ramakrishna and the devotees experienced great bliss.

It was Sunday the sixth day of the dark fortnight in the month of Jyestha. This day Sri Ramakrishna had come to Surendra's garden house at Kakurgachi, a suburb of Calcutta. Nearby was Ramchandra Dutta's garden house, where about six months ago Ramakrishna had attended a similar festival. This day it was about nine o'clock in the morning, and Ramakrishna had been conversing with the devotees. There had been much merriment.

Surendra's house was in the middle of a lovely garden near the bank of the Ganga. Devotees were crowding around the house on all four sides. Within was a large central room where the professional musicians were seated. The floor of the room had been covered with white sheets, and bolsters were scattered throughout for the devotees to lean against. To the west and to the east of the central room were other rooms, and on the north and south sides of the house were verandas.

South of the house was a beautiful flower garden. A path winded through the garden to the north side of the house. On both sides of the path were other paths beautifully landscaped with orchid-like flowering plants. Another path, paved with red brick and lined on both sides with flowers, threaded through the garden to the north of the house. To the south and to the west of the house were the kitchens used to prepare food for the festival. There was a lot of noise emanating from the kitchens that day, as cooks prepared a huge meal for Sri Ramakrishna and all the devotees.

Suresh and Rama had been continually discussing intricate details of Hindu philosophy. The veranda of the garden house was densely crowded with many seated devotees. From early in the morning the devotees had been singing kirtan, and the professional singers had been singing songs depicting the gopis' ecstatic love for Sri Krishna. There was much discussion of the love of Radha for her beloved Krishna. Sri Ramakrishna was intoxicated with divine love and often lost all external consciousness.

In the main room of the house, where the kirtan was in progress, was a great crowd of people. Bhavanath, Niranjan, Surendra, Rama, M., Manimacharan, Mani Mallik, and many other devotees of Ramakrishna were present as well as a great number of Brahmo devotees.

As the singing began, they first sang songs in praise of Gauranga, depicting Gauranga's life, intense devotion, and renunciation. Gauranga had become a sannyasi, a monk. He had become virtually mad with love for Sri Krishna. Inspired by his unparalleled example, many residents of that region of West Bengal, which was known as Navadvip, had become devotees of Krishna and followers of Gauranga. The singers, taking the role of Gauranga's devotees, sang the bhajan, "Oh Gauranga, come with us to Nadia at least this once." Then they sang about the love of Radha for Krishna. Ramakrishna was in bhava.

With great love, Ramakrishna stood up and began to sing very sweetly. He himself kept the beat and sang, "Oh, my Beloved. Oh, my Beloved. Oh, my Beloved. Bring my Beloved to me. He is the Beloved of my life. Bring me to him and put me in his presence." Ramakrishna assumed the role of Radha, who was overcome by her love of Krishna. While thus singing, he lost all consciousness of the external world. His body was motionless. His eyes, focused in the middle of his forehead, were only partially open. His breath had become completely still. He was in samadhi. After a long time, he returned to waking consciousness and sang in a beautiful voice. "Oh, my Beloved, you have purchased me, and I will become your servant. You taught me about the love of Krishna. You taught me how to surrender my life. You are the strength of my life."

The kirtan continued with Ramakrishna in the role of Radha. "Oh, my Beloved, I will not go again to bring water from the Jamuna. It was there that I saw my Beloved among the flowering branches of the kadamba tree, and I lost all consciousness of the world." Again Ramakrishna was filled with bhava, and it was with great difficulty that he began to speak. "Ah, ah, ah." As the kirtan was proceeding, he was totally consumed with the attitude of Radha. "The breeze cools my body, heated by hearing the name of Krishna."

Ramakrishna began to keep the beat of the kirtan. "My ornaments have no more value to me. All those wonderful times are gone, and now bad times have come. I have lost my Krishna, and I no longer care for this world." He began to clap his hands as he improvised the line, "Won't Krishna come again?" Then the musicians sang an improvised line, "So much time has passed. Won't he come today?" The kirtan continued.

> I will die, I will die, my friends,
> definitely I will die.
> How shall I leave Krishna,
> who has every quality?
> Do not burn Radha's body.
> Do not submerge it in water.
> See that no one burns this body,

this body which played with Krishna,
Do not submerge it in water,
this body which played with Krishna,
Do not give it to the flames.
Tie this corpse-like body
to the branch of a tamal tree.
Keep it tied there so it will touch
the black of the tree.
Krishna is black, the tamal tree is black.
Since my childhood
I have very dearly loved the color black.
My body is devoted to Krishna.
See that it is not parted from Krishna.
Radha is in her last stage.
She has fallen in a faint.

Song improvised:
Radha has become unconscious
while repeating Krishna's name.
Radha, oh friend, is the play complete?
Beloved, how did it happen in this way?
Just a little while ago she was speaking.
Some friends apply sandal paste
to Radha's body.
Some friends cry with loud sounds.
Some friends sprinkle water on Radha's face.
Maybe she will return to life.
Can water bring her back to life,
one who dies from her love of Krishna?
Seeing Radha unconscious,
her friends begin chanting Krishna's name.
The name of Krishna
brought her back to consciousness.
Seeing the black color of the tamal tree,
she thinks that Krishna has come before her.

Song:
Revived by Krishna's name,
Radha's eyes wander.
But failing to see Krishna,
she weeps inconsolably.
She says, "Where is he?
Bring him to me at least once."
Seeing the black color of the tamal tree
she says, "There is my Krishna."
Seeing the peacock on the tamal tree
she says, "I see Krishna's crown."
After consulting together,
Radha's friends send a messenger to Mathura.
There the messenger meets a woman
of her own age, who asks for her introduction.
The messenger, Radha's friend, says,
"I don't have to call Krishna.
He will come of his own."
The woman of Mathura takes
the messenger to Krishna.
And she weeps distressingly calling on Krishna,
"Oh Lord! Where are you?
Oh life of the gopis! Oh beloved of our hearts!
Oh beloved of Radha!
Oh Hari, who removes the pain of devotees!
Show yourself once.
I have proudly told these people
that you will come of your own desire."

Song:
The woman of Mathura turns around
and smiling says,
"Oh poor Gopi, how can you go
in the dress of a beggar?
The king dwells beyond the seven gates.
How can you go there?

I feel shame seeing your bravery.
Oh how can you ever go there?"
The maiden cries in grief,
"Beloved Krishna! Soul of the gopis!
Save the life of this servant
by showing yourself to me.
Where are you, oh life of the gopis?
Oh Lord of Mathura, show yourself!
Oh beloved of our hearts,
Oh beloved of Radha!
Save the life and mind of this servant
by showing yourself!
Where are you, O Hari, Destroyer of our pain?
Save the honor of your servant
by showing yourself!"
The messenger cries inconsolably,
"Oh Beloved, oh life and treasure of the gopis!"

Hearing the words, "Where are you," "the life of the gopis," "the beloved of our hearts, " Ramakrishna went into samadhi. After the kirtan, the musicians were singing aloud in chorus. The Master was standing again absorbed in samadhi. Slowly regaining consciousness, he said in a voice barely understandable, "Kitna! Kitna!" (Instead of "Krishna! Krishna!") He was so immersed in the bhava that he could not utter the name of Krishna distinctly.

Radha and Krishna were united. The musicians sang songs conveying that mood:

See! There stands Radha!
There she stands with her body swaying.
Radha stands to the left of Krishna.
To the left of Krishna Radha stands
like a creeper wound around the tamal tree.

Afterwards they began chanting "Hare Krishna." The musicians sang to the accompaniment of drums and cymbals, "Victory to Radha and Krishna!" All the devotees were frenzied. The Master was dancing in the center. The devotees were dancing wildly, going around him and chanting, "Hare Krishna, Hare Krishna!"

Second Discussion

> Swamiji: On simplicity and the attainment of godliness and on serving God and serving God's creation.

After the kirtan Sri Ramakrishna began to speak with the devotees. Niranjan arrived and made a full prostration. When Ramakrishna saw Niranjan, he stood up. His face was filled with bliss and joy.

Ramakrishna: Oh, you have come!

Ramakrishna (to M.): This young man is very simple. It is impossible to be so simple unless you have performed much tapasya in your previous lives. If one is very shrewd, if one is scheming and calculating and always looking to win and for advantage, that person will never find God.

Don't you see that wherever God takes birth as an avatar, an incarnation of God, there is simplicity in the family? How simple was the nature of Dasaratha, the father of Rama. People said of Nanda, Krishna's father, "Oh, what a simple nature he had." Look, this young man, Niranjan, is of the same quality. Devotees are always simple.

Niranjan is so simple, because God Himself has become an avatar again.

Ramakrishna (to Niranjan): Look, I see a darkness in your face. Have you taken a job? Are you working in an office? Are you required to keep the accounts and to do all kinds of work? You must keep the presence of God with you, when you are in the office and performing your duties. You are doing worldly work just like other people in the world. Bu there is a difference. You have accepted employment for the benefit of your mother. Mothers and gurus are to be respected. They are the living forms of God. If I heard that a mother has had to go to work for the sake of her children, I would think that to be contemptible.

Ramakrishna (to Mani Mallik): Look, this boy is very simple, but these days he occasionally tells lies. That is his one fault. One day he said that he would visit me, but he did not come. (Ramakrishna said this looking directly at Niranjan.)

Rakhal (to Niranjan): You said you would come. Why didn't you?

Niranjan: I had only just begun visiting the Master, only a few times.

Ramakrishna (to Niranjan): M. is the headmaster of a school, and you went to visit him.

Ramakrishna (to M.): Did you send Baburam to see me the other day?

Third Discussion

Swamiji: Sri Ramakrishna and the love of the gopis.

Sri Ramakrishna was sitting and conversing with two or three of his devotees in one of the rooms to the west of the large meeting room. There was a table and a chair and a few other pieces of furniture in that room. Ramakrishna was half leaning against a bolster.

Ramakrishna (to M.): Ah, what depth of feeling the gopis had for Krishna! Whenever they saw a dark tamala tree, they became mad with love, because it reminded them of Krishna's dark complexion. Radha had such a fever of longing for Krishna that it dried up her tears as they fell from her eyes. At other times no one could notice the intensity of her longing, just as an elephant entering a large lake may go unnoticed. However, if it enters a small pond, there is a great commotion.

M: Yes, it was similar with Chaitanya Mahaprabhu. Whenever he saw a forest, he would at once remember Vrindavan. When he saw the ocean, he would think of the sacred Jumuna.

Ramakrishna: Ah! If anyone has even a drop of such love, what feeling, what joy! It is not one hundred percent. It is one hundred twenty-five percent! This is called being mad with love. In a word, you have to love God. One must be sincere and focused and really determined. You can choose a path with form or without form. If you choose a path with form, it can be the form of a human avatar or the form of a deity. If you have that intensity of feeling, then no matter what path you choose, you have achieved everything. Then the Divine Spirit, in whatever way He chooses and whatever time He chooses, will make Himself known to you. If you have to be crazy, why be crazy for the things of the world? If you must be crazy, be mad for God.

Fourth Discussion

Ramakrishna came again to the main hall. There was a bolster placed next to his asana to lean against. Reciting the mantra, "Om tat sat," he touched the bolster before taking a seat. Many types of people come to the garden house, and so he purified the pillow. Bhavanath and M. were sitting nearest to Ramakrishna. It was getting quite late in the afternoon, and no food had been served. Ramakrishna was in the attitude of a child. He called out, "Hey, no one has brought me anything to eat yet! Where is Narendra?"

A devotee came up to Ramakrishna and said, "Sir, Ram Babu is in charge. He's looking after everyone." This caused all the devotees to laugh. Ramakrishna was overcome with laughter as well. He said, "Ram Babu is in charge? Then it will be like this." A devotee said, "Wherever Ram Babu is, this is the way things go." All laughed.

Ramakrishna: Where is Surendra? Surendra has a wonderful inner nature now. He is a very pure devotee. His words are truthful, and he is never afraid to speak the truth. He fears no one. He is always joyful, always laughing. He is very giving, very generous. Anyone in need who goes to him will not come away empty handed.

Ramakrishna (to M.): Did you ever visit Bhagavan Das? What did he look like?

M: I went to see him in Kalna. He was very old and couldn't hear well. One had to speak very loudly. When I saw him, it was night, and he was lying on a carpet. Someone brought him prasad and began to feed him. As I said, he doesn't hear well. But when he heard your name, he assured me that I have nothing to worry about. He said, "The highest Divinity is present in that place."

Bhavanath (aside to M.): It has been many days since you have gone to Dakshineshwar. He even asked me about you the last time I was there. He said, "Why is M. staying away? Has he lost all desire to visit me?"

Bhavanath laughed. Sri Ramakrishna had been listening to their conversation, and he also laughed.

Ramakrishna (to M. with great love): Why haven't you come to see me for so many days?

M. became tongue-tied and couldn't give a coherent answer.

Just then Mahima came in and prostrated. Mahimacharan Chakravarti was a person of independent means who had great faith in Sri Ramakrishna and visited him at every opportunity. He posed as a student of both Sanskrit and English literature, but his weakness was for name and fame. Ramakrishna always showed him great love, though he often gently reproved him for his failings.

Ramakrishna: Oh, I see that a large steamship has arrived! Here we are only small boats.

Charity is good, but it is not appropriate to feed untruthful people. Where untruthful people and those who have committed various heinous crimes sit to eat, the earth is polluted seven feet deep. Hriday fed some people in Sihore, and among them were a lot of very bad people. I said to him, "Look, Hriday, if you feed such folk as these I won't be able to stay in your house when I come here."

Ramakrishna (to Mahima): I heard that you used to feed a lot of people. You used to spend quite a lot of money doing that. (All laugh.)

Fifth Discussion

The meal was to be served on the south veranda. Ramakrishna was waiting with many of the Brahmo devotees to begin.

Ramakrishna (to Mahima): Please go and see what is causing the delay. You can help with the serving yourself if you like.

Mahima: First, I'll bring your meal to you Sir, and then maybe I'll help with the other serving.

With obvious reluctance Mahima moved slowly toward the kitchen area, but in a short time he returned. As the meal was served, Ramakrishna and the devotees began to eat with great delight. After the meal was over, he returned to the room where a cot had been prepared for him to take some rest. He sat down on the cot, and the devotees strolled down to the bank of the Ganga to wash their hands after the meal. There they chewed some pan and then walked back to Ramakrishna's room and took their seats.

It was afternoon at about two o'clock when Pratap came in and saluted Sri Ramakrishna. Pratap Chandra Mazumdar was a physician and a prominent minister of the Brahmo Samaj. He had been educated in England and America. Though he criticized the West as being overly materialistic, he along with the Brahmo Samaj disbelieved in the Hindu deities and the worship of images.

Ramakrishna (returning the greeting): Namaskar.

Pratap: Sir, I went to the mountains all the way up to Darjeeling.

Ramakrishna: But your body is not so strong. You went to Darjeeling in order to recover, to gain some strength. You didn't get any benefit from going there. What illness were you suffering from?

Pratap: I have the same disease that Keshab died of.

Pratap (speaking of Keshab): Even in his youth he had dispassion toward worldly things. As a student at the Hindu College, Keshab was great friends with Satyendra (Devendranath Tagore's son) and through him became acquainted with Devendranath, who was also the father of Rabindranath, the poet. Keshab practiced yoga meditation and also bhakti, devotion to God. Sometimes his devotion became so great that he fainted. The foremost objective of a householder is to practice dharma, or righteousness, in their lives. Keshab was a great example of how that is to be done.

The subject turned to the egoism of worldly people.

Pratap: Even some of the women of our country have traveled to other countries. One Marhatta lady went to England to study and later even became a Christian. Sir, did you ever hear of this lady? Do you know her name?

Ramakrishna: No, but from what you say, I can understand that she has some desire for eminence in the eyes of society. That kind of attitude is not good. The concept "I am the doer" comes from ignorance. The belief "Oh, Lord, You alone are the doer" is born of wisdom. God is the doer. No one else does anything. How much pain we suffer from saying "Me, me, I, and I."

Consider the life of a calf, and you will understand. A young calf says, "Hamma, hamma -- me, me." Look at all the suffering the calf must experience. From early in the morning until late at night, it has to pull the plow. In the burning sun as well as the drenching rain, it must continue to work. After a long life of labor, it is killed by the butcher. Then it is skinned, and people will eat the meat. The skin is tanned and made into shoes which people will use to walk on the hard ground. Even then its suffering is not over. Drums are made from the skin, which are continually beaten. Finally, the entrails are taken to make strings for the cotton-carding machine. When the machine operator pulls the strings to card the cotton, it makes a droning sound, "tuhu, tuhu, you, and you." Then only is the calf liberated. It does not have to return to this land of karma any more.

When an individual comes to this knowledge, this understanding that "You alone, oh Lord, are the doer, I am not the doer, you are the Craftsman, and I am merely the tool," then all the pains of this ocean of worldliness cease. Then that individual experiences liberation and never has to return to this field of karma again.

A devotee: How does one get rid of the ego?

Ramakrishna: Until you have the vision of God, the ego will remain. If you find someone who is without ego, surely they have had the vision of God.

A devotee: Sir, what are the signs of one who has realized God?

Ramakrishna: There are indications as to whether one has had the vision of God. In the Srimad Bhagavatam it says, "There are four signs of one who has seen God. He sometimes acts like a child, sometimes like a ghoul, sometimes he is inert, and sometimes he acts like a crazy person.

Those who have seen God have the nature of a child. They go beyond the three gunas. They are unattached to any of the qualities. Sometimes they behave like a ghoul because to them purity and impurity are equal. Sometimes they are like crazy people. They have no sense of shame or modesty. They may take off all their clothes, put them under their arm, and walk around naked. Sometimes they just sit down silently and still, like inert matter.

A devotee: After the vision of God, does the ego completely go?

Ramakrishna: Sometimes God just takes the ego and completely erases it, like when we are in samadhi. In other cases, He keeps a little bit of ego and protects it. That ego can commit no fault. It is like the ego of a child. A five-year-old child says, "I, I," but he doesn't want to do anything evil or cause harm to another being. If you touch the philosopher's stone to iron, the iron becomes gold. Even an iron sword becomes gold. The form of the sword remains, but it can't cause harm to anyone. You don't injure anyone. You can't fight in a battle with a golden sword.

Sixth Discussion

> Swamiji: The worship of materiality in foreign countries. Is the purpose of life to do work in the world or to realize God? In the Kaliyuga which is best, the path of union through action or the path of union through devotion?

Ramakrishna (to Pratap): You have visited England. Please tell me what you found there?

Pratap: In foreign countries the people worship material wealth. Certainly there are a few very good people there as well. There are various kinds of people, but most are bound by rajas. I saw that very much in America also.

Ramakrishna (to Pratap): It's not true that worldly ideas are only found in foreign countries. They are present everywhere. Activity and work are only the first stage in sadhana. The highest quality, or guna, is called sattva. Sattva is the quality of balance, truth, devotion, discrimination between what is real and what is unreal, renunciation, and compassion. Rajas, which motivates activity, is the quality of desire and enjoyment. That is why we see that rajas often degenerates into tamas, the quality of darkness, bondage, and confusion. When one is involved in many works, it is easy to forget about God and higher ideals. Then all your desires and attachments will bind you.

There is no need to renounce all action. In fact, your very nature will make you act. With or without desire you will be required to act. That is why it is said to work with all your energy, but don't long for the fruits of the work. It is like performing religious disciplines, worship, japa, and austerities. You don't perform these to impress other people. They are done for the spiritual benefit alone. Work and activity in the world can be done in exactly the same way. This is called karma yoga. It is difficult, especially in the Kaliyuga. We may think that we are doing good works with no personal motivation, but selfishness creeps in, from where no one knows.

Even I did a great worship. I gave many alms to the poor, and I served those who were in need. I thought that I was doing a very noble deed without any selfishness, but from where did the idea come that I would get status in the eyes of my fellow men? At that time it was impossible for me to renounce all my selfishness. Only when I had had the vision of God could I give up all sense of self.

A devotee: If one hasn't had the vision of God, then what is the way? How can one just stop all the worldly thoughts?

Ramakrishna: In the Kaliyuga, the path of devotion is appropriate. Sing the name and glories of God as Narada and others did. With the utmost devotion and sincerity, sing the names of God, recite His glories, and always pray to God. Pray, "Give me wisdom, give me devotion, show yourself to me!" It is very difficult to unite with God through action. That is why you must pray, "Oh God, please reduce the necessity for my activities in this world. As for the work that You have given me, please let me always remember that it is only through Your grace that I have the privilege of doing work for You. Please don't give me a lot of desires to bind myself with more karma. I am unable to renounce all this activity."

When someone thinks "I am meditating," this also is karma. When you get true devotion, all the worldly thoughts will leave of their own accord. They won't want us any more. Once one has tasted sugar candy, he no longer has any taste for common jaggery.

A devotee: They say that in foreign countries the people are very industrious. They just keep acting and acting.

Ramakrishna: The objective of human life is to realize God. Karma is one part, only the first part. Karma cannot be the objective of human life.

However, karma without attachment and desire is the means to spiritual attainment. Shambhu Mallick said, "Please bless me that I can use all the wealth that I possess for the poor and for public services and for the benefit of society." I said to him, "If you can do all those things without any selfishness creeping in, then it will be fine, but it's very difficult. The objective of human birth is to attain God. It is not to build hospitals and dispensaries. If God appeared before you and said, "Ask a boon of Me," what will you say to Him? Will you say, "Oh, Lord, please give me hospitals and dispensaries to run?" Won't you say instead, "Oh, God, give me pure devotion to Your lotus feet?"

Ramakrishna: These hospitals and dispensaries are transitory. God is the only true, pure, and eternal Reality. All else is passing.

If you attain to God, you will understand that He alone is the doer. We are not the doers. Why would you leave God and go after all these other works in the world? If you can realize Him and if He has the desire, He can create lots of hospitals and dispensaries. That is why I am saying that karma is only the first step. It is not the objective of life. If you do your spiritual practice and go forward, ultimately you will know that God is the one true reality. Everything else is transitory. The realization of God is the objective of life.

There was once a woodcutter who went daily to the forest to cut wood. One day he met a brahmachari who said, "Go forward." The woodcutter went home and began to think about it. "Why did that brahmachari tell me to go forward?" Some days passed. One day while taking a brief rest from work, he remembered the words of the brahmachari. He said to himself, "Today I will go farther."

That day the woodcutter went deeper into the forest than he had ever gone before. There he found a whole grove of very valuable sandal trees. With great delight he took out many, many loads of sandalwood. He went to the market-place and became a very wealthy man.

In this way the time passed, until one day he again remembered the brahmachari and what he had been told. He thought, "Why did the brahmachari say to go forward?" So that day he went even farther into the forest, and he came to the bank of a river where he found a silver mine. He could not imagine such a thing even in a dream. He began to extract silver from the mine, and he took it to the market where he sold it. He became fabulously rich. He then said to himself, "This is why he asked me to go forward."

Living a life of great wealth, it was quite some time before the words of the brahmachari began to ring in his ears again. "Go forward!" The woodcutter began to think. "The brahmachari didn't tell me to stop at the bank of a river; he told me to go forward." So the next day he returned to the forest and crossed the river. There he found a gold mine. Later, he even found a diamond mine. Then he became as wealthy as the Lord of Wealth.

That is why I am telling you that whatever you do, go forward, and you will find better things ahead. Do not think that the light you see from a little japa is all that you will get to see. But action is not the purpose of life. If you go forward the action can become free from selfish desire. But action which is free from selfish desire is very difficult, which is why it is recommended that with sincere devotion you pray, "Oh God, give me true devotion to your lotus feet, and reduce my necessity to act; and that amount of action which you leave for me, let me perform without selfish attachment!

If you continue to go forward, you will attain to God. You will get His darshan. You will be able to converse with Him.

Now the conversation turned to the dispute as to who would occupy the dias in the temple since Keshab had ascended to heaven.

Ramakrishna (speaking to Pratap): I heard there was a dispute with you as to who would occupy the dias. Those who fought with you were unqualified people (any Tom, Dick or Harry). Everyone laughed.

(To the devotees): Look, people like Pratap and Amrita sound loudly like conch shells! The others try to sound, but no noise comes out at all.

Pratap: Great Sir (Mahashay), if you talk about making a sound, well, even a mango pit can make a sound.

Seventh Discussion

Swamiji: Instruction to Pratap and the other members of the Brahmo Samaj.

Ramakrishna (to Pratap):   Look, upon hearing the lectures of the Brahmo Samaj, one can understand quite a lot about the organization. Someone once took me to a lecture by a Brahmo preacher named Samadhyayi. He said God by Himself has no feeling, no love. It is we who give God these feelings by means of our devotion. When I heard that, I was astonished. It reminded me of a story. There was a boy who said, "In my uncle's cowshed, there are many horses." Now, horses are not kept in a cowshed. When people hear this ridiculous story, what are they to think? They will think that the uncle has no horses. (All laugh.)

A devotee: They may think that he has no cows either! (All laugh.)

Ramakrishna: How can one say that God, who is of the very nature of love, can be devoid of feeling and love? One can understand from the preacher's teaching that he himself knew nothing about God or about devotion to God either. The concept that "one is the doer" is born of ignorance. The objective of life is to submerge oneself in the ocean of God's loving presence.

Ramakrishna (to Pratap): You see, people tell me that you are a very wise and literate man. You and Keshab were just like the two brothers Gaur and Nitai. For a long time you have given countless lectures and writings. It is time to cultivate devotion to God, to go towards God.

Pratap: What you say is true, Sir. I also want to do so. I only keep working as I do in order to perpetuate Keshab's name.

Ramakrishna (laughing): You have spoken correctly. You are working to perpetuate his name, but how long will that name last? Let me tell you a story. There was a man who lived in a house on top of a mountain. It wasn't much of a house, but he had built it with great labor. One day a great storm came, and the house began to shake in the wind. He became very concerned and pondered how he could save it. He thought for a while, and then he remembered that Hanuman is the son of the Wind God. So he went out into the storm and cried out, "Oh, great and mighty Wind God, don't break down this house. It belongs to Hanuman, your son!"

Nothing much happened except that the wind began to blow even more strongly, and the house shook violently. The man thought again and had another idea. He said, "Oh, Wind God, this house has been built by Lakshmana, Rama's brother. Please don't destroy it!" Again there was no result, and the house began to shake as though it would fall at any moment.

The man became desperate with concern. He shouted into the storm, "Wind God! This house belongs to Rama himself. Don't break Rama's house. It will be a calamity for you if you do!" No one seemed to hear. The house was swaying to such an extent that it began to crack and break in various places. At this point the man had to flee away from the house just to save his own life. As he did so, he cried out, "The devil take this miserable place. It's not worth dying for!"

Ramakrishna (to Pratap):   You don't have to protect Keshab's name. Know that Keshab's fame and influence has existed only because it was God's will. All that happens is a result of the will of God. It is His will that we are all acting as we are in the present. Your duty now is to give your whole mind to God. Dive deep into the ocean of God's love. In his melodious voice, Ramakrishna began to sing a song.

> Oh, mind, dive deeper and deeper
> into the ocean of God's holy form.
> If you descend to the deepest depth,

there you will find the jewels of love.
If you search and search, you will find that
within your own heart is the blissful Vrindavan.
Light your heart with the lamp of wisdom.
Let it burn there illuminating your whole life.
Who will paddle your boat
across the ocean of this world?
Kabir says, Listen and hear me.
Keep your mind and heart
at the feet of your beloved guru!

Ramakrishna (to Pratap): Did you listen to the song? You have given enough lectures. You have had enough organizational disputes and philosophical debates. Now, it is time for you to submerge yourself in the love and the presence of God. If you dive into the ocean of God, you will have no fear of death. It is the ocean of the nectar of eternal bliss. Never think that if you say the name of God too many times you will go crazy. I told Narendra the same thing.

Pratap: Sir, who is Narendra?

Ramakrishna: Oh, he is just a young boy. I told Narendra, "Look, God is the ocean of nectar. Don't you have the desire to dive in and swim in the ocean of eternal bliss? Think that your mind is a fly, and it comes upon a whole container of honey. Where will you sit to drink the honey?" Narendra said, "I will sit on the edge and reach down and sip the honey." I asked him, "Why, why will you sit on the edge?" He said, "If I fall in, I will sink, and I will lose my life." I said, "No, that is not how it is. This is the ocean of the bliss of immortality, true existence, consciousness, and bliss. You have nothing to fear. If you submerge yourself in this ocean, you need never fear death. It is eternal life. You will not be lost by becoming mad for God."

Ramakrishna (to the devotees):   What is ignorance? Ignorance is the concept of "I and mine."   I hear many people say these words, "Rani Rasmani built this beautiful temple for Kali."   I do not hear anyone say that God made this temple for the Goddess.   You say in the Brahmo Samaj that such and such a person has been accepted into the community of the Samaj.   No one ever says that it was God's will that the person enters the congregation and becomes a member.   The idea that "I am the doer" is ignorance.   The thought "Oh, God, You are the doer. I do nothing at all. You are the craftsman. I am merely the tool in your hands."   That is wisdom.   "Oh, God, I have nothing. This is not my temple. This is the temple of the Goddess Kali. This is not my congregation.   It is all Yours and Yours alone."   This is wisdom.

When one speaks of one's possessions and feels love for those possessions, this is known as illusion.   The love of everyone and everything equally is known as compassion. To love only the members of one's own congregation or of one's immediate family is illusion.   To love only the people of my own country is illusion.   The love of all people, of all communities, of all religions and sects, of all cultures, creeds and castes, this is known as compassion.   By means of illusion, human beings are bound and move farther and farther away from God.   By becoming compassionate, we attain to God.   Sukadeva, Narada, and other great saints and rishis all practiced compassion.

Eighth Discussion

Swamiji: The Brahmo Samaj and desires and attachments.

Pratap: It is evident, Sir, that those who are able to live with you are making rapid progress toward God realization.

Ramakrishna: What is the fault of living one's life in the world? Live in the world as a servant in the master's house. This is the attitude and the spiritual discipline for house-holders. The servant maid always speaks of the master's home as her own home, and she says to other people, "This is our house." She knows very well that it is not her own house, but she feels like it is hers. Her house is in another section of the city.

She raises the master's children as though they were her own, and she says to them, "Oh, my child, how have you grown so big? My child doesn't like to eat his vegetables." She says, "my child this and my child that," but she knows all the while that it is not her child at all. It is the son of the master.

That is why I say that those who live in the world of attachments and desires should do all their duties and have all the interactions of life, but always remember that none of this is your own. Do your duty with your whole mind focused on God.

Once more the conversation turned to foreign countries. A devotee said, "Sir, is it true that foreign scholars of our day do not believe in the existence of God?"

Pratap: Whatever they may say, I do not think that any of them are atheists. They all have to admit that behind the workings of the universe there is a greater power.

Ramakrishna: Then let them say what they will. But they do believe in shakti (energy). Why should they be called atheists?

Pratap: Besides that, European scholars believe in the moral government of the world, that there will be rewards for good actions and punishment for sinful actions.

After much discussion, Pratap was about to take his leave.

Ramakrishna: What else can I say? A devotee of God doesn't remain where there is fighting and dissension and many conflicting opinions. Desires and attachments take one away from God. They do not allow one to proceed toward God. Everyone is busily engaged in enhancing the status of their own families. (All laugh.) Whether the family be good or bad, if you ask, "What kind of a family do you come from?" all will answer "I come from a good family."

Pratap took his leave from Sri Ramakrishna.

Ramakrishna (speaking of Pratap to the devotees): As of yet, the instructions that I gave to Pratap have not settled in his heart.

Ramakrishna's words about renunciation of desires and attachments and the love of God were so filled with nectar; there was no end to the instructions conveyed through his wonderful discussions. Ramakrishna began to describe the leaves on the trees in Surendra's garden and how they make a whispering sound in the southern breeze. He described this in such a way that everyone was mezmerized and deeply stirred by his words. Then everyone went back inside, still listening to the sound of the whispering of the leaves.

After a little while Manilal Mallik said to Ramakrishna, "Sir, it is getting late. It will soon be dark, and the ladies of Keshab's family are to meet you at Dakshineshwar this evening. They will be very sad if they miss you." It had been some months since Keshab left his body. His mother, grandmother, and other women of the household had arranged to visit Sri Ramakrishna at Dakshineshwar for his blessings and instructions.

Ramakrishna: Please sit down again. I can't hurry. If they arrive before I have returned, they will enjoy a walk through the garden.

After a little while, Sri Ramakrishna was about to depart for Dakshineshwar. Before leaving, he first walked through all the rooms of Surendra's house, chanting the names of God in his sweet voice to purify and protect the house. Then as he was standing there, he said, "Oh, I didn't have any puris with my meal. Please bring me some now." Puris were brought, and he ate a very small portion of one. Then he said, "There is a meaning in this. If I had left without having any puris, I would have had to return to fulfill that desire."

Mani Mallick: Well, that would have been very good, for then we would have all come with you. (All the devotees began to laugh.)

Chapter 11

Wednesday, June 25, 1884

Calcutta

First Discussion

Today was the celebration of Rathayatra, the festival of the pulling of the cart. It was Wednesday the twenty-fifth of June 1884, the bright fortnight in the month of Aashadh. Sri Ramakrishna and all the devotees had been invited to celebrate the festival at Ishan's house in north Calcutta. Ramakrishna had greatly desired to meet the pundit Shashadar Tarkachudamani for quite some time. It was decided that Ramakrishna would visit the pundit later in the afternoon, since the pundit was staying nearby at Chaturji House on College Street. It was now about ten in the morning, and Ramakrishna was sitting in Ishan's parlor with some of his devotees as well as two or three of Ishan's brahmin friends. Also present were Ishan's sons, a Bhagavata pundit, and a Tantrika devotee of the Divine Mother. The Tantrika devotee had a red mark of sindhur on his forehead. Ramakrishna was delighted to see the Tantrika worshiper and joyfully exclaimed, "He has a red mark on his forehead!"

Before long M., who had previously been informed of the visit to Ishan's, and Narendra arrived. M. bowed down respectfully to Sri Ramakrishna.

Ramakrishna (to M.):   Exactly where do you live in Calcutta?

M.:   I live near the school in Talimpukur, which is a suburb of Calcutta.

Ramakrishna: And today you didn't go to the school?

M.: I took leave because of the Ratha festival.

Narendra had been in great financial difficulty since the sudden death of his father. He was the oldest son and had younger brothers and sisters. His father had been a lawyer, but had left nothing for the family, so Narendra had been looking for a job.

Ramakrishna had previously spoken to Ishan and other devotees about helping Narendra, and Ishan knew a gentleman who held an important post in the comptroller general's office.

Ramakrishna (to Narendra): I spoke to Ishan about your difficulties.

It was about eleven o'clock, and Narendra was about to sing. The devotees were enjoying themselves and laughing. The Bhagavata pundit was entertaining the others with a humorous Sanskrit verse.

Bhagavata pundit: The poetry of the rishis is full of nectar compared to which the Vedanta, the Sankhya, and the Patanjala are very dry. Religious songs are even more beautiful. They can melt one's very soul. However, if a beautiful woman walks by, even the singer of such songs may stop, along with all his listeners, to admire her beauty. When one realizes God and attains liberation, one has no further interest in scripture, song, or women. Then one's whole attention goes to God and God alone.

Ramakrishna (laughing): His words are full of nectar!

Narendra now began to sing. As he did so, Ramakrishna rose to go to another room to take some rest. Suresh and M. followed him. Kedarnath had prepared the room which was upstairs next to the road.

M. (introducing Suresh): He is a student of the scriptures and has a very peaceful nature. When he was a young boy, we used to study together frequently. Now he has become a lawyer.

Ramakrishna: Is it possible that people like this become lawyers?

M.: By mistake some people do go down that path.

Ramakrishna: I see that Ganesh has also become a lawyer. He used to visit me occasionally at Dakshineshwar. Now he is a handsome man and chews pan, but within he is still a simple man.

Suresh (to Ramakrishna): God is infinite and beyond the grasp of the mind, yet it is said that He has created all of this. Then how can the names and qualities which we attribute to God be correct? How can we contemplate the infinity of God?

Ramakrishna: There are many mango trees in the orchard and countless branches on the trees. On each branch there are innumerable leaves. You came to the orchard to eat mangos, did you not? Then what will you gain by counting all the leaves and branches on the trees? It is to love God that mankind has taken human birth. So eat the mangos and go home. Does one visit the tavern to learn how many kinds of liquor there are there or how many bottles are on the shelves?

Why would you need to know this? One glassful is enough for you. Why try to measure the Infinite? You cannot. In the same way, you cannot know all of God's qualities and activities.

Ramakrishna was silent for a moment as a brahmin entered the room and took a seat. Then he began to speak again, referring to the brahmin.

Ramakrishna: In this world of objects and relationships there is nothing worth being attached to. If your children take a lot of ganja and other intoxicants and waste their lives in that way, you will have only problems. All the members of Ishan's family are good. One doesn't see that very often. Only two or three times have I seen such a harmonious family. Generally there is fighting and discord as well as illness, grief, and mental afflictions of all kinds. Look at the difficulties in which Narendra has found himself. His father has died, and there is not even enough for the family to eat. He is trying to find a job and cannot. What can he do? He is running around like a crazy man.

Ramakrishna (to M.): You used to visit me frequently, but now you hardly come at all. Is it because you are thinking too much about your family? What can be done? From every direction there are desires and attachments. If one has the capacity, one should never enter into this worldliness.

Ramakrishna (after a thoughtful pause): We have made a mistake. Narendra is singing, and we have left the room.

Second Discussion

It was about four o'clock in the afternoon, and Sri Ramakrishna was about to board a carriage to visit the pundit Shashadhar. The Master's appearance was very beautiful, and he was handsomely attired. He had difficulty walking on the path. If he did not have a carriage, he could not walk even a short distance. As he entered the carriage, he entered into bhava samadhi. A very light rain began to fall. It was the rainy season, and the sky was filled with clouds. The paths were very muddy.

The devotees all surrounded the carriage and walked slowly along with it. They took leaves from the trees and fashioned them into horns to make noise in celebration of the Ratha festival.

The carriage arrived in front of the house where the pundit was staying. The owner of the house and his family came out to welcome Ramakrishna and invited him in. There were stairs going into the house at the top of which was a sitting room. Ramakrishna climbed up to the top floor where he found Shashadhar waiting to welcome him.

When Ramakrishna met the pundit, he could recognize at once that he had been studying the scriptures since his youth. Shashadhar was very fair skinned and had a rudraksha mala around his neck. With great humility he bowed down to Ramakrishna and then ushered him into the room. All the devotees also entered and took their seats. All waited with great anticipation and sat as close as possible to hear the nectar that would flow from Ramakrishna's mouth. Narendra, Rakhal, Ramchandra, M., and various others were present. Hazra had also come along with Ramakrishna from Dakshineshwar.

From just sitting and gazing at the pundit, Ramakrishna became filled with bhava. Suddenly he laughed, and with great joy said to the pundit, "Enough, enough! What kind of lectures do you give?"

Shashadhar: Oh, Sir, I try to explain the meaning of the scriptures.

Ramakrishna: In the Kaliyuga the path of devotion as taught by Narada is appropriate. Nowadays who has time to study the scriptures? These days there are so many ideas in people's heads that they become beset with illness. In fact, the fever is so acute that the old herbal folk remedies are too slow. The patient will die unless the modern fever mixture is used. So I say to people, "You don't need all these mantras to perform your worship. If you do a mala of the Gayatri, it will be sufficient." You will find only a very few like Ishan who perform regular sadhana.

You can give a thousand lectures, and yet it will never change those who are filled with thoughts of the world. Is it possible to drive a nail into a stone wall? You only bend the nail by trying to pound it into stone. The wall is not penetrated in the least. If you try to pierce a crocodile's thick skin with a sword, what will happen? A sadhu's begging bowl gets filled at the four holy places of pilgrimage, but it still remains the same begging bowl. The teachings you give in your lectures don't change many people. People must evolve step by step. A little baby can't stand up all at once. It falls down and then stands up again. Slowly it learns to stand and walk.

If you attain to God, then your work will be filled with the spirit of renunciation. If you work without attachment or desire, it will lead to samadhi. Those who are filled with thoughts of the world cannot recognize a devotee of God, but it is not their fault. In the confusion of a great storm, one can't distinguish between a tamarind tree and a mango tree.

Until you realize God, you can't hope to renounce all work. How long must one perform formal worship? Until tears of love fall from your eyes whenever you sing the name of God. When you can utter the name of Rama just once and tears fall, you can know that your karma has come to its conclusion. Then formal worship is no longer necessary for you. When the fruit appears, the flower falls. The fruit is love of God, and activity in the world is the flower.

When the housewife becomes pregnant, she reduces her work somewhat. As time passes, the mother-in-law takes even more of her responsibilities until after eight or nine months she is hardly doing any work at all. Then when the baby is born, all she does it rock the baby and play with it. She has no other responsibilities or duties to perform.

As one repeats the Gayatri mantra during worship, everything dissolves. The Gayatri dissolves into Om which dissolves into samadhi. It is like the sound of a bell, "taaamm." The gross sound dissolves into the subtle, and that dissolves into the silence of God. In samadhi all the various elements of the formal worship are dissolved. In the same way, the wise renounce their karma.

Third discussion

> Swamiji: One who is a mere pundit devoid of discrimination and renunciation must practice sadhana.

As Ramakrishna was speaking about samadhi, his mind was drawn inward. In that state, his face was suffused with divine light. All the devotees who witnessed the scene were amazed. He had no consciousness of the outer world. No sound came out of his mouth whatsoever. His gaze was fixed, his eyes unmoving. The devotees had no doubt that he was in direct communion with the Lord of the Universe.

After a long time he came back to the waking state and said, "I would like some water." In an ecstatic mood, he began to speak. "Oh Mother, You showed me Vidyasagar. Mother, I wanted to meet another pundit. Is that why You brought me here?" He looked at Shashadhar and said, "Baba, increase your strength, and do sadhana for some days. You have hardly begun to climb the tree, and you think that you can already reach the fruits. I know that you are working only for the good of others." Then he bowed to the pundit.

Ramakrishna: When I first heard about you, I thought, "Is this pundit just a pundit, or does he have discrimination and renunciation as well?"

If you don't have authority from God, you can't become an effective teacher. Pundits who are devoid of discrimination are not true pundits. There is no harm if people learn from those who have received God's authorization. Then no one can defeat them in discussion. If even a small ray of light from the Goddess of Knowledge touches them, even the greatest of pundits becomes like a worm beside them.

When the light is shining, the moths are attracted and come of their own accord. Teachers who have the authority of God do not have to call people to come to them. When they are to give a lecture, they don't have to advertise. They have such an attraction that people come on their own to hear. Then kings and the rich and important people of the city come to listen and learn. They will say, "What can we offer you? I have brought mangos and sweets. I have brought new shawls. I have brought money. Will you please take something from me?"

I say to people, "Go away. I don't need any of this! I don't want anything." Does the magnet say to the iron, "Will you come to me, please?" It doesn't have to say anything at all. The iron comes to the magnet of its own accord.

If one must proclaim one's own greatness and ability to teach, then one is not a true spiritual teacher, not authorized by God. By the will of God, even a stone will become wise. Just proclaiming your own wisdom does not make you wise. True wisdom comes from God Himself and is without end. When the harvested rice is weighed, one person holds the scale while another person keeps pushing the rice onto it. In the same way, a true teacher gives the teaching, while the Divine Mother stands in the background and gives him the nectar to share. Her Wisdom is never-ending. Once you have seen the Divine Mother, can you ever be devoid of wisdom? That is why I am asking if you have received the authorization to teach.

Hazra: Yes, certainly he has the authorization to teach.

Hazra (to the pundit): Isn't that true? You are authorized, aren't you?

Pundit Shashadhar: No, I haven't received authorization from God.

The owner of the house: If you did not receive divine authorization, you are doing your duty by giving lectures.

Ramakrishna: What can one gain by listening to the lectures of one who does not have divine authorization? There was a teacher who was giving a lecture about God. The teacher said in the course of his talk, "My friends, I used to drink so much liquor. I used to do this and that." All the people listening to the lecture said, "You wretched person. What do you mean by saying you used to drink and do such things? Then your life makes a mockery of your words about God."

So you see, people who are not of good character cannot teach effectively about God and spiritual matters. A wealthy businessman from Barisal once said to me, "Sir, if you will only consent to give lectures, I too will take up the task of teaching." Upon hearing this, I told him the story about the Haldar pond in the village where I was born. Some people used to answer the call of nature on its banks. Others who came there to draw water would shout at those who did the deed, but their scolding yielded no results. The next day the same thing would happen. Finally they appealed to the owner of the pond. He sent a worker who posted a sign forbidding the defilement of the pond. Then it stopped at once.

So I am saying if ordinary people try to deliver lectures about God and spiritual life, what will it accomplish? It will bear no fruit. Only if an authorized person gives an order will people act on it. Without authorization from God, one cannot be an effective spiritual teacher. For that one needs divine power. There are many great wrestlers in Calcutta, and you will have to wrestle with them all. By comparison these devotees sitting around us now are mere sheep. Chaitanya Deva was an incarnation of God. How much remains now of what he accomplished? Can you imagine how much remains from those who are not authorized by

God to teach?   That is why I am saying first become
intoxicated with love for the feet of God.

Ramakrishna was speaking with such love that he began
to sing

> Oh, mind, submerge yourself.
> Sink deep into that Ocean Beyond All Form.
> If you search in the very deepest depths,
> you will see the treasures there,
> the jewels of love.
> If you sink in this Ocean,
> you will not die.
> You will find the Nectar of Eternal Bliss!

Fourth Discussion

Swamiji: The paths to attain to God are
infinite.   In this Kaliyuga the path of devotion is
supreme.

Ramakrishna: There are innumerable paths that lead to
the Ocean of the Nectar of Immortality. Follow any path that
you can to reach the Ocean of Immortality. The goal is to
somehow touch a drop of the Nectar of Immortal Bliss to
your lips. Whether you dive into that Ocean or are pushed in
or walk slowly down the stairs into it, the result is the same.
If one takes just one drop of that Ocean of Bliss, one becomes
immortal. There are many paths leading to that Ocean: the
path of wisdom, the path of action, and the path of devotion.
Whichever path you take, ultimately you will find God.

Those who follow the path of wisdom, jnana yoga,
discriminate by saying "Not this, not this." They believe that
the Supreme Divinity alone is real and that the entire
perceivable universe is only an illusion. By contemplating

the truth alone and denying the illusion of this world, they ultimately attain Nirvikalpa Samadhi and thus merge with Brahman, the highest divinity.

The followers of the path of action, karma yoga, perform every action as an offering to God. All actions thus become a form of yoga, and every work leads to union with God. One's work may be that of a teacher, or one may practice meditation and pranayama. That also is work. If a worldly person is able to surrender with devotion the fruits of all his actions to God and thus work without attachment to the results of his work, that is called karma yoga. The objective of karma yoga is union with God.

In the practice of bhakti yoga, the path of devotion to God, one sings the names of God and contemplates His divine qualities and infinite attributes. In this age of darkness, the Kaliyuga, it is the easiest and most recommended path. Union with God through love is the highest ideal of spiritual perfection for this age.

It is very difficult to realize God by means of karma yoga alone. Where is the time to do all the prescribed actions? In the Kaliyuga one's life span is very short. Working in the world without attachment or selfishness is very difficult. It is very difficult for one who has not realized God to work in the world and remain free of selfishness. One does not notice how subtly the selfish desires and attachments creep in.

It is also very difficult to practice jnana yoga in this time period. All life now depends upon food, and all life is short. Attachment to one's body does not leave. Without rising above identification with the body, jnana (wisdom) is impossible. A jnani declares, "I am not the body. I have gone beyond hunger and thirst, disease and old age, sorrow and joy, pleasure and pain, birth and death." If our personal experiences of pleasure, pain, disease, etc. remain strong, how can we follow the path of wisdom and become a jnani?

If I cut my hand, blood flows, and it hurts very much. A follower of the path of wisdom must say, "There is no cut and there is no pain. Nothing has happened to me." Therefore, the paths of karma and jnana are not the ideals for this age. The path of union through love of God, bhakti yoga, is appropriate for this age. Bhakti is the easiest path to attain to God. That does not mean that devotees will go to one place, and the followers of action and wisdom will go somewhere else. It means that whoever desires realization of the Supreme Divinity may attain this oneness by means of devotion.

By means of bhakti yoga, the path of the love of God, one may realize the same divinity that a follower of jnana yoga or karma yoga realizes. A devotee wants to see God with form and desires to have a personal relationship with Him, to talk to Him. A devotee does not desire the knowledge of Brahman, the Supreme Divinity.

The same God is the creator and fulfiller of all the yogas. My Divine Mother is supreme. She is the fulfiller of all yogas. When She is pleased, She can grant a devotee what-ever he desires. She gives devotion, and She also gives wisdom. If you go to Calcutta, you will see all the high society, pomp, and wealth. The only question is how to get to Calcutta. If you find the Mother of the Universe, you will find both devotion and wisdom. In bhava samadhi you will experience Her Divine Form. In nirvikalpa samadhi you will go beyond form and experience Sat-Chid-Ananda (Truth, Consciousness, and Bliss). Then the "I" of the devotee disappears into the formless God.

Ramakrishna (continuing): The devotee says, "I have great fear of all these worldly duties. In all this work in the world, selfishness becomes intermingled. Even when I try to act unselfishly, there is still desire for the fruits of the work. It seems impossible to get rid of every last trace of selfishness. If I do perform work with desire, that work will create bondage for me causing me to forget You. So please reduce my need to work in this world so that I can attain to You. Whatever activities that You give to me to do, please bless me that I can perform them without any personal desire. May my every act express only my pure love for You. Please don't increase my worldly duties as long as I have not attained Your Grace. When You instruct me to do so, I will do Your work, and if You don't instruct me, I won't do anything."

Fifth Discussion

Swamiji: About pilgrimage and giving spiritual teachings.

A pundit asked Ramakrishna how many places of pilgrimage he had visited.

Ramakrishna: I saw many places.

Ramakrishna (then, laughingly): But Hazra went further and rose very high. He even went to Rishikesh. (All began to laugh.) I didn't go that far. I can't go that high. The vulture soars very high in the sky, but its gaze is always on what is down below. (All laugh again.) Below lay attachments and desires. If you can sit in one place and acquire true devotion, then what is the necessity of going on a pilgrimage? I went to Benares, and there I saw the same tamarind trees. If you go on a pilgrimage and fail to acquire true devotion, then the purpose of your trip is unfulfilled. Devotion to God is the purpose and the only real necessity.

Do you know the nature of the vulture? There are many kinds of people. Of them some are filled with pride and speak with big words. They say, "Of all the actions prescribed by the scriptures, I have done many." Their minds are filled with worldly thoughts. They are full of selfish attachments -- money, name, fame, gain, and comforts of the body. Their minds are very busy contemplating all these things.

Pundit: I agree, Sir. Once a man went on a pilgrimage and lost his emerald but found a diamond.

Ramakrishna: You know, you can give a thousand teachings, but until the time is right, they will bear no fruit. A young child was being put to bed by his mother when he said, "Mother, when I need to go to the bathroom, please wake me up." The mother answered, "My child, when you need to go to the bathroom, that need will wake you up all by itself. Don't worry about it at all. You will get up yourself when it is time." (All begin to laugh.) In the same way, if you have a sincere desire to realize God, everything will happen at the right time.

God is a fountain of compassion. There are three kinds of doctors. The average physician examines the patient, prescribes the appropriate medicines and herbs, and then says to the patient, "Take these medicine," and he leaves. This is the worst kind of doctor. Similar to this, there are many spiritual teachers whose lectures are full of instructions, but they never bother to see if their students are applying the teachings correctly or to good effect.

Another kind of physician not only prescribes the medicine but follows up with the patient to see how the treatment is progressing. If he finds that the patient does not want to take the medicine, the doctor admonishes him and explains the necessity to follow the treatment. This is the middling type of physician. There is a middling type of spiritual teacher as well. This kind of teacher will explain at great length the need to follow the teachings and practices which he has given.

Then there is the really great doctor. If such a doctor finds that the patient is not listening to his sweet words, he will use force when necessary. He will even grab the patient by the chest and pour the medicine down his throat. In the same way, there are great spiritual teachers who in order to bring their students to God are authorized to use force if necessary.

Pundit: Sir, if one has the company of a great teacher, why doesn't spiritual attainment come of its own accord? Why do you say that wisdom must wait until the proper time?

Ramakrishna: That is true, but please consider this. Until the patient has swallowed the medicine, it could fall out of the mouth of a semiconscious patient. Then what can the doctor do? He can do nothing. The medicine must be swallowed and assimilated by the body before it can have its effect.

A teacher must examine the student carefully, and then decide what kind of instructions to give. You see, you don't discriminate between those who you accept as disciples. If a young man comes to me, I ask him first about the state of his family at home. If I find that his father has passed away and that the family is deep in debt, how can I expect him to give his mind completely to God? He cannot. Are you listening to me?

Pundit: Yes, I am listening to everything.

Ramakrishna: One day a number of Sikh policemen visited the Kali temple. As they gazed through the entrance into Mother Kali's shrine, one man said, "God is the embodiment of compassion." I said, "Nonsense! Why do you say such a thing?" They replied, "What do you mean, Sir? Why do you say that? God is protecting us. He gives us food and shelter." I replied, "What wonderful compassion is that? God is the Father of all. If the parents do not provide for their children and care for them, who will? Will the other members of the community watch over them?"

Narendra: Then should we not say that God is compassionate?

Ramakrishna: Did I forbid you from saying that? My meaning is that God is our very own. He is not an outsider.

Pundit: Your words are beyond value.

Sixth Discussion

Swamiji: Taking leave of Pandit Shashadhar.

Sri Ramakrishna wanted a glass of water. There was water right beside him but he said, "Please bring me another glass of water." Later we learned that a person of immoral character had touched the glass from which Ramakrishna would not drink.

Pundit (to Hazra): You stay with him day and night. You are very blessed.

Ramakrishna (in a joyful mood): Today was a very enjoyable day! I saw the new moon. (Everyone laughs.) Do you know why I say "the new moon?" Sita said to the demon Ravana, her abductor, "Ravana, you are like the full moon, while my husband, Rama, is merely like the new moon." Ravana did not understand the real meaning of her statement, so he was extremely happy. What Sita really meant was that Ravana's power had increased as much as it could. He had reached his limit. From now on his "moon" would wane. Rama, on the other hand, was like a new moon that would continue to wax each day.

Sri Ramakrishna now rose, and as he was leaving, everyone offered him their pranams. Pundits, visitors, and devotees all offered their pranams.

Seventh Discussion

It was now afternoon, and Sri Ramakrishna had returned to Ishan's house along with several devotees. He took a seat in the parlor on the first floor. Present there was a Bhagavata pundit, as well as Ishan and his children.

Ramakrishna (laughingly): I said to pundit Shashadhar, "You have hardly begun to climb the tree, and you think that you can already reach the fruits. Practice more sadhana and sing more to God, and then you may give your lectures."

Ishan: Everyone thinks that he is qualified to teach many people. The firefly believes that it illuminates the whole world, but all it really does is make the darkness seem even darker.

Ramakrishna (laughing): Shashadhar is not merely a pundit. He has some discrimination and renunciation as well.

The Bhagavata pundit was about 70 or 75 years old and lived in a section of Calcutta called Bathpara. He had been staring at Sri Ramakrishna with a one-pointed gaze, when he suddenly said, "You are a great soul!"

Ramakrishna: You can say that of Narada, Prahlada, Sukadeva, and others like them, but I am like your own son. However, one can also say that in one sense the devotee is bigger than God, because devotees always carry God in their hearts. (All were filled with bliss on hearing these words.) In Vaishnavism, a devotee may consider himself as large and God as small. Krishna's mother, Yashoda, bound her child Krishna with a cord so that he couldn't wander off to the other village families. You see, she believed that she alone knew best how to care for him.

Ramakrishna: Sometimes God is like a magnet, and the devotee is like a piece of iron. God irresistibly attracts the devotee. Sometimes the devotee is like a magnet, and God is like a piece of iron. God is so attracted by the devotion of the devotee that He becomes intoxicated with his love and must Himself rush to the devotee.

Sri Ramakrishna was ready to return to Dakshineshwar. In the parlor on the veranda, he turned to Ishan and the others to give these last inspiring words.

Ramakrishna: Whoever can call on God even in the midst of this life in the world, which is like an ocean over-flowing with attachments and worldly relations, is most certainly a true devotee. Those who have renounced the world will of course call on me and serve me. What is the greatness in that? If a renunciant doesn't call on me, others will speak disparagingly of him. He who calls on me even while living in the world is truly great. He is a hero.

The Bhagavata pundit: The same thing is written in the scriptures, Sir. Once the meditation of a hermit sadhu was disturbed by the cawing of a crow. When the hermit looked in anger at the crow, the bird was at once burned to ashes. Feeling proud of his attainment, he went to beg his daily meal at the house of a pious woman whose custom it was to serve her husband as God Himself. She served her husband day and night. When he came home from work, she washed his feet with water and dried them with her hair. When the sadhu arrived to beg his meal, she told him that she was cooking her husband's meal just now and that he would have to wait until she had finished. The sadhu was hot tempered and at once cursed her with these words, "There will be no welfare in this house!" The devoted wife answered, "Oh, sadhu, I am not a crow to be burned to ashes by your curse. You just wait a while, and I will soon serve you as well." The sadhu was astonished by this reply and at once became the woman's disciple.

In another story a Brahma jnani was a butcher. In the day he sold meat, and after work he devotedly served his elderly parents. A brahmin seeker had heard that a sage of the highest attainment lived in that house, so he went there in search of enlightenment. The brahmin was astonished and horrified to discover the profession of this knower of God. He thought, "This man is a butcher who sells meat that he has killed and cut up himself. How can such a person lead any-one to enlightenment?" In truth, the butcher was a great sage, and the brahmin became his disciple.

Sri Ramakrishna was ready to sit in the carriage. The family of Ishan's father-in-law lived in the house next door, and they were standing on the porch to hear Ramakrishna's parting words.

Ramakrishna: Live in the world like the ant. In this world the eternal and the transitory are mixed together like sand and sugar. The ant is able to take only the sugar and leave the sand. Be like the swan. The true and the untrue are mixed together like milk and water. The swan is able to drink only the milk of divine bliss, while leaving the water of worldly pleasures behind.

Chapter 12

October 19, 1884

Calcutta

First Discussion

Today, Sri Ramakrishna has come to attend the great autumn festival of the Sinthi Brahmo Samaj. It is the day after Kali Puja, the first day of the bright fortnight, the nineteenth of October, 1884. The festival is being held at the beautiful garden house of Benimadhav Pal, located in Sinthi, about three miles north of Calcutta. Beni Pal, a Brahmo devotee, is present, along with the whole assembly of the Brahmo Samaj.

Early in the morning the congregation had completed their spiritual practices and performed their worship. Now, at about four o'clock in the afternoon, Sri Ramakrishna arrived. His carriage drove to the center of the garden and stopped. It was surrounded on four sides by the Brahmo devotees. He proceeded to the large assembly hall of the house where a platform had been arranged upon which he was to sit. He took his seat on the platform and leaned back against the wall next to the platform. On all sides were the devotees of the Samaj. Trilokya and Vijay were present, as well as a judge, who was also a Brahmo member.

It was a bright afternoon and many flags of various colors were flying. There was a lovely lake directly beyond the open doors of the hall, and in the garden a fragrant breeze was blowing through the countless leaves on the trees. Even the bees seemed to be dancing about the flowers of the many fruit trees which grew throughout the garden.

Everyone present felt a divine bliss in experiencing all this beauty and the company of the great saint of Dakshineshwar. All were thinking, "Today we will will listen to the words of the Vedas from the mouth of Sri Ramakrishna. These are the same words of wisdom spoken by the Aryan rishis in ancient times to their disciples, who hearing them, became illumined with the knowledge of Brahman, and all the pain of their lives vanished forever. They were filled with devotion; they became incarnations of devotion, just as the twelve disciples of Jesus were devoted to their Master. Even the fish listened to those vedic words of truth. They were the same words that Krishna spoke to Arjuna on the battlefield of Kurukshetra as recorded in the Bhagavad Gita, and to which Arjuna listened with the greatest reverence." All the devotees felt that Sri Ramakrishna was about to speak to them in the same way that Krishna spoke to Arjuna, and the Vedic seers spoke to their disciples in ancient India.

Sri Ramakrishna took his seat. He sat on the beautiful raised dias and gazed at the adoring devotees that surrounded him. On this dias it was the custom of the Brahmos to give lectures and discussions on the subjects of the highest divinity. It seemed to the devotees that this place devoted to discussions about God, and now graced by the presence of the great Master from Dakshineshwar, had become the convolution of all the holy places of pilgrimage.

Trilokya began to sing:

> Mother, You are mad.
> Make me, your devotee mad as well.
> Make me mad with pure divine love for You!
> I have no other karma remaining
> except to love You.
> Take me, your devotee,
> and submerge me in the ocean

of Your divine love.
This world is a madhouse, a lunitic asylum;
some are laughing, some are crying,
and some are dancing in bliss.
Jesus, Chaitanya, and Mohammed
were all mad with your love
and danced in their madness.
They became unconscious with love.
When will I be so blessed?
When will I dissolve and be lost in You forever.
Just as the guru is, so is the disciple.
Who can understand this play of love?
You are the One who makes us mad.
You are the epitomy of Madness!
And You bless us with pure love.
I am Your servant in life after life.

As Sri Ramakrishna listened to this song he went into deep bhava samadhi; all his pranas merging into one, he went beyond the pranas, and became one with the Self. His organs of action and knowledge, his mind, intellect, ego, all were transcended. Everything was erased, vanished, only the body remained sitting there, like an inert doll. Once, Krishna entered such a state. It was at the end of the great war of Kurukshetra. As Bhishma lay dying on his bed of arrows, Krishna went into deep samadhi, and Yudishthira and the Pandavas thought, "Now Krishna also will leave his body!" And they began to cry.

Second Discussion

Swamiji: The Brahmo Samaj and meditation
on the formless God.

After some time of being in deep samadhi, Sri Ramakrishna returned to consciousness of the outer world, and began speaking to the Brahmo devotees. It is extremely rare to see someone submerged in samadhi. At first Ramakrishna's words were unclear, but as he regained normal consciousness his speech became more coherent. He spoke in a state of divine love.

Ramakrishna: Mother, I don't want to become one with the source of bliss, I want to enjoy bliss. Nor do I want occult powers. If a person has even one of the eight siddhis, that person will not find God. Krishna explained to Arjuna how to make oneself small or large at will. Then he said, "If you see someone with even one of these powers, you may know that he will not attain to Me." Why? Because with powers comes egotism; there is always much talk about one who is able to manifest occult power. And if even the smallest tail of the ego remains, God is unattainable.

There are also devotees who spend a lot of time in conspicuous worship. They wear a mala in a prominent way, they also put a big tilak on their forhead. In various ways they show others what great devotees they are, and how far they have advanced. But, if one truly wishes to go toward God it is better show very little outwardly. A true devotee who sincerely wishes to have the vision of God, calls on the Divine from within. He repeats the Name silently and his external manner is also very simple and unassuming.

What is the state of one who has attained God? Without a doubt, when one knows that his soul is one with God and that God alone does everything, that one has seen God. When one has not only seen God, but communicated intimately with Him, then one can be said to have attained to God. Such a person will have a relationship of profound love. One will have the attitude of a child of God; another the attitude of a friend. Others, with a relationship of great sweetness, will commune with God.

One person may have faith that there is fire in wood. But another brings the fire out and cooks his rice and is nourished by that rice. These are two different things. One devotee knows that God exists, but the other is fully nourished, satisfied, and at peace. There is no end to the infinite manifestations of God. God comes to one who is sincere. Increase your faith, continually call on Him with sincerity, feel the loving presence of God, and you will realize Him. Then, if it is your wish, you will attain to the formless God as well.

(To the Brahmo devotee): Be fixed in your faith. Whether it be God with form or without form, you must be steady in your sadhana. Then, when you receive God's grace, all your doubts will vanish. Those who have faith in God with form will have the vision of God, and those who believe in the formless God will also attain to Him. If you sprinkle sugar on bread it will taste sweet, and if you throw away the bread and eat the sugar plain, it will also taste sweet. (All laugh.)

The main thing is to make your mind fixed, constant. You have to pray with great sincerity. When an ordinary devotee contemplates God, do you know what it is like? There is a fine gentleman strolling in the garden, and he picks a flower and says to his friends, "Look, God has created such a lovely flower." His thought of God lasts only for an instant, like a drop of water on a hot frying pan. It evaporates immediately.

Your faith and practice must be steady as well. If not, you will not be able to find the gems and jewels which lie on the bottom of the sea of love. If you just float on the surface you will never find them. And, saying this, Sri Ramakrishna began to sing a song that intoxicated all the devotees. Everyone understood, just as though they were sitting in

Vaikuntha listening to the words of Vishnu.

> Oh my mind, submerge yourself in this ocean
> of God's wonderous Form.
> You may search the worlds from low to high
> and you may find a wealth of jewels;
> But if you look within your heart
> you will discover God's everlasting realm.
> Light the lamp of illumination upon the altar
> of your heart, and keep it shining always.
> As you row your boat
> across the sea of worldliness,
> guide your course
> with the compass you received
> at the feet of your beloved Guru.

Third Discussion

Swamiji: The Brahmo devotees and their
exclusive worship of the transcendental, formless
aspect of God. Study and true longing.

Ramakrishna: Dive deep.   Learn to love God
sincerely. Become intoxicated with divine love. You see, I
have heard about your worship, but why is it that you
emphasize the formles aspect of God so much? "Oh God,
You made the heavens, You made the sky. You made the big
ocean. You made the moon and the sun and the stars. You
did everything." Why do you talk so much about all this?
People come to this beautiful garden house, and they say,
"Oh, look at the trees, look at the flowers. What sort of
pictures are hanging inside the house?" Everyone is so
impressed, but how many desire to meet the owner of the
garden? Only two or three will go in search of the owner. If
you search for God you will find Him. Make a relationship
with God. Speak with Him, just as I am speaking with you
right now. I am telling you the truth; if you desire it, you will

see God. But, to whom can I tell these words? Who will believe me?

If you study the scriptures, will that take you to God? By reading and studying Sanskrit, you will learn about grammar, the different meters, and so forth. But, until you dive deeply you will not see God. If you dive deep into true practice, God will let Himself be known by you, and all your doubts will vanish. You may read a thousand scriptures, and memorize ten thousand verses, but if you do not dive deep with tremendous sincerity you cannot hope to see God. Just being a pundit is not sufficient. A preacher can tell others about the existence of God, but he himself will not find God. What will you gain by collecting a lot of books and scriptures? Until you receive the grace of God, nothing will avail. God bestows His grace on those with whom He is pleased. Therefore try with great sincerity to earn God's grace. When grace comes, you will have His vision and He will talk with you personally.

A businessman: Sir, does God give His grace more to one person than to others? If that is true then God is just like a businessman.

Ramakrishna: What are you talking about? All belong to God, the horse is His and the pig is His. The great Bengali philosopher, Vidyasagar, said the same thing to me. He said, "Sir, does God give more power to one person than to another?" I said to him that God is hidden within all beings. He dwells within me in the same way that He dwells within an ant. But some have a greater capacity to receive the divine power. If we were all the same, and everyone were equal in regard to power, then why do we come to see you, Vidyasagar? Do you have two horns growing out of your head? Is that why we are here? That is not the reason, you are compassionate, you are intelligent. These are the qualities which have made you well known. That is why your name is famous in Bengal. There are some scholars who are able to defeat a hundred others in argument. And there are some who hear just one verse and run away. If you do not have a special power, then why do so many people respect you and hold you in such high regard? This is also why people respect Keshab Sen so highly.

In the Gita it is written that when you see someone who is worthy of great respect because of his intellect, or musical talent, or ability to speak well in front of groups, you may know without a doubt that God has endowed him with a special power.

A Brahmo devotee (To the businessman): You should listen carefully to what he is saying and accept it.

Ramakrishna (Displeased): What are you saying? What kind of person are you? Do you mean that without testing the truth of my words and becoming convinced, he should just accept them? People like you are likely to be deceived by a fraud. Don't accept so quickly. (The Brahmo devotee felt very much embarrased.)

Fourth Discussion

The businessman asked: Sir, do we have to renounce all worldly concerns?

Ramakrishna: No, why should you renounce? You must cultivate a spiritual life within the world that you know. But from time to time you need to retire to a quiet, solitary place to call on God. You can make some arrangements to live near your home and go to your house for meals, and then return to your place of retreat.

"Once Keshab told me, 'Sir, we should live like King Janaka of olden times, but I told him that it is very easy to speak of King Janaka. But what did he do?

Though he was king, he spent a great deal of time in solitude, and performed tremendous spiritual disciplines. He stood on his head for years while repeating the name of God. So first, do something, then we will speak of living like King Janaka.

A poor villiage boy once learned to read and write in English, and subsequently became very well educated. Could he achieve this all at once? He was a poor son of the village. He would cook at someone's house and then eat the leftovers. It was with great difficulty he educated himself, and now he can read and write fluently because he did that hard work.

I also told Keshab that if a worldly man doesn't go into solitude from time to time, how can he cure the disease of worldly desire? It is like a man living in a room full of jars of pickled mangos. Look, even the thought of pickled mangos is making my mouth water! (All laugh.) If the person with the disease of worldliness eats all the pickled mangos, then his disease will only increase. So he must stop eating them, and he must go to a place away from the pickles.

If you remain continually in contact with objects and relationship of your desire, what will happen? The taste for desires has no end. For men, women and wealth are the pickled mangos. The taste for worldly desire is a disease that makes us beggers. So it is necessary to go to a solitary place away from objects of desire for some time and do spiritual practice. Then you can return to your environment, and desires and attachments will not bind you. A time will come when you will be free from all attachments just like King Janaka. But at first you must be very careful. First, you must retire into solitude and pray to God with a longing heart.

When we plant a sapling of the peepal tree we put a fence on all four sides so that goats and cows will not destroy the plant. But when the roots become very strong and the tree grows high, there is no need to protect it any longer. Then you could even tie an elephant to that tree and have no worry at all. If you do spiritual discipline in solitude you will acquire true devotion to the lotus feet of God. Your strength will increase, then you can go to your home and interact with all the concerns of your world, and no desire or attachment will bind you.

The practice of devotion is like churning cream into butter. The knowledge of God is the butter. You can take that butter and put it into the water of samsara, and it will float on the surface. But if the mind is not purified by devotion, it is like mixing the unchurned milk with water. The milk becomes diluted and is lost. Such a mind cannot remain unaffected by worldly attachments.

> Shree Maa says: Maybe we need to call a swan at such a time; the swan is the only one that has the discrimination to take the milk and leave the water.

From worldliness we want to achieve godliness. With one hand hold tightly to the lotus feet of God, and with the other do the work of the world. When you have earned your holiday from the work in the world, then with both hands you can hold onto God's feet. Then once again you will remain in solitude and you will only think of God and serve God.

The businessman was very pleased, and said, "This is a very beautiful talk. I would like to do spiritual practice in a solitary place, but I forget to. Sometimes I think that all at once I will become a King Janaka." (Sri Ramakrishna and the others laugh.) "But, when I hear that there is no great necessity to renounce the world, and that I may stay home and find God, my mind becomes very peaceful and I feel very happy."

Ramakrishna: Why should you leave your home? Wherever you may be in time of war you have to fight the battle. You have a battle with your senses, hunger, thirst, all these various desires have to be fought with. You can fight from within a worldly setting. In the Kali Yuga one's life depends on food. If you have nothing to eat, your desire for God will dissolve. One person said to his mother, "Mother, I will renounce the world and become a sadhu." But his mother was very wise and she said, "My son, why do you want to tour and wander all around the world? If you don't have to beg at ten houses to fill your stomach then go ahead. But why should you renounce? There is a great advantage to staying at home. There you will have regular meals, and if you become ill there is someone to care for you." King Janaka, Vyasa Deva, and Vashishtha were all house-holders who lived in the world and still attained to God. They drew their swords and fought the battle. On one side was spiritual wisdom and on the other karma, activity in the world.

Businessman: But Sir, how will I know when I have attained to spiritual wisdom?

Ramakrishna: When you have achieved true wisdom, then you don't see God as far away from you. You know Him as one with your true Self. God resides in the hearts of all beings; you can see Him in your own heart. He is within all, and whoever will sincerely search will find Him.

Businessman: Sir, I am a sinner. How can I say that He is within me?

Ramakrishna: Why do you people all talk so much about sin? I understand that this is the Christian view. One man brought a Bible, and I listened to a little of it. But I only heard that one word over and over: sin and sin and sin. When you repeat the name of God, when you say the name of Hari or the name of Rama, leave off all this talk of sin. If you have faith in the greatness of the name of God, that is sufficient to chase away any sin.

Businessman: But Sir, how does one attain such faith?

Ramakrishna: You must learn to feel the presence of God. One of your own songs says, "Oh God, is it necessary to do austerities and worship if I feel sincere love for You?" But who loves God for Himself? Countless people cry to God because they have lost their health, or their wealth, or because they have problems at home. But who cries to God just to know God? Who cries to God for Himself?

Fifth Discussion

Trailokya: Sir, when do we have time for spiritual practice? We have to work for the English rulers.

Ramakrishna: If you turn over your responsibilities to a trustworthy person, he will manage everything correctly. So, with great faith, give all your responsibilities to God. Then, with no worries in your mind, just do whatever work He has assigned to you.   Kittens do not worry about what is expected of them; they just cry out, "Mew, mew!" Wherever the mother cat places the kittens, there they stay. They just cry "Mew, mew." When she puts them somewhere to sleep, they remain in that place and continue to call to their mother.

Businessman: Sir, we are householders, how long must we continue to perform our duties in the world?

Ramakrishna: You have responsibilites no doubt. You must care for your children until they are grown. You have to supply your wife with all her needs, her clothing, her ornaments. You would be called a heartless person if you didn't do so.   Sukadeva and other sages were all compassionate.   One who is not compassionate is not a human being.

Businessman: How long must one take care of one's children?

Ramakrishna: Until they have attained responsibility and are independent. When the little bird has grown big, the mother pushes it out of the nest. (All laugh.)

Businessman: What is my responsibility to my wife?

Ramakrishna: As long as you live, speak to her about spiritual matters and practice righteousness. Care for her needs as long as you live, and, if she is faithful, arrange for her livelihood after your death. The case is different how-ever, if you become mad with love of God. Then you would have no further responsibilites.   God would take your responsibilities. You would not have to think of tomorrow. When one becomes intoxicated with love of God, God Himself will care for your family. If a wealthy landlord dies, the court will appoint a guardian to care for the estate and any minor children there may be. But these are legal matters; you know them all.

Shree Maa: Better you should have a goal before you get married, and live your lives with that sankalpa.

Businessman: Ah!   That is a wonderful statement: "Those who comtemplate God with one-pointed devotion become intoxicated with God and mad with love. Then God

Himself will take on their responsibilities. Of His own accord, all their responsibilities will fall to God." And when will this situation come about? Whoever attains such a position is very fortunate indeed!

Trailokya: Sir, as long as we are bound to this world of objects and relationships, is it ever possibile to realize such a state of bliss? Can we ever attain God?

Ramakrishna (Laughing): Why not? You can sing 'Doe Rae Mi'. (All laugh). If you keep your mind steadily focused on God, you will still have the world around you; it will continue to exist. Where would it go? What is the result of doing sadhana while still in the world? It is the same realiziation of God...liberation while living.

Trailokya: What are the signs that a person living in the world has attained to God?

Ramakrishna: Your very body becomes alive with the name of God. Your body tingles when you hear the name of God, and tears fall from your eyes. As long as worldly thoughts remain, as long as you are filled with attachments and desires, your sense of the body will not leave you. You will always be thinking, "I am the body." But to the degree that your worldly thoughts diminish, to that degree you will search for the true wisdom of the soul, and there will be a corresponding reduction of your attachment to the body. When worldly thoughts completely vanish, the wisdom of the soul is attained. Then you will have discrimination, and the understanding that the soul is very different from the body.

Until all the water dries up in the green coconut, the meat does not separate from the shell. When the water has dried up, you can shake the coconut and hear that the kernel inside is separate from the shell outside. The description of one who has attained the highest degree of divine wisdom is that he had become like the kernel of the coconut, separate from the shell. His awareness of the shell, his attachment to the body, completely vanishes. He is not concerned with the pleasures of the body, and he does not desire or pursue them. He conducts himself as a great renunciate, one who is liberated while living. (Quoting from a text): "The devotee of Kali is a jivanmukta and dwells in eternal bliss."

When tears fall from your eyes while repeating the name of God, you may know that attachments and desires are coming to an end and God realization is not far off. If the matchstick is dry, one strike of the match will cause it to ignite. If it is wet, you may strike it fifty times and nothing will happen. You will just have to throw away the matches. If you are sitting in the midst of worldly thoughts, your matchsticks are wet. Your mind is saturated with the juice of desires and attachments, and you will not be able to ignite the Divine within you. You may try a thousand times, it is just wasted effort. But, as soon as the water of worldly thoughts dries up, your matchstick can ignite.

When you know beyond a single doubt that She is your Mother, it can happen immediately. She is not someone else's Mother, She is ours. She is our own. You must call on Her with great sincerity and great intensity. The child is pulling on the mother's cloth, asking for money to buy a kite. The mother is talking and gossiping with the other ladies. At first, the mother does not want to give any mind to the pleas of her child. She says, "No! Your father has said that you cannot have a new kite. Maybe when he comes home we can talk about it. When you get a new kite you run around out of control, so he said, 'No kite.'" But the child begins to cry, and will not stop for anything, so the mother says to the other ladies, "Please wait a moment, I have to attend to this child." Then she takes out her keys and opens a box and gives her little child money to buy a kite.

So, you must complain to your mother. Certainly she will give you what you want if you persist. I told this to a group of Sikh businessmen who once came to the Kali temple at Dakshineshwar. They were sitting in front of the temple, so I joined them. We sat down and began to talk. They said, "God is the manifestation of compassion." I said, "What kind of compassion do you mean?" They said, "Why sir, He always sees our needs and gives us what we need to live. He gives us the economic necessities by which we can live in this world. He feeds and clothes us." I answered, "What kind of compassion is that? If your own parent doesn't care for His own child, what then? Must the other people of the neighborhood do so?"

A businessman: Then Sir, should we not feel that God is compassionate?

Ramakrishna: I did not say that. I only mean that She is our very own. You can even force your demands on your own mother.

Sixth Discussion

Egotism and the businesman

Ramakrishna (To the businessman): If you are full of pride and worldly attachments, you cannot have spiritual wisdom. The worldly ego gives rise to tamas, spiritual darkness, and it is born from ignorance. Because of this self-centeredness, we are unable to see God. The various expressions of the worldly ego are worthless; the concepts, "my body," and "my wealth" -- none of this will remain.

Once, a crazy person came and saw the clay image of the Goddess that is made and worshiped for the few days of the Durga Puja. He saw how profusely She was decorated with silks and ornaments, and said, "Hey Mother, you may like to wear all those fancy clothes and jewels now, but even so, they are going to take you to the Ganga in a couple of days and throw you in." (All began to laugh.) So I am saying to you that whatever you may become in this life, it is only for a few days. Knowing this, one should renounce vanity and worldly desires."

People have various characteristics which are determined by different mixtures of the three gunas, sattva, rajas, and tamas. Egotism, sleep, excessive eating, lust, anger, and so forth, are the expressions of a preponderance of tamas.

Those with a preponderance of rajas, feel that they have much to accomplish in this world. They are very concerned with their apparel and personal appearance. Their home must be clean to an excessive degree. In the parlor and sitting room there must be a picture of the Queen of England. When they pray to God and perform worship, they wear a fancy silk cloth or sari, a rosery with alternating gold beads. If a guest comes to see their worship hall, they say, "Oh, there's so much more to see! Come and see this; come and see that." Their altar is made of marble and is very elaborately decorated. They make liberal gifts and donations to charity in order to show others the extent of their devotion.

People with a preponderance of sattva are very peaceful. They wear whatever clothing is convenient and available. They work only enough to support their simple needs and lifestyle. They prefer to remain independent by not accepting gifts or loans from others. There is nothing extravagant or for show in their home. They do not dwell continually on what their children must become in life in order to uphold the family name. They are not concerned about their personal status or social position. They spend all their time in contemplation of God. Their meditation and devotions are done in private, with no show or display. If they make charitable gifts, they do so out of the public view. They meditate in their room in the early morning. When others see them later, they suppose that they hadn't slept well that night and so were late in rising.

Sattva is the last step on the stairway to the roof. The next step is the roof. When one has become sattvic to this degree, you can know that he is very near to having the vision of God. If he goes only a little further he will find God. (To the businesman): You Brahmos believe that everyone is equal, but now you can see that there are many varieties of human nature.

And there are others as well. There are a special few who are called nitya siddhas, eternally free. They are never caught is the net of this world. There are also those who have struggled hard and attained liberation. And of course there are those who are bound to the world. Sages like Narada and Sukadeva are the nitya siddhas, the eternally free. They are like a large steamboat that can carry many human beings or even elephants across the river.

Those who are trying to become liberated are like fish who have been caught in a net and are being dragged to shore. With great earnestness and determination they struggle to free themselves; and a few among these are able to leap over the net and become free.

The bound souls are bound by their desires to this world, this samsara. Their consciousness is not clear, and they have no ideal beyond the pleasures of the world. They are caught in the net and they do not even know of their danger, so they do not try to escape. If they happen to come upon someone speaking of God, or someone repeating God's Name, they run away. They feel that they have more important things to do. They say, "I will repeat the Name of God at the time of death. Why should I spend time doing it now? I have many duties to attend to." But, when the hour of their death does arrive, rather than thinking of God they say to their children, "Turn down the flame in those lamps! You are burning too much oil." The children and wife are standing nearby, weeping, and the dying man can only think, "What will happen to them when I am gone?"

Bound souls suffer greatly in their lives. They are like the camel which eats the leaves of the thorn tree. Even though its mouth is cut and bleeding from the thorns, it continues eating from the tree. In this world everyone is suffering. Not a single home is without grief. One man has lost his child to death, and yet he continues to have more children every year. He gives his daughter in marriage, and it nearly bankrupts him, and there are more daughters on the way. He says, "What can I do? It is just my fate." If the family goes on a pilgrimage to a holy place, he has no time to contemplate God, he is constantly busy watching that the children behave respectfully, and to see that nothing is lost. When they reach the temple, proud of his family and worldly success, he makes large donations to the temple deity, flaunting his wealth in order to impress others. In this way, time passed, and his life draws to its close.

Bound souls are servants to their own stomachs and to the needs of their families. They are not servants of Truth. They are reduced to acquiring life's necessities by any means. Others contemplate God and become intoxicated with the love of God in their spiritual practices. Bound souls look at them and say, "They are crazy people!" (To the business-man) So look at how many kinds of human natures there are. You say that are all equal, but some have more of the divine power and some less.

At the time of death bound souls cannot remember to repeat the name of God. With attachment and desire for the objects and relationships of the world, on their deathbed they speak only of the world. They may have done some japa in their life, and had a bath in the Ganga, and gone to a place of pilgrimage, but what of that? These were only formalities. At the time of their death their selfish attachments and desires will allow them to think only of this world. They cannot remember God.

A parrot can very easily learn to repeat the name of Rama or Krishna, but when the cat catches it by the throat it forgets the holy name and can only squawk. In the Gita, it says that what we are thinking at the time of death will determine our next life. Bharata, a great king, had become attached to a pet deer, and could only remember his pet deer as he left his life. So he took birth as a deer. If you are able to comtemplate God at the time of leaving your body, you will go to God. You won't have to return to this world again.

A Brahmo devotee: Do you mean to say, Sir, that even if we have meditated on God during our lifetime, that, if at the time of dying we are unable to do so, we will have to come back to this world of pain again? Why don't we get credit for the times when we did contemplate God?

Ramakrishna: No doubt that in your life you think of God. Many individuals think about God. But they don't have full faith and so they forget. They become bound to this world again by selfish desire. It is like when you give a bath to an elephant; after the bath the elephant at once lies down in the mud again. The mind also loves to lie in the mud of this world. But, if you can tie the elephant in a clean place, it won't become muddy again.

Those who can think of God at the time of their death have purified their mind. Selfish desires do not arise in such a mind. If you do not have a burning faith in God, then you will have to enjoy the fruits of many different kinds of experience. People say, "When you take a bath in the Ganga, all your sins are washed away." But, in fact, they merely fly up, like crows, into the trees that grow along the bank of the river and wait. Then, when you have completed bathing and come back to the shore, all your sins fly back down to you again. (All laugh.)

When you leave your body, you should remember God. But you must prepare for that moment in advance. The way to do so is to practice. If you practice thinking of God your whole life, you will surely remember Him, even at the time of death.

Brahmo devotee: Your words are very beautiful, Sir. You have said many worderful things.

Ramakrishna: Oh, these are just mere words. But do you know my inner feeling? "I am the tool, and She is the craftsman. I am the house, and She is the resident. I am the car, and She is the driver. I am the machine, and She is the mechanic. Just as She guides me, just so do I move. She alone causes me to act, and so do I act.

Seventh Discussion

Ramakrishna singing in bliss

Trailokya sang again, accompanied by drums and cymbals. Sri Ramakrishna danced intoxicated with God's love. While he was dancing he went into samadhi several times. He was even in the state of samadhi while standing. His body was completely still, his eyes were steady, and his mouth was smiling. He was standing with one hand on the shoulder of a beloved devotee. Coming out from samadhi, again he danced like a mad elephant. When he regained his outer consciousness, he improvised words to the music.

Mother, dance around
the gathering of devotees.
While You dance, oh Mother!
make them dance.
(I repeat,) oh Mother! Dance at least once
in the lotus of my heart.
Dance, oh the Energy of the Supreme Divinity!
with your world-bewitching beauty.

What an indescribable scene! The divine child, intoxicated with love, was dancing with his heart given to Mother! The Brahmo devotees dancing around him were attracted like pieces of iron by a magnet. Chanting the names of the Supreme Divinity again and again, the names of the Divine Mother, they were filled with bliss! Many wept like children crying, "Mother! Mother!"

After the singing ended, they all sat down. The group's evening worship had not yet been performed. Suddenly all the rules had been forgotten in the bliss of singing the divine names. It had been arranged that Vijay Goswami would sit on the dias that night. The time was nearly eight o'clock in the evening.

All were seated, including Sri Ramakrishna. Vijay was in front. Vijay's mother-in-law, grand-mother, and other female devotees wanted to see Ramakrishna and talk with him. They sent a message to him. He went into a room to meet them.

After some time he returned and told Vijay, "What love of God does your mother-in-law have! She says, 'There is no need to tell you about the world. A wave goes and another follows!' I said, 'What's that to you? You have acquired wisdom.' Your mother-in-law replied, 'What wisdom have I got? I have not yet gone beyond vidya maya and avidya maya. It is not enough just to go beyond avidya maya; one has to go beyond vidya maya as well. Then only will true knowledge dawn. Don't you, yourself, say that?'"

While this conversation was in progress, the respected Beni Pal made his appearance.

Beni Pal (to Vijay): Sir, now please get up. It has already become very late. Please begin the worship.

Vijay: Sir, what is the necessity for more worship? In your place the desert is served first and then comes the main course.

Sri Ramakrishna (laughing): Devotees make arrangements according to their own capacities. The sattvic devotees will offer rice pudding. The rajasic devotees will offer fifty dishes to the Deity. The tamasic devotees will offer sacrifices of goats and other things.

Eighth Discussion

> Swamiji: Thakur gives advice to Vijay when he lectures in the Brahmo Samaj on the duties of the teacher, reminding him that God alone is the guru. Vijay was contemplating whether or not he would conduct worship on the dias.

Vijay: If you accept, I will teach from the dias.

Sri Ramakrishna: If you have no ego then it will be accomplished. It will be fine if you don't have any superior attitude like, I am lecturing while you are the listener. Is ego the product of wisdom or ignorance? Who is free from ego has wisdom. Rain water drains off from a high place and collects in a low place.

As long as a man has ego, he does not have wisdom or freedom. He has to come back to manifested existence again and again. The calf bellows, "Hamba, Hamba, (I, I,)." That is why it suffers so much. It is slaughtered by the butcher. Then shoes are made out of its hide. The hide is also used to make drums, which are struck frequently by sticks. There is no end to its misery. Finally the entrails are made into the strings of a carding machine. When the strings of the carding machine sing the sound of "Tuhun, Tuhun, (you, you)" then comes relief. It no longer says, "I, I." It says, "You, you." It means, "Oh God! You are the doer. I am not. You are the craftsman, I am the tool. You alone are everything.

The words guru, father, master, prick me like thorns. I am His son, I am always a child. How can I be a father? God is the doer, I am not. He is the craftsman, I am the tool.

If somebody addresses me as Guru, I say, "Get away, you scoundrel! How can I be a guru? There is no other guru except Satchidananda, truth, consciousness, bliss. There is no other refuge but Him. He alone is the ferryman who takes us across the ocean of worldly existence.

(To Vijay): It is very difficult to act as a teacher. It causes harm. Finding that even a small group people respect him, he crosses his legs and says, I will talk and you people listen. This is a very bad attitude. That is all it takes! Just a little respect, and then people will say, "Ah, Vijay Babu spoke very well. The man is so wise!" I pray that She does not make me wise in this way. I say, "Mother, you are the craftsman, I am the tool. Just as you cause me to do, just so I perform. Just as you make me speak, just so I speak."

Vijay (humbly): If you give me your permission, I will sit on the dias.

Sri Ramakrishna (laughing): What shall I say? The Moon is the Uncle of all the children. You ask Him. If you are sincere there is nothing to be afraid of.

Requested again by Vijay, Sri Ramakrishna said, "Go and complete the system of worship. If there is sincere love for Him, it will be all right.

Vijay then sat on the dias and performed the worship in accordance with the rules of the Brahmo Samaj. During the worship Vijay called, "Mother, Mother," again and again, which melted the minds of all.

After the worship was completed, arrangements were made for feeding the devotees. The mats and carpets were removed, and plates made of leaves were placed on the floor. All the devotees took their seats. Ramakrishna also sat down and was offered luchis, kacuri, papad, and various sweets prepared by Beni Pal, along with yogurt, sweet rice pudding, and other offerings which were made during the worship. With great bliss they partook of the consecrated food.

Ninth Discussion

> Swamiji:After realization of the highest wisdom there is no distinction between Mother, Kali, and Brahman: .

After dinner they chewed on pan with betel nuts. They all made preparations for returning home. Before leaving Sri Ramakrishna engaged in a conversation with Vijay. M. was also present.

Sri Ramakrishna: You prayed to God addressing Him as Mother. This is excellent! It is said that a mother's attraction for the child is stronger than the father's. One can apply pressure on the mother, but not on the father. Once they were taking wagon loads of money from the estate of Trailokya's mother, accompanied by many guards wearing red turbans and armed with sticks. Trailokya had been waiting on the road with his people, and snatched all the money away by force. One can apply a great deal of force when it is about his own mother's wealth. They say that it is not so easy for a mother to make a case against her son.

Vijay: If Brahman is Mother, is It in that case with form or without form?

Sri Ramakrishna: That which is Brahman is also Kali, the Mother, the energy. When it is inactive, it is called Brahman. When it creates, preserves and transforms, and performs all these actions, we call it shakti, or energy. Still water is an example of Brahman. Water when it is moving is an example of shakti or Kali. What does Kali mean? She who communes with Mahakala (Brahman) is Kali. Kali has form and She is also without form. If you believe in formless divinity, meditate on Kali as that. If you meditate on any particular form with stillness, She will let you know what She is. If you reach Shyampukur you will also be familiar with Telipara.

Then you will realize that God is not just pure existence. He will come near you and talk to you, just as I am talking to you. Have faith and everything will come to you. Another thing: if you believe that God is formless, believe it with firmness. But do not be dogmatic. Never say that He can be only this and not that. Say, "I believe he is formless and that he can also be so many things. He only knows what He is. I do not know. I do not understand. Can the nature of God be understood by the ounce of intelligence that man has? Can a pot which holds two quarts of milk contain a gallon? Only if He reveals himself to his devotee and makes him understand from His grace, then alone one can know. Otherwise one cannot know."

> Swamiji: That which is Brahman, is also energy, and that again is the Divine Mother.

Ramprasad says, The truth is
who I regard as Mother,
Should I reveal this secret in the market place?

Oh mind, grasp it from the hints I have dropped.
Shyampukur and Telipara
are neighboring places.
Who I regard as truth, that is,
it is me who conceives the truth.
It is that truth that I address as Mother.

Again Ramprasad says the same thing, "Knowing the secret that Kali is Brahman, I have given up both dharma and adharma (the ideal of perfection and its opposite)."

Adharma means actions contrary to the ideal. Dharma means actions that bring us to perfection. As examples, one should give to charity, one should feed the learned. These are righteous acts of dharma.

Vijay: What remains when both dharma and adharma are given up?

Sri Ramakrishna: The pure love of God. I said to Mother, "Mother! Here is your righteousness and here is your unrighteousness. Take them both. Please give me pure love. Here is your knowledge and here is your ignorance. Take them both. Please give me pure love." You see, I did not even ask for knowledge. I did not ask for public recognition either. When you renounce both dharma and adharma, what remains is pure love: pure, desireless and unselfish love.

A Brahmo Devotee: Are they different -- He and his energy?

Sri Ramakrishna: Upon the attainment of full knowledge one realizes their unity, just as the jewel and its luster are not different from each other. If one thinks of the luster of a jewel, one cannot but think of the jewel. Again it is like milk and its whiteness. You have to think of the other as soon as you think of the first one. But this knowledge of non-duality does not arise before the realization of true wisdom. Samadhi is attained upon the realization of true wisdom. One goes beyond the twenty-four principles. Therefore, there is no longer the principle of ego.

What happens in samadhi cannot be put into words. One can only give a faint hint after coming out from it. When I repeat, "Om, Om," after coming out from samadhi, I have come down at least a hundred cubits. Brahman is beyond Vedic principles. There exists neither I nor You.

As long as I and You exist, as long as there is the feeling that "I" am praying or meditating, so long also exist the feeling You, God, are listening to my prayers, and also the awareness that God is a specific being. The feeling that You are the master, and I am the servant, You are the whole, I am a part, You are the Mother, I am the child, will remain. This feeling of difference is as follows: I am one and You are another. God himself makes us feel that way. It is on account of this that we recognize the differences between man and woman, light and darkness, and so on. As long as there is the perception of this difference, one has to admit energy or a personal God. It is He who has installed the ego in us. You may reason a thousand times, but the ego never disappears. And as long as ego exists, we maintain this individuality.

Therefore, as long as the ego persists, as long as there is the feeling of difference, one can never assert that Brahman is formless, without attributes. One has to admit Brahman with attributes. The Brahman with attributes has been declared by the Vedas, Puranas and Tantras as Kali or the primary energy.

Vijay: By what means can one have vision of this primary energy and the knowledge of Brahman without attributes?

Sri Ramakrishna: Pray to Him with the sincerity of your heart and cry. In this way your heart will be purified. You will see the reflection of the sun in clear water. You will see the Brahman with attributes, the primary energy, in the reflection of the ego. But the mirror must be wiped perfectly clean. There will not be a clear reflection if it is dirty.

If you seek the knowledge of Brahman without attributes, first perceive the reflected sun and then see the real sun. If you pray to the same Brahman with attributes who listens to prayers, He will give you the knowledge of Brahman without attributes. Because He who is the Brahman with attributes, is himself the Brahman beyond attributes. That which is energy is also Brahman. The realization of non-duality comes upon the attainment of complete wisdom.

Mother also bestows the knowledge of Brahman without attributes. But a true lover of God does not crave for the knowledge of Brahman without attributes.

There is another path: the path of union through knowledge. It is a very difficult path. You who belong to the Brahmo Samaj are not actually followers of the path of knowledge. You are devotees, lovers of God. Those who follow the path of knowledge believe that Brahman is the reality. The world is unreal, like a dream. I, you and everything else are like a dream.

God is the inner knower of all. Pray to Him with a pure mind and sincere heart. He will allow you to understand everything. Renounce your ego, take refuge in him. You will find everything.

> Oh mind! Dwell within yourself,
> Do not go into anyone else's house.
> Whatever you will want,

You will find without moving.
Search in the sanctum within you.
The philosopher's stone, God within,
Is the supreme treasure.
It can give whatever you ask for.
So many gems lie strewn
All over the outer court
of the philosopher's stone.

Whenever you meet with people who do not belong to your group, love them all. Be one of them in their company and never entertain any malice toward them. Don't maintain any conflicting attitudes saying, "He believes in God with form, and does not believe in a formless God. That one believes in God without form and does not believe in God with form.

This one is a Hindu and that one a Muslim, and he, again, is a Christian. God has given different understanding to different people. Know that people are of different natures. Mingle with all with this understanding, and love them all. Retiring into your inner sanctum afterwards, you will enjoy peace and bliss.

Light the lamp of wisdom in your room,
See the face of the Divine Mother,
the embodiment of Brahman.
See your true Self within your own room.

When the cowherds go to the fields to graze their cattle, the cattle all get mixed up. They all form one herd. But when they return to their sheds, they become separated again. They remain separate alone in their sheds.

Swamiji: Sannyasins should not save for the future. This was a good use of resources by Beni Pal.

It was after ten o'clock at night when Sri Ramakrishna got into a carriage to return to the Kali Temple. With him were a few accompanying devotees. The carriage was standing under a tree in deep darkness. Beni Pal came forward with some luchis and sweets to send with Ramakrishna for his nephew Ramlal.

Beni Pal: Sir! Ramlal could not come. With your permission I want to send some Prasad for him.

Sri Ramakrishna (anxiously): Oh Babu Beni Pal! Please do not send those things with me. It will be harmful for me. I cannot store anything extra to take with me. Please do not mind.

Beni Pal: Just as you wish, Sir! Please bless me.

Sri Ramakrishna: We have shared great happiness today. See, he alone is a man who makes wealth his servant. Those who do not know the proper use of money are not men, even though born as human beings. They have the figure of a man, but the conduct of an animal. You are blessed. You have filled many devotees with bliss.

Chapter 13

October 26, 1884

Dakshineswar

First Discussion

Swamiji: This is a discussion between
Thakur, the respected Manmohan, devotees at
Dakshineswar, and a description of his activities
with the devotees

"Come on, brothers! We're going to have darshan again
of that great man. We're going to look at that child. He does
not know anything except the Divine Mother. He's taken on
a body just for us. He's going to tell us how we're going to
resolve all the great difficulties of wearing a body in this lifetime. He is going to tell it to the sannyasis. He's going to tell
it to the householders. He is an avatar, an incarnation of God.
In the Kali temple of Dakshineswar he is waiting for us.
Come on, come on, everybody let's go! We're going to see
him! He wears infinite qualities. He is the image of
satisfaction. When you hear the words flowing from his
mouth, tears will fall from your eyes. Come on, brothers! He
is the ocean of infinite qualities, of compassion and grace.
He is the vision of love. Day and night he is absorbed in the
vision of God. He has taken a human body so we can
experience his divine nature and his beautiful countenance."

Today is Sunday the twenty-sixth of October, 1884. It is
winter. It is the seventh day of the bright fortnight in the
month of Kartik (November). It is in the second prahara of
the evening (early evening). Ramakrishna is sitting in that
same old room and talking to the devotees. On the western
side of the room, half of the moon is shining onto the
veranda. To the west of the veranda is a path that leads to the
garden. The path extends to the north and to the south. To

the west of the path is the garden full of flowers that will be offered to Maha Kali. To the west are the pure flowing waters of the Ganga. There are many devotees present because today is going to be a day of great bliss. The very embodiment of bliss, Sri Ramakrishna, is going to mesmerize and hypnotize the devotees assembled with the love of God. What a wonderful sight! It's all bliss. The devotees reflect the intoxication of the bliss of their master.

Down in the garden the leaves of the trees are exuding a fragrant scent. The rays of the setting sun are reflecting on the waters of the Ganga. This entire scene is giving bliss to all who perceive it. What a wonder! This is the truth of all truths. This is the sweetness of the indivisible kingdom. Even the dust and dirt in the garden are filled with bliss. I have a secret desire to mix with the dust of the earth because it contains so much bliss. I have the desire that I could stand on one side of the garden all day and take darshan. My desire is to hug all the leaves, flowers, shrubs, and trees in the garden with love and affection. Can you imagine that Sri Ramakrishna walks on this earth with his own feet? Can you imagine that he walks along beside all these creepers, trees, plants, and flowers? I have the desire that I could just sit in this breeze and gaze at the moon because I am seeing that on this earth all the inhabitants are laughing with joy and love. The pujari of the temple regards everyone as a relative, as part of the family, because for a long time there has been great sweetness exuding from the holy presence of Ramakrishna. In the atmosphere, in the Ganga, in the temple of the Gods, along the path of the garden, in the trees, in the flowers -- all the devotees are feeling united with all of creation. The whole of creation is comprised of the same components as Ramakrishna. It's like a garden made of wax. The leaves, the trees, the fruits, the path, the gardener, all the inhabitants, even the beautiful house situated there, all are made of wax. It's all made of bliss!

Sri Manmohan, M., and a few others were present. On the eastern side were Hazra, Ishana, and Hriday. Balaram and Rakhal were in Vrindavan. At this time, new devotees came and went -- Narayan Poltu (Little Naren), Tejo Chandra, Vinot, and Haripot. Baburam sometimes came and stayed. Rama, Suresh, Devendra, and other devotees often came. Some came for one week, some for two. Latu stayed all the time near the house of Jogin and came often. Narendra came occasionally, but when he came, it was so beautiful. We had a lot of fun. Narendra sang with such a beautiful voice, and he sang the name of God. Ramakrishna often went into samadhi when Narendra sang. It was like a great festival going on all the time. Ramakrishna wanted his children to stay with him day and night, and why not? They had pure hearts and pure souls. As yet, they hadn't been bound by married life with its worldly obligations and responsibilities. He asked Baburam to stay when he was able, and occasionally he did stay. Adurshen often came. Many devotees were sitting inside the room. Ramakrishna, like a little child, stood up. What was he thinking? All the devotees were watching.

Individuals and the Whole

Ramakrishna (to Manmohan): God is looking at everything. I see Rama everywhere. You all are sitting here, and I see Rama has become each and every one of you.

Manmohan: Has Rama become all of this, just as you are saying? You are Narayan, and the water is Narayan. Which water shall we drink? With some water we wash our faces. With some water we wash our utensils.

Ramakrishna: Yes, but I am actually seeing that He has become all. He is this entire perceivable universe, and He lives inside it. (Saying this again and again, he sat down on the small cot.)

Hold on to Truth and Leave All Your Doubts

Ramakrishna (to Mahimacharan): Hey, you! You have to hold on to truth. You have to perform every action with a pure attitude and dedication. If I suddenly say, "I won't eat," then even if I get hungry, I won't take food because I said I wouldn't eat. If I say I have to give some water to an individual, then I'll take the water. If somebody else takes them the water, I have to tell them to come back. What happened? Is there no other way? If you take something along with you, even if you have a small desire like wanting something to drink, you can't save up things for the future.

At that time, someone came up and said, "Oh, Great Sir (Mahashay), Hriday has come to the garden of Jadhu Mallik. He's standing near the gate and wants to see you."

Ramakrishna (to the devotees): I'm going to go see him for a few minutes. You sit here.

He said this and took the darkly polished shoes, put them on, and went to the eastern side. M. went with him through the garden along the red brick path. Hriday bowed down to Ramakrishna. On the south side was a door, and on the left a sitting room, a blue hut. Gajitohla was a bit to the southern side, and Pushkarini ghat (the steps to the Ganga) was right there. On the left side was the house for the doorman, and on the south side was an altar for tulsi. If you looked just outside the garden, you could see Hriday standing by the entrance to Jadhu Mallik's garden.

Second Discussion

Hriday was standing close by in an extremely respectful attitude ready to perform seva. On the path in front of Ramakrishna, the devotees did danda pranam, while Hriday did a full pranam. Ramakrishna told him to get up, and

Hriday stood up with his hands folded like a little child and began to cry. How fantastic! Ramakrishna himself was crying. One could see the tears falling from the corners of his eyes, but he wiped them away hoping no one would see. What was this? This Hriday who gave him so much pain and so much trouble, he was crying for him.

Ramakrishna: You just got here?

Hriday: I came to see you. To whom else can I explain the pain of my heart?

Ramakrishna (laughing): In this world of objects and relationships, you will experience many kinds of pain. If you go to do this worldly business, you will experience pain.

Ramakrishna (to M.): These people come all the time. They listen to two or three words about God and they have some peace of mind.

Ramakrishna (to Hriday): What pain do you have?

Hriday (crying): When I'm not with you, I have pain.

Ramakrishna: But you said, "You stay in your own attitude, and I'll stay in mine."

Hriday: Yes, I said it, but what do I know?

Ramakrishna: So you are here today. Come another day, and we will sit down and talk. Today is Sunday so a lot of people are here who want to talk to me. Tell me, how was the rice harvest in our village?

Hriday: Oh, about average.

Ramakrishna: You come another day.

Hriday again made full pranam to Ramakrishna with great respect and then Ramakrishna returned by the same path as he had come. M. went along with him.

Ramakrishna (to M.): As much seva as he did for me, that's how much pain I experienced. The more I ate, the more I became skin and bones. I couldn't digest anything, and he would say to me, "Hey, look at how I'm eating. You can't eat due to the qualities of your mind." Then he said again, "What a fool! If I don't stay here, you don't have the attitude of a sadhu at all. Without me you won't be a sadhu." One day he gave me so much trouble that I wanted to go to the Ganga and jump in!

When M. heard this, he was taken aback. He thought, "This is fantastic! For these kinds of people his tears are falling?"

Ramakrishna: He did so much seva. How did he become like that? He raised me just like one raises a child. I used to stay unconscious in the night and in the day. There were many days when I was ill. He used to protect me in such a way that however he put me, that's the way I stayed.

What could M. say? He was quiet. He began to think, "Well, I guess Hriday wasn't truly doing selfless seva without his own selfishly motivated desires creeping in." While they talked, Ramakrishna arrived at his room where many devotees awaited. Ramakrishna sat on his cot.

Third Discussion

Along with the devotees and various other individuals, Ramakrishna was going to discuss the attitudes and the hidden meanings of the principles. Mahimancharan and several devotees had come. One man was talking to Ramakrishna for some time. He was a devotee from Kronnagar.

Devotee: Oh, Great Sir (Mahashay), I hear you have this great attitude of samadhi. Why does it happen? In what form does it happen? Will you please explain to us what this attitude and samadhi is?

Ramakrishna: It's just like Radha's great attitude. If any of her friends came to touch her, then the other friends would say, "Don't touch her. She's got Krishna's love on Her skin. Krishna resides in her body." If you don't feel God, you can't have this great attitude. If you go to catch the fish from the bottom of a deep pond, the water splashes just as you catch the fish. That is why the bhava is like laughing, crying, dancing, and singing. You can't stay in the bhava for a long time. If you just sit in front of the mirror and look at your own face, people will think you are crazy.

Devotee: Oh, Great Sir (Mahashay), please show us what it's like to have the darshan of God.

Ramakrishna: If you haven't done the sadhana, if you haven't done the karma, you can't get a vision of God. You have to be completely surrendered or dependent upon God. What will humanity do? If you repeat His names, sometimes tears will fall and other times not. If you go to meditate on God, sometimes you go very deep and other times nothing happens. First you must do the karma. Then you get the darshan.

Ramakrishna (continuing): One day I was in a great mood, and I went to see the Haldar pond. I saw that there was a lot of scum on the surface of the water. A man was pushing it all out of the way so he could get to the clear water. He kept lifting up the water and looking at it. Since the moss and scum didn't stick to the water, he couldn't see anything. If you don't do the actions, you can't achieve devotion. You can't see God. You have to do meditation and japa. This is the action required. You have to sing the names of God and speak of His qualities. This is the karma. You have to be generous in giving. You have to do yajnas. This is all karma yoga. If you want butter, you have to first make the milk into cream. Then you have to put it in a quiet place. Later, when the cream has become congealed, you need to churn it with a lot of effort. Only then can you get the butter out.

Mahimacharan: Oh, yes, we have to do the karma. We have to produce the effort. Then we can gain the experience. We have to read and study an infinite number of scriptures. First comes knowledge. Then comes contemplation of wisdom. Then afterwards comes the vision of God.

Ramakrishna (to Mahimacharan): How many scriptures are you going to study? Do you think that just by thinking about it, it's going to be done? You have to produce the effort in order to achieve Godliness. You have to have faith in the words of your guru, and you have to make the effort in accordance. If the guru is no longer here, then you have to pray with deep sincerity. What is She like? She will let you know. What will you know from reading books? As long as you're marching to the marketplace, you're going to produce a great noise. As soon as you arrive, it becomes quiet. You can see clearly. You can hear clearly, "Give me the potatoes. Take the money."

Ramakrishna (continuing): When the ocean is far away, you make a lot of noise in your effort to get there. When you get there, you can see how many ships are out in the sea and how the birds are rising in the air and how the waves are rising and falling. You can see it. If you read a book, can you understand and feel what it means to be on the shores of the ocean? There's a big difference between reading the book and having the experience. Reading all these scriptures doesn't have the same nectar or the same taste as having the experience. It's necessary to discuss with others who have had the experience.

When you speak to a rich man, you ask, "How big is your house? How many trees are there and how big is your garden? How many companies do you own?" Before you even meet him, why are you so concerned with his accounts? If the servants go to the master, he doesn't even allow them in the same room. What do the papers explain about the company? You must make an effort to go and meet with the owner of the company. Then, when you discuss with him, he will give you the full account. After you've talked to the owner, all the employees will salute you when you come out.

Devotee: How do you get to meet the owner of the company? (Everyone laughed.)

Ramakrishna: That's why you need to do the work. If you just say, "God is that" and just go sit down and do nothing, then you're not going to get there. You have to go with great vigor and great effort. Go to a quiet place and pray to Him, saying with great sincerity and longing in your heart, "Reveal Yourself to me."

You run after your attachments and desires with great fervor, but for once be a little bit crazy for God. Some people may say that such-and-such a person has become crazy for God. Good! Let them. Leave all things and just call on God. If you say, "He exists and I know it" and then do nothing, what will happen? There's a great big fish in the pond. If you just sit on the banks, will you get to eat fish? When you throw your net into the pond and the fish swims into it and you see the net moving, you get a lot of delight. You can even see the fish from time to time. The fish is constantly jumping. When you see Him, you have even greater bliss. One person wants to see the king who is very far away. He went a long way in one direction but did not find the king. Where is the king? After many tribulations you cross a great distance and find where the king is.

The Means of Success of

Attaining Godliness: Sincerity

Mahimacharan: By what path or activity can we achieve Godliness?

Ramakrishna: By pure unselfish activities you can get to Him. It's not true that there is only one way to get to Him. Become completely dependent on the grace of God. Then with great sincerity, do whatever activity is appropriate in your particular circumstance. If you are deeply sincere, you will get the grace. You need an excellent means of union. Stay with sadhus. Have discrimination. Get a true guru. It may be that the oldest brother took responsibility for the entire household. His wife was very dharmic and had lots of intelligence. She had no consciousness that she was a married woman. Even though she was married, she did not engage in worldly activities. She had no attachment to the samsara, and with this dharmic union she was able to attain the grace of God and unite with Him. First we need the darshan of the saints. Then we need to develop proper discrimination. We must surrender to a true guru. These are all the grace of God.

Ramakrishna (continuing): In somebody's house someone was very sick and on their deathbed. One sadhu gave the prescription to save the patient, "In the Shati Nakshatra, a certain period of astrology, some rain will fall. If you catch some of the rainwater in a skull and mix it with the venom of a snake who tries to catch a frog, and put that mixture in the patient's mouth, he will be saved." The relatives in the house where the patient was living looked at the astrological signs, and went to try their best to save their patient. With great sincerity they went to search for the ingredients. In their minds they were calling on God, "Oh, God, if you would give us all the ingredients to make this medicine, we will be successful in saving our beloved relative."

In this way, they were going and going until at last they
found a skull. While looking at the skull, it started to rain.
One individual shouted "Oh, Guruji! I have found the skull!
It's the perfect astrological configuration, and the rain is
falling. Just see the rainwater has fallen into the skull. Please
give me your grace, and give me the other ingredients!" In
this way, they were calling with deep sincerity. After some
time they saw a great big snake coming. They felt great
delight in their hearts. They were so sincere that their hearts
were pounding in their chests. They said, "Hey, Gurudev,
even the snake has come! Many of the ingredients are
present. Please give us your grace and whatever else is
needed to fulfill our objective. Please bring us the remaining
ingredients." While saying this, he saw a frog. The snake
went after it. The frog jumped over the skull and fell on the
other side. The poison from the snake fell into the skull. The
seekers were so delighted they began to dance. That's why I
say that if you are deeply committed and deeply sincere, all
the ingredients will come together. Om.

Fourth Discussion

Renunciation and Living a Householder's Life

Attaining Godliness and Renunciation

Who Is a Real Sannyasi?

Ramakrishna: If you have not renounced all the
attachments of your mind, then you cannot attain to
Godliness. Sadhus and birds don't store up goods for the
future. When you wash your hands with mud, you don't take
the mud along with you. The sadhus don't take things along
with them for the future. When Hriday was giving me a lot
of pain, I thought I would go to Benares. I thought, "I'll take
a cloth. How will I take some money?" That's why I didn't
go. (All laughed.)

Ramakrishna (to Mahiman): You are worldly people. You say this and you say that. You protect your worldliness and also your dharma.

Mahimacharan: Even if we save it, does it stay? It doesn't stay at all.

Ramakrishna: Near the Panchavati on the banks of the Ganga, I was contemplating that mud was the same as money, and money the same as mud. Thinking this way, I threw the money into the Ganga. Then I became afraid. I thought, "Have I become without any Lakshmi at all? What would happen if Mother Lakshmi closes Her cashbox? Then I'll have to become a businessman like Hazra! Mother, you please stay in my heart."

One person was doing tapasya. When the Goddess became pleased with him, She said, "Take a boon from me." He said, "Mother, give me the boon that I'll eat at my grandson's house from a golden plate." So receiving this boon from the Goddess, the grandson got all kinds of wealth and golden utensils! (All laughed.)

When you have renounced all attachments from your mind, then your mind goes to God. Your mind just goes and stays there. He who is bound cannot be liberated. When you are away from God, you are bound. With all your worldly attachments and karma you fill up your bowl leaving no room for God.

Why do children cry when they are born? They say, "I was in the womb! I was in union! Where did I come to? I was so happy contemplating God! Where am I now?" Without selfishness you should renounce all desires in your mind and then perform your work in the world.

Is It Necessary to Renounce the Whole World?

Mahiman: If you keep your mind on God, does this worldliness stay with you?

Ramakrishna: Eh? How is that? If the world doesn't remain, where will you go? I see that wherever I stay, I'm in Ayodhya with Rama. This whole world of objects and relationships is Rama's Ayodhya. Ramachandra went to his guru in order to get wisdom and said, "I am going to renounce this world of objects and relationships." He sent Vasishtha (his guru) to Dasarath (his father). Vasishtha saw that Rama had extreme renunciation. He said, "Rama, first reason with me and then you can leave all this worldliness, ok? Let me ask you, is this world without God? If it is, then you have to renounce it!"

Then Rama saw that this entire perceivable universe and all the individuals in it are manifestations of God. "Because of the Truth of God, all of this is true, and I understand it to be true." Then Rama was silent. In this world we have to fight against our desires and our anger and our passion, all these limitations of our individuality.

We have to make war with all the desires. We have to fight against our tendency towards selfishness. After fighting with all these limitations, we have some ease. From the house it is efficient to fight. You get your food. Your spouse gives you all kinds of help. In this age of darkness, there are various forms of life. Rather than roaming around to various places, sitting in one spot is more efficient. That's why one should stay in one's house like a fortress and fight from there. If you stay in your own world and fight against worldliness, the storm will pass. Sometimes the storm blows old dry leaves in through the window in your house. Whichever direction the wind blows, in that direction the leaves will go. Sometimes they land in a good place and sometimes in a bad place. God has thrown us into this world of objects and relationships. Now it's fine. Just stay where you are. Again God will pick you up with the breeze and blow you to a nicer place.

In this world of objects and relationships, we want to surrender our soul. This is God's desire. He has placed us in this world of objects and relationships. What can we do? We want to surrender it all to God, even our own souls. If we do so, there is no more confusion or conflict. Then you will see that He is doing everything. Everything is God's desire.

Devotee: What is the story of Rama's desire?

Ramakrishna: In one village there was a very dharmic weaver. Everyone believed him and liked him. He would go regularly to the market to sell his cloth. If anyone asked him for the price of the cloth, he would say, "It's Rama's desire. I spent one rupee for the thread by Rama's desire. I put in about twenty-five paisa of labor, also Rama's desire. I will take fifteen paisa as profit. The price of the cloth is Rama's desire. I will charge one rupee and six annas." (There are sixteen annas to a rupee.)

Everyone had so much faith in this man that they would immediately lay down their money and purchase his clothes. He was a great devotee. Every evening after his meal, he would sit for a long time in the temple of Chandi and think about God. He would sing about the qualities of God. One night very late, he was not able to sleep. He just sat and smoked tobacco. At the same time a band of thieves came down the path. They needed someone to carry the stolen load so they grabbed him and took him along with them. Then they went into a house and stole all the goods and put it on the weaver's head. Just then the police came, and all the thieves fled. The weaver was the only one left. They took him to jail for the night. In the morning he went before the magistrate. All the villagers found out and came to the court house. They said to the magistrate, "He cannot be a thief!" The magistrate said to the weaver, "Tell me what happened." The weaver said, "Oh, Great Sir (Mahashay), it was all Rama's desire. I ate rice that night, and that was Rama's desire. I was sitting at the Chandi temple because of Rama's desire. It was very late, and by God's grace I was thinking about Him and singing His qualities and His names. By Rama's desire a whole band of thieves came walking down the path at that time. They grabbed me by the scruff of my neck and took me with them, and that was Rama's desire. They stole all the goods from this one house, and that was Rama's desire. They put all the goods on my head, and by Rama's desire the police came right then. I was caught, and by Rama's desire the police put me in jail. Then by Rama's desire they brought me to you this morning." When the magistrate saw what a religious man he was, he ordered the weaver's release. Then the weaver said to all his friends, "According to Rama's desire, they let me go."

So you see, whether you conduct worldly business or you are a sannyasi, it's all Rama's desire. Just give it all to God, and in this way you can do your worldly activities. If you don't give it all to God, what will you do with it?

A clerk went to jail. When his sentence was up, he got out. Will he dance or will he work? If an individual is liberated while doing worldly actions, he will contemplate that he can live in this world without selfishness. He who attains to wisdom has a mind that does not float here and there. All places are equal. That which is over there is also right here. That means that God is in every place. Om.

Fifth Discussion

Swamiji: How to remain unattached while living a householder's life.

Mahimacharan, Manomohan, M., and several other devotees were enjoying the nectar of Sri Ramakrishna's words in his room at Dakshineswar. It was afternoon, and the devotees were mesmerized by the endless flow of gems and jewels flowing from Sri Ramakrishna's mouth. All felt a strange heaviness that did not allow them to move from their seats. In the minds of the devotees there was not the slightest thought or worry. Their workaday world had completely vanished as the Master's nectar-like words brought resolution to all the concerns and difficulties of their lives.

Over the years many renowned scholars and pundits had visited the Master and had been astonished by his wisdom. Padmalochan, Narayan Shastri, Gauri Pundit, and Dayananda Saraswati, to name a few, had come and stood in awe of the unlearned saint of Dakshineswar. Dayananda had said, "We have studied so much of the Vedas, Vedanta, and all the scriptures, but on seeing this great soul, we are now receiving the fruit of all that study, and we have the proof of the promise of the scriptures. After all the churning of the milk of our studies, we are only drinking the whey and water. He alone is eating the butter."

When Keshab Sen and other notable teachers of the time, who had received English educations, met Sri Ramakrishna, they were confounded by his wisdom. They said, "How wonderful! It is as though Christ has returned to Earth in human form. In his village dialect he is teaching through stories in such simple language that even a child can understand the highest spiritual truths!"

As Jesus called on his Father in heaven, Sri Ramakrishna called on his Divine Mother. Both demonstrated that wisdom is not in the letter of the scripture but in the spiritual fact of a living faith and divine realization. The Master of Dakshineswar is a true renunciant. That is why his words have such compelling power. Were those enmeshed in the world to say the same words, they would not carry the same power. It is through renunciation and living faith that the power to impact the worldly mind arises.

Keshab Sen and other spiritual leaders of the day were profoundly impressed by Sri Ramakrishna's spiritual presence and simple teachings about God and spiritual life. How could such an illiterate man have acquired such wisdom that the greatest scholars of the day came to his feet to learn? He respected all religions and sects and quarreled with none. His mind was entirely free of desire, passion, and anger. He had nothing himself. He lived a life of perfect renunciation, and yet he never asked others to renounce the world. Rather, he advised his devotees to remain in the world. He said, "Your life in the world is like a fort behind whose walls one can pray to God. When a prisoner is released from jail, he will return to the same job or profession he had before his imprisonment. When a devotee becomes liberated, he will remain in the world. Where else will he go?"

Ramakrishna: In the beginning of spiritual life, you must retire to a solitary place from time to time. It is necessary to put a fence around the newly planted tree so that animals will not destroy it. Later, the fence can be taken away with no worry. When I first saw Keshab Sen, I said, "His tail has fallen off." When a tadpole loses its tail and becomes a frog, it can live on land as well as in the water.

I wanted to see Devendranath Tagore, so Mathur Babu took me to meet him. When I first met him, he seemed a little egotistical. I said to Mathur, "One who has egotism cannot have true knowledge of God. Pride is a sign of ignorance. Those who have seen God are very wary of egotism. 'I am a scholar. I am a wise man. I am wealthy.' Can that kind of idea remain in one who has seen God?"

As I was speaking with Devendra, I went into samadhi. When I am in that state, I don't know what people see. From inside of me, a kind of "Ha, ha" laughter bubbled up. That was the condition I was in. At that time I have no regard for a pundit or a learned man. If I see that a person is without discrimination and renunciation, I regard him as mere straw. A vulture may fly very high in the sky, but its eyes are always on the ground below. In that state I saw that Devendra had yoga as well as bhoga, enjoyment of the world. He had many children, and a doctor was in the home tending to some family member. I understood that even after attaining spiritual wisdom, he still had to remain in his worldly environment. I said, "You are the King Janaka of this age. Janaka drank his milk from two glasses, the glass of yoga and the glass of worldly enjoyment. Even though you are living in the world, you have kept your mind on God. It is for this reason that I wanted to visit you. Please tell me something about your understanding of God."

Devendra quoted from the scriptures. Then he said that the universe is like a chandelier, and the individual beings are like lights on the chandelier. When I used to meditate in the Panchavati, I had a similar vision so I knew that Devendranath was authentic. Do you understand the meaning of this? God has created man in order to reveal His greatness. If the lights do not remain, everything will be in darkness. You won't even see the chandelier.

Devendra invited me to come to the festival of the Brahmo Samaj, but I said, "That depends on the will of God.

You see my condition. I don't know what attitude God will put me in at any time." Devendra insisted. He said, "You must come! When you come, wear proper clothing. If you arrive unkempt and disheveled, I will feel personally insulted."

Ramakrishna (continuing): I answered, "I'm afraid I can't assure you of that. I have not been able to become a gentleman." (All laughed.) The next day a young man arrived with a letter from Devendra saying that I should not come to the festival, that I might do something improper or wear my clothing incorrectly.

Captain, Devotees, Householders, and

Improprieties of the Brahmo Samaj

Ramakrishna (to the devotees): Captain is active in the world, yet he is a great devotee. You should go and meet him. Captain knows the Vedas, the Vedanta, and the Bhagavad Gita by heart, as well as many other scriptures. He is also very devoted to me. I was walking on a path in Baranagore, and he held an umbrella over my head. When I went to his house he served me with great devotion. He fanned me and massaged my feet. He also served me many delicious vegetarian dishes. When I was in the bathroom, it happened that I went into an ecstatic state and couldn't take care of myself. He cared for me there even though he is so orthodox in his conventions about ceremonial purity.

Captain has a lot of expenses. His brothers live in Benares, and he manages all their financial needs. His family told me that he doesn't like all this worldliness. He says repeatedly that he will leave the world. Every member of his family is a devotee. His father was an officer in the army and fought in a war. He would worship Shiva with one hand while holding a sword in the other. He is strictly orthodox in following his religion. That is why he stopped seeing me for a month when he heard that I would visit Keshab Sen. He said, "Keshab has violated the conventions of Hinduism. He doesn't follow the traditional ways any more. He eats with English people and has joined his daughter in marriage to a family of a different caste. His unorthodox behavior has cost him his own caste."

Ramakrishna: I said to Captain, "What do I care for such things. He chants the name of God. I only go to him to hear about God. I only eat the fruit of the tree. I don't care about the thorns!" Still Captain would not leave me alone. He said, "You mean that you will continue to see Keshab?" Then I became a little upset and said to him, "At least I don't go there for money! I see Keshab in order to hear the name of God. You go to the homes of the wealthy. Why do you go there? They are not orthodox Hindus!" After I said this to him, he remained quiet.

But Captain is truly a great devotee. When he performs the arati, he burns camphor. After his worship he sits on his asana and sings devotional songs. Then he becomes like another person. He has no consciousness of his body.

Sixth Discussion

Vedanta, Maya, and Ramakrishna

Ramakrishna (to Mahimacharan): According to Vedanta, this world is only an illusion that obscures the true reality. The world is merely a dream. The supreme soul is ever awake and present in the three states: the waking state, the dreaming state, and the state of dreamless sleep as in deep meditation. In each of these states, the true self is fully awake and aware.

I will tell you a story that suits your own attitude. There was once a farmer who lived out in the countryside. After many years he was blessed with a son. He named the child Haru. Both the parents loved Haru very much. The farmer was a very righteous man, and his neighbors, even those in the nearby villages, held him in great respect and loved him dearly.

One day as he was working in the fields, a neighbor came to tell him that his son had suddenly come down with cholera. Upon hearing this dreadful news, he left at once for home to care for the boy. In spite of the best treatment available in the small village, his son died that very day. Everyone in the house was filled with grief, except the farmer who showed no sign of sorrow at all. He merely asked the others, "What is the fruit of your grief?" Then he went back to the fields to work.

That evening when he returned from the fields, he saw that his wife was crying even more. She said to him, "What kind of cruel father are you? You didn't even shed one tear over the loss of your son!" The father, in a thoughtful mood, replied, "Shall I tell you why? It is because last night I had a beautiful dream. I dreamt that I was a king who had eight sons. I had all the comforts a kingdom could provide, and my subjects loved me dearly. Then when I awoke this morning, all of that disappeared, and I went as usual to the fields to work. Now I ask you. Should I grieve for the eight sons who were lost in the dream last night or for the one son who died today?"

The farmer was a jnani, a man of spiritual wisdom. He knew that not only was the dream false, but the waking state is a dream as well. The only true, eternal, and unchanging reality is the soul. For the jnani all three relative states of the soul have dissolved: the waking state, the dream state, and the state of dreamless sleep. There is only the Supreme Self and maya, which obscures the Supreme Self. The jnani has dissolved the three relative states of the soul. One who clings to these three relative states of consciousness can never move beyond them.

Devotee: But why must one renounce the three states?

Ramakrishna: To realize the Supreme Divinity, one's individuality as well as the perceivable universe must be transcended. By discriminating through the process of "not this, not this," the individual soul transcends ego identification and attachment to the relative universe. As long as the "I" remains, one will feel that it is God who has become everything: the universe, the individual self, and the twenty-four cosmic principles of the Sankhya philosophy.

When you buy a belfruit, you pay for the whole fruit including the seeds and the skin as well as the pulp and the juice. When you get home, you discard the seeds and the skin and keep only the eatable portion. If you want to know the weight of the whole fruit, you must include the seeds and the skin also. That is why I say that all this is my Eternal Mother's drama. I can't call it a mere illusion and throw it to the wind. The weight would be less.

Om and Union with the Eternal Drama

Ramakrishna (to Mahimacharan): When you explain the sacred syllable "Om," you refer only to the "A," the "U," and the "M."

Mahima: A-U-M means creation, preservation, and transformation.

Ramakrishna: Well, I give the illustration of the ringing of a large bell, "t-a-a-u-m-m." The lila, the great drama, dissolves in the Nitya, the Great Cause. The gross, the subtle, and the causal bodies merge into Turiya, that pure consciousness which is beyond the three states of waking, dreaming, and deep sleep. When the bell is struck, it is as if a heavy object has fallen into the ocean. Then waves arise, and ripples circle outward. Thus, from the Eternal the divine drama begins. From that Great Ocean arise the realms of the causal, the subtle, and the gross. From the Great Cause, from that which is beyond all manifestation, arises the universe of gross or material experience, the universe of subtle experience, and the universe known only through meditation leading to intuitive experience. Then the ripples of creation subside once again into the Great Ocean. If you think of the Nitya, the Eternal, you come to the lila, the drama of relativity; and if you think of the lila, the drama, you come to the Eternal, the Nitya. Therefore, I understand Om through the "t-a-a-u-m-m" of a bell. I have actually seen this. She has shown it to me. There is no end to the Ocean of Consciousness. From that Ocean all the drama has evolved, and into that Ocean it will dissolve again. In the ether of consciousness, tens of millions of creators have taken birth, and they will dissolve into that infinite expanse once again. I don't know what is written in the books about all this.

Mahima: Those who have seen such things don't write books. They remain immersed in ecstatic joy. When would they have time to write books? One who writes must be attentive to worldly things. He must take care of his accounts. He must budget his time and so forth. Others have heard from those who have had personal experience and have written about it.

Swamiji: The world of objects and relationships demands motivated action until we attain the wisdom of the Supreme.

Ramakrishna: People ask, "In the world of objects and relationships, why do the selfish attachments and desires remain?"

When we attain to that supreme wisdom, then selfishness will depart. If you experience the bliss of that Supreme Divinity even once, your mind will never again run towards the pleasures of the senses and worldly attachments. Once the moth has seen the light, it doesn't return to the darkness. Once someone asked Ravana, "Why take the trouble to abduct Sita? Why not just appear to Her in the form of Her husband Rama?" Ravana replied, "If I took the form of Rama, I would be lost in the knowledge of Brahman, the Supreme Divinity. Then how could I think of something of so little consequence as abducting another man's wife?"

To the extent that your devotion to God increases, your attachment to the small self and its worldly desires will diminish. Chaitanya lost himself in divine love. For one to achieve this, it is necessary to practice spiritual discipline. The more you meditate on God and increase your devotion to His lotus feet, the more the pleasures of the body and worldly desires will recede. Finally, all attachment to the world and bodily enjoyment will disappear. You will not look at others with attachment. You will see all women as your own mother. Then the relationship between spouses becomes a partnership in spiritual evolution. One's animalistic nature subsides, and one's divine nature reveals itself. Then even if you remain in the world, you will move through it as a jivanmukta, one who is free even while living. The disciples of Chaitanya were unattached even while living their lives in the world.

Seventh Discussion

Ramakrishna and Hazra and

Service to the Divine Mother

Hazra was sitting on the eastern veranda of Ramakrishna's room doing japa. He was about 46 or 47 years old and came from the same rural area of India as Ramakrishna. He had attained the spirit of renunciation for a long time. Sometimes he went on pilgrimages, and sometimes he stayed at home. He owned some land on which his house was built, the income of which supported his wife, daughters, and sons. Yet he still had some outstanding debts which caused him much worry. He was always wondering which debtor to pay in each month and how to find the means to do so. He traveled to and from Calcutta frequently and often stayed at Ishan Mukerjii's house while in Calcutta where he was treated like a sadhu. When he stayed at Dakshineswar, as he often did, he served Sri Ramakrishna as the opportunity arose. For instance, he would buy a new cloth for the Master if he saw that the old one was torn. He was always eager to receive news of Ramakrishna.

But Hazra also loved to discuss and debate the scriptures and had a somewhat inflated opinion of his own spiritual stature. He presented himself as a jnani, a follower of the non-dual Brahman, the highest form of divinity. While staying at Dakshineswar, he somewhat conspicuously sat for long periods on the veranda outside the Master's room doing japa. Recently, news had reached him that his mother had fallen ill. She had asked Ramlal to request Hazra to come to her and to tell him that she anxiously desired to see her son. The other devotees had departed. Only Mahima, Hazra, and M. remained with Sri Ramakrishna in his room.

Ramakrishna (to Hazra): Go to your home and see your mother at least for a few days. If you cause pain to your mother, your sadhana will be of no avail. Go to her at least for a short time. Then you may return here.

Mahima: Sir, why do you ask Hazra to go home? He has no desire to return to his family.

Ramakrishna: His mother has expressed her pain to Ramlal. That is why I say so. He should go there for three days at least, and then he can come back here. When I was staying at Vrindavan, it suddenly occurred to me that my mother was crying for me at home, so I came straight back with Mathur Babu. In any case, what is the harm for a "jnani" like Hazra to return to the world for a few days?

Mahima (laughing): Sir, that would be a good point if Hazra were a jnani.

Ramakrishna (smiling): Oh, Hazra is a jnani all right. Only he has just a touch of desire left for the world. He has children at home and a few outstanding debts. As the saying goes, "Auntie is now in perfect health; only she is a little ill." (All laugh.)

Mahima (smiling): Then where is his jnana?

Ramakrishna: Oh, don't you know? Everyone believes Hazra is special. He lives in Rani Rasmani's temple garden. He is a renowned person. Many people around here speak only of him. (All laugh.)

Hazra: Sir, you are beyond form and attributes. That's why no one can understand who you are.

Ramakrishna: Exactly! The formless is beyond all action. So why should anyone speak of me?

Mahima: Sir, he knows nothing himself.   Whatever instructions you give him is what he is following.

Ramakrishna: Oh? You had better ask him about that. He has said to me that I have nothing to give to him, and he has nothing to learn from me. He is always arguing, and occasionally he even gives me instructions. (All laugh.) When he tries to debate with me, I give him a scolding and leave him to himself. Then that night remembering how I spoke to him, I don't sleep well. I have to get up in the night to go and give my salutations to him. Only then am I at peace.

Vedanta and the Pure Atman

Ramakrishna (to Hazra): Why do you refer to God as the pure Atman? The Atman is beyond all action. When I think of the activities of creation, preservation, and destruction, I call the atman Ishvara, the personal God. What is the pure Atman like? It is like a magnet which is itself motionless but makes a sewing needle placed near it move.

Eighth Discussion

Talking to Ishan

It was evening. M. was sitting alone in a somewhat troubled mood, thinking. Ramakrishna came over to him and very lovingly said, "Please bring me two pieces of inexpensive cloth. I can't wear clothing brought by just any-one. I thought that I would ask Captain, but it is better if you bring it to me." M. at once stood up and said, "Certainly, Sir, I will bring them."

As the evening deepened, M. was lost in contemplation of the temple activities.   Frankincense was brought to Ramakrishna's room. The Master was repeating the name of

God, and then he began to sing. Outside the room all of nature was beautiful. It was the seventh day of the bright fortnight of the month of Kartik (November). The waves of the Ganga were singing, as it were. The beautiful strains of the songs of the evening arati in the temples merged with the sound of the holy river, the sound of whose waves seemed to be chanting, "Kali, Kali." All the concerns of the day soon dissolved in the blissful sound. The arati was being performed in all three temples: Kali, Vishnu, and Shiva. And now, at each of the twelve Lingam temples of Shiva, worship was being performed. The priests moved from one temple to the next, performing arati at each. In their left hands they held a bell, in their right, the five lights. In front was the assistant priest who carried a brass gong.

In the southwest corner of Ramakrishna's room, songs in various ragas were being sung. To M. it seemed as though the bliss of the eternal had become manifest in this festival of worship. In this joyful setting it was natural for devotees to remember their true nature. No one experiencing this could be without bliss. All of one's worldly pleasures and pains became insignificant in this divine joy. The children of the servants of the garden did not enjoy fine food or clothes, and their homes were dilapidated. No matter. Mother was in their hearts. They knew that their Mother was present here and that She was taking all responsibility for them. She was not a vague or distant mother. She was real and present, here and now.

M.'s contemplations deepened with the darkening shadows of the evening.

M. (thinking): Who am I? From where have I come? What will happen to me in this lifetime? Where will I go? What will I experience? Only Mother knows, and She knows everything. What human being cares for me even a particle as much as my Divine Mother? She is my true Mother. She has given me my body, mind, vital force, and soul. I don't need to know any more than that. If there is something that She wants me to know, She will tell me. Who else cares for me so much? Truly, Mother's children live in unbroken bliss.

Outside the Master's room the moonlight was laughing, as it were. Within the room Sri Ramakrishna was sitting immersed in the bliss of divine love.

Later Sri Ramakrishna was sitting in his room with several devotees. Ishan had come from Calcutta, and the discussion naturally turned to spiritual matters. Ishan had great faith in God. He had said, "If you repeat the name of Durga even once upon leaving your house, She will walk with you every step of the way protecting you with Her trident in Her hand. What fear can you have? She will surely protect you."

How to Perform Yoga through Karma

Ramakrishna (to Ishan): You have great faith. I don't have that much faith. (All laugh.) By such great faith one can realize God.

Ishan: If you say so, Sir.

Ramakrishna: You are sitting by the fire performing homas, japa, fasting, and so on. All of these activities are very good. If you have an inner urge to realize God, God Himself will make you perform such disciplines. If you can perform these activities without desire for their relative fruits, you will attain to God without a doubt.

You are presently following the activities and rites prescribed by the scriptures. This is called vaidhi-bhakti, the devotion through knowledge. There is also another form of bhakti, devotion through feeling. In this bhakti, one follows the subtle feeling of the love of God. This is the path shown by Narada. If that form of devotion comes to you, you will not need to follow the vaidic karma any more, but may do so for sheer delight.

Ninth Discussion

The Heart of the True Devotee

Before evening M. took a walk and was thinking that the story about the will of Rama was very appropriate. It reconciled the incessant conflict between predestination and free will, between liberty and necessity. "I was smoking by the will of Rama, I was taken by robbers by the will of Rama. I assisted in committing robbery by the will of Rama. I was caught by the police by the will of Rama. I have become a sadhu by the will of Rama. I am praying, 'Oh Lord, do not give me impure intelligence -- do not make me commit robbery.' This also is by the will of Rama. He is giving both good desires and bad desires. But there is a question here. Why should He give us bad desires? Why should He give us the desire to steal?

In answer the Master replied, "As the Lord has created tigers, lions and snakes among animals, as He has created poisonous trees among vegetation, in the same way he has created thieves and robbers among men. Who can tell why he has done so? Who can understand God?"

But if he has created everything then what happens to the sense of responsibility. Why should it go? Without direct knowledge of God, without His darshan, no one can have complete faith in Rama's will. Without realization of God, this will be remembered only from time to time and then will be forgotten again. Until one does not have complete faith, the sense of virtue and vice and the sense of responsibility must remain without fail. The Master explained that it is not enough to repeat, "It is Rama's desire," from your mouth by rote like a parrot. Until God is not realized, until His will and my will do not become one, until the ego is not understood to be an instrument, until then God maintains in man the dualistic feelings of virtue and vice, of pleasure and pain, of purity and impurity, good and bad, and the sense of responsibility. If He did not do so, how would this ocean of worldliness be able to function?

The more I contemplate the Master's devotion to God, the more I feel amazed. Keshab Sen chants the names of God and thinks of God. This is enough to send him running to visit the Master. Immediately Keshab became one of his own. He did not listen to Captain's objections. All the accusations against him, that he went to England, ate with English men, gave his daughter in marriage to a different caste, were ignored. I eat the plum fruit; what do I need with the thorn? The thread of devotion to God unites those who believe in God with form with those who believe in God without form. It unites Hindus, Muslims and Christians. It unites the four castes. Victory to devotion to God! Blessed is Sri Ramakrishna! Victory to you! You made manifest once again the universal spirit of the eternal religion. That is why your attraction is so great! You embrace the devotees of all the religions as your very own. Your one criteria is devotion to God! You only see if one has love of God and devotion in one's heart or not. If it is there, the person is your very own. If you see a Hindu who has devotion to God he at once becomes your own. If a Muslim has devotion to Allah he also is your very own. If a Christian has devotion to Jesus he also is your own. You say that all the rivers coming from diverse regions flow into one ocean. The goal of all is the same ocean.

The Master does not say that this world is a dream. You say that argument is without merit. This is not the doctrine of Maya, that the world is an illusion. It is the doctrine of qualified non-dualism. This philosophical doctrine does not say that the living beings and the universe are illusory or delusions of the mind. God is true, and again man is true and the world is true. Living beings and the universe are the Supreme Divinity. If you omit the seeds and the shell, you can't have the whole bel fruit.

I heard that the universe of change arises out of the great ocean of consciousness and disappears in it in time. Waves are rising in the vast ocean and in time are subsiding in it. Endless waves sport in the ocean of bliss. Where is the beginning of this game? And where is the end? One cannot speak of it or think of it. How little is man and how little is his knowledge. I have heard that great saints have seen the primary consciousness in the state of samadhi. They have seen the ever-playful Lord. They must have seen Him because Sri Ramakrishna is also saying the same thing. But they could not have seen with these eyes of flesh. Perhaps they saw with divine eyes, the divine eyes with which Arjuna saw the cosmic form, the eyes with which the rishis saw the Self, the divine eyes with which Jesus used to see his heavenly Father. How can one have those eyes? I heard from the Master that one can have that kind of vision through sincere yearning. Now, how can I have that kind of sincerity? Will I have to leave the world? But that is not what he said today.

Chapter 14

Swamiji: Ramakrishna was visiting the house of some devotees accompanied by Narendra, Girish, Balaram, Chunilal, Latu, M., and Narayan. The devotees were discussing pure and spiritual topics with great delight.

First Discussion

In a Devotee's Home with the Devotees

It was the tenth day of the dark fortnight in the lunar month of Falgun, and the moon was in the Purva Nakshatra. The solar day was Wednesday the eleventh of March 1885. It was around ten o'clock in the morning. Ramakrishna had come from Dakshineswar, accompanied by Latu and other devotees. They stopped at Balaram's temple and partook of prasad from the Jagannath temple in Puri.

Ramakrishna: Balaram, you are blessed. Your light today is illuminating the field of divine action.

There were many new devotees, and Ramakrishna welcomed them all. How he sang and danced with the devotees, just like in the temple of Gauranga Mahaprabhu, where everyone sang and danced in ecstatic bliss.

Sri Ramakrishna sat crying in the Kali temple of Dakshineswar. He was looking inside himself and feeling an extreme, burning, sincere desire to see his most intimate devotees. In the evening he had become so restless he couldn't sleep.

Ramakrishna (to Mother): Maa, Balaram has great devotion. Draw him to you. Bring him here. If he can't come, then you take me there. I want to see him.

The very next day Ramakrishna immediately took off for Balaram's house.

Ramakrishna (to all the assembled people): Balaram has been performing seva for Jagannath for some time and has grown very pure in the process. I invited Narendra, Balaram, Rakhal, and Bhavanath to visit his house with me so that they may be fed by him. You see, they are not just ordinary devotees, but they are actually parts of divinity made flesh. If you feed them, it's like feeding God. You will earn a lot of good merit. When you feed pure souls, your own soul benefits greatly.

It was during a visit to Balaram's house that Ramakrishna had met Girish Ghosh for the first time. The Rath Yatra, where everybody pulls the carriage that carries the deities, had been celebrated at Balaram's house. There had been much merriment on that occasion. It was like a festival of love. Everyone had felt great delight, singing and dancing to express their devotion. Now devotees had gathered once again in the home of Balaram with great bliss.

M. was teaching at a school nearby. When M. heard that Ramakrishna was visiting Balaram's house, he took time off and came to pay his respects. Upon arrival, M. at once bowed down to Sri Ramakrishna in reverence.

Ramakrishna had just completed his meal and was sitting in the parlor taking rest. He was eating pan masala and some sweets. He was flanked on all four sides by some youthful devotees.

Ramakrishna (to the devotees): How have you young people come to see me? Don't you have school today?

M: We all came as there is no special work going on in the school today.

A devotee: No, Sir, that's not true. He fled from the school! (Everyone laughed.)

M: Some irresistible energy has pulled me here.

M. seemed quite concerned for Ramakrishna. He sat right beside him, and they began to talk

Ramakrishna: My little towel is soaking wet. Would you put it someplace to dry? Put my shirt someplace where it can dry as well. My feet pain me. Please massage them a little.

> Swamiji: M. as yet had a reluctance to do seva. That's why Ramakrishna started to teach him how to serve properly.

M. finished his appointed tasks very quickly and then started to press Sri Ramakrishna's feet with his hands. Ramakrishna began to talk about many subjects, like who is a sannyasi, what is renunciation, and how does one cultivate divine qualities.

Ramakrishna (to M.): For the past several days, I have been feeling something strange in my body. Do you happen to know the reason? I can't touch anything metallic. Once I touched a bowl, and I felt as though I had been stung by a scorpion. My hand ached tremendously. I am not even able to touch the metal water pot next to the toilet to wash myself. That's why I thought, "I'll wet down my towel and take it with me. I'll see if I can't grab it with the wet towel." When I put my hand there, my hand began to pain me very greatly. Great pain came up! Ultimately, I prayed to the Divine Mother, "Mother, please don't make me take any kind of action. Please excuse me."

Ramakrishna (continuing to M.): Little Naren visits here quite often.

M: He has grown both physically and spiritually.

Ramakrishna (to M.): Yes. When little Naren hears any-thing divine, it stays with him. He remembers everything. When he was a young boy he used to cry that God didn't show himself to him.

While Ramakrishna and M. were talking about little Naren, one devotee remarked, "M. aren't you going to go back to the school?"

Ramakrishna: What is the time? Oh! It has become 1:10 pm.

Ramakrishna (to M.): You better go as you are getting late. You have left your work.

Ramakrishna (to Latu): Where's Rakhal?

Latu: He went home.

Ramakrishna: He left without seeing me?

Second Discussion

Definition of an Avatar and

How Ramakrishna Conforms to That Definition

Ramakrishna was sitting in Balaram's parlor amidst the devotees having a good time. He was laughing sweetly, and his laughter radiated in the bright faces of the devotees.

M. came back into the room and bowed to Ramakrishna. Ramakrishna made M. sit next to him again. The respected Girish Ghosh, Suresh Mitra, Balaram, Latu, Chunilal, and various other devotees were present in the room.

Ramakrishna (to Girish):   Talk with Narendra and find out the different ideas that he likes to discuss.

Girish (laughs):   Narendra says, "God is infinite. Whatever we see and hear are all a part of God. We don't have the capacity to extol all the qualities of God, the infinite ether, the infinite sky. It doesn't have parts. How do you divide the sky?"

Ramakrishna: It is true that God is infinite. He is as great and as vast as can be, but if He desires, He can dwell in the form of a human. He comes in the form of an avatar, an incarnation of God. You can feel all the attributes of this manifestation of divinity, but you cannot understand it intellectually. You want to see it with your own eyes. You want to assume some of those qualities and practice them in your own life. If you touch the horns of a cow, you've touched the cow. If you touch the foot or the tail, you have still touched the cow. For us the real essence of the cow is in the milk that comes from its udder. In the same way, in order to teach us love and devotion, God comes in the form of an individual human being.

Girish: Narendra asks how you can comprehend all of these different aspects fully. God is infinite.

Perception of the Infinite

Ramakrishna (to Girish):   Who can contemplate the infinity of God? You can neither feel nor have the attitude of the totality of divinity. You can neither feel nor have the attitude of the smallest part of God. What necessity is there in thinking about God? It is enough if you can see him with your own eyes. If you see an incarnation of the divine, then you have seen the divine. When people go to the Ganga River and touch the water, they say that they have had the darshan of Mother Ganga. It is not necessary to go from

Haridwar to Ganga Sagar and touch every drop of water in the river in order to say that one has seen the river. (Everyone laughed.)

Ramakrishna: If I've touched your foot, I say that I've touched you. (Everyone laughed again.)

Ramakrishna: If you go to the ocean and touch some of the water, then you've touched the ocean. The principle of fire is everywhere, but it is most predominant in wood. (At that, Girish began to laugh.)

Ramakrishna: Wherever I find fire, that's my place. (Ramakrishna began to laugh.)

Ramakrishna: The principle of fire is manifest most predominantly in wood. In the same way, you must look inside humanity if you want to search for the principle of divinity. His illumination is most prevalent in humanity. If you look at a human that is intoxicated with love for God, you will know for certain that this individual has become an incarnation of God.

M. was looking at Sri Ramakrishna with one-pointed vision and listening with one-pointed attention.

Ramakrishna: That is divinity. Sometimes that energy is greatly manifested and at other times quietly hidden away. There is a great illumination inside the incarnation of God. Sometimes that energy is full and complete, and that energy becomes the incarnation of Divinity. The individual's mind is illuminated with light. This is the pure mind. This is not about intellect. It's about pure intellect. When attachments and desires and selfishness go away, the pure mind and the pure intellect demonstrate themselves. When the pure mind and the pure intellect are one, this is called the pure mind. Haven't you heard of the rishis and munis? They stood before consciousness and actually perceived consciousness.

Girish (laughing): Narendra was defeated in debate by me.

Ramakrishna: No. He told me that Girish believes in avatars. Now what shall I say? If he has that kind of faith, then there's nothing more to say.

Girish (laughing again): Oh, Great Sir (Mahashay), all of my questions have been resolved, but M. is sitting here so quietly. What could he possibly be thinking upon listening to your talk? (Ramakrishna began to laugh.)

Ramakrishna: Narendra is a very deep soul. You have to be very careful with these kinds of people. Also be careful with people who talk too much. Inside they are very silent. No matter how deep you go, you will never be able to understand their minds. They stick tulsi leaves in their hair so that everyone will think they are a devotee. This is the meaning of the poem that he was reciting.

Chunilal (to Ramakrishna): People are talking badly about M. because he brought his students Little Naren, Baburam, Narayana, Paltu, Purna, and Tejacandra to you. They are doing poorly in their studies as a result. In a way, he is at fault.

Ramakrishna: Who will believe their words?

While this conversation was going on, Narayan arrived and bowed down to Thakur. Ramakrishna loved this boy very much. Narayan was a very fair-complexioned young man about 17 or 18 years old and a student. Ramakrishna would often become restless, sit in Dakshineswar, and cry if he could not see Narayan. He would say that in Narayan he could actually see God.

Girish (looking at Narayan): Who gave him the news that Ramakrishna is visiting here? I see M. has been creating more trouble. (Everyone laughed.)

Ramakrishna (with great laughter): Be careful! Be quiet! They will start saying bad things about M. again.

Worrying about Food is a Wonderful Subject and the Results of the Brahmin's Acceptance of Gifts

Once again a discussion arose about Narendra.

A devotee: Why does he not come these days?

Ramakrishna: The worry for food is wonderful indeed. Even Kalidas (the great writer and poet) lost his mind thinking about it. (Everyone laughed.)

Balaram: Narendra frequently visits Shiva Guha's eldest son, Ananda.

Ramakrishna: Yes, along with Ananda, Narendra often goes to one officer's house where they have meetings of the Brahmo Samaj.

A devotee: That officer's name is Tarapada.

Balaram (with great laughter): The brahmins say that Ananda has a great ego.

Ramakrishna: Don't listen to everything the brahmins say. You know what kind of people they are. You are judged good or bad depending on how much you give them. (Everyone laughed.) I know Ananda. He is a good person.

Third Discussion

The Bliss of Singing in the Company of Devotees

Thakur has declared his desire to listen to songs (bhajans or hymns). Balaram's parlor was filled with people eager to observe Ramakrishna and listen to his words.

> Tarapada began to sing:
> Oh, Keshava, give grace to the lowly.
> You who roam in the groves of Vrindaban.
> Oh, Madhava, who mesmerizes all minds
> while holding that mesmerizing flute.
> Oh, my mind, sing the name of Hari!
> Sing the name of Hari!
> Sing the name of Hari!
> Oh, young boy of Vrindaban,
> who took away the fear of the snake Kaliya,
> take away the fear from all.
> Oh, You with large round eyes,
> with a crown of peacock feathers,
> You are the delight of Radha's heart.
> Oh, You who are adorned with wild flowers,
> who raised the mountain Govardhana,
> it is you who destroyed the pride of Kamsa.
> Oh, Dark One, You play with the gopis
> with great delight.
> Oh, my mind, sing the name of Hari,
> Hari, Hari!

Ramakrishna (to Girish): Ah, he sings very well. Did you write all the songs?

One devotee: Yes, Girish wrote all the songs of the Chaitanyalila drama.

Ramakrishna (to Girish): This particular song has come out very well.

Ramakrishna (to the singer): Can you sing a song about Nitai?

Then Tarapada sang a song about Nitai:

> Come and take the love of the youthful,
> for the waves of love have risen.
> The love is flowing in a hundred streams.
> Come and take as much as you desire!
> Taste the love given freely
> by this youthful girl in love.
> For the love radiating from Radha
> inspires us to sing the name of Hari!
> It is Love alone that gives us life,
> and the waves of love
> cause life to dance in ecstasy.
> From Radha's fount of love
> flows the name of Hari!
> All come and chant
> the name of Hari, Hari, Hari!
> Come, come, come, come!

Then he sang a song about Gauranga:

> Oh, Gauranga, with whose bhava
> did you fill my life?
> A hurricane has risen in the sea of love.
> My thoughts no longer remain my own.
> My mind has been filled with Gauranga.
> In the midst of Vraja (the area of Vrindaban),
> You appeared as a cowherd
> tending to his cows.
> You played that mesmerizing flute
> stealing the hearts and minds of the gopis.
> By lifting Mount Govardana,
> You saved Vrindaban.
> You showed Your respect
> to the gopis by touching their feet

while shedding tears of love.
My mind has been filled with Gauranga!

Everyone requested M. to sing a song. M. was embarrassed and whispered into Ramakrishna's ears.

Girish (laughing, to Ramakrishna): Oh, Great Sir (Mahashay), it looks like M. doesn't want to sing any song at all!

Ramakrishna: He goes to school and shows his teeth but to sing a song he puts on a dark face!

Suresh Mitra was sitting a little farther away. Ramakrishna looked at him with a puzzled glance and then pointing to Girish Ghosh asked Suresh, "Who are you? He is Girish."

Suresh (laughing): He is my older brother. (They all began to laugh.)

Ramakrishna: Mahima Chakrabarty has read many scriptures. He is much respected.

Girish: Yes, he has great knowledge. I haven't forgotten him.

Girish (to Ramakrishna): I didn't study well when I was a child, and yet some people say that I'm smart.

Ramakrishna (laughing): Do you know the kind of attitude we need to have with books and scriptures? They are all here to help us to reach God. They are like road maps. They are here to teach the path and to show the means of attainment. How many books and scriptures do you need? You have to do the work yourself.

One man received a letter from his family asking him to buy some items. There were many things written down, but he misplaced the letter. He began to search high and low and got everyone involved to find out where he had put the letter. When he finally found it, his delight knew no bounds! With great care he opened and read the contents. In it was written that he had to send five kilos of sweets, a roll of cloth, and a few other things. Then he threw it away as there was no more need for the letter. He purchased the sweets, the cloth, and all the other things that were on the list. So, for how long was the letter necessary? Just so long as he couldn't remember the sweets, the cloth, and the other things on the list. Once he knew what was needed, it was time for the implementation.

The scriptures describe the way to attain God, but after you've learned all the ways to attain to Godliness, you have to begin the work. Only then can you get to God. Just being a pundit is not sufficient. The pundits can memorize many verses and know many scriptures. However, they have selfishness in their worldly dealings and great love for their desires and attachments. Just carrying the scriptures is of no use to anyone. Even if it is written in the almanac that it is going to rain today, you won't get even a drop of water by squeezing the almanac. (Everybody laughed.)

Girish (jokingly): You mean if you squeeze the almanac, you won't get even one drop of water? (Everybody began to laugh.)

Ramakrishna (laughing): The pundits talk, talk, talk! What do they really know? Where is their perception? All that they really seem to care about are their desires and attachments, the comfort of their bodies, and the collection plate. The vultures fly very high in the sky, but their perception remains focused on the earth looking for dead animals.

Ramakrishna (to Girish): Narendra is a very good boy. He sings and is active in sports. He is smart and a good student. He has conquered his senses. He has discrimination and renunciation. He speaks the truth. He has many good qualities. What do you think? Am I right?

Girish: Yes.

M: He is.

Ramakrishna: Look, M. has a great feeling for Girish. They have bonded.

M. is looking at Girish with one-pointed attention. Girish has known M. for just a few days but says that by the way that M. looks at him, he feels as though it is an old relationship. He feels as though they have been friends for a long time or like they are close relatives. It looks like they have been stitched together with the same thread. They are jewels out of the same group.

M. and Girish (to Ramakrishna): Sir, won't you sing for us?

Ramakrishna (with a beautiful sweet voice began to sing of the divine qualities):

> Protect the Divine Mother in your heart.
> May you see Her as I see Her and nobody else.
> You take away all of my desires
> and my anger and my passion.
> I am seeing with great deep intensity,
> and I am keeping that sweet nectar within.
> Again and again I pray to the Divine Mother.
> Maa, don't give me bad desires,
> and don't give me inauspicious thoughts.
> Send them all far away from me.

> Give me the eyes of wisdom as protectors
> so that I am always protected
> and always be careful not to accede
> to bad desires and bad thoughts.

His singing intensified expressing an overwhelming love for Divine Mother and utter disdain for worldliness. He was going deeper and deeper inside while continuing to call on Divine Mother with great love and affection:

> Maa, You are the Mother of all bliss.
> Don't make me devoid of bliss.
> Mother, fill my mind with Your two lotus feet.
> I don't want to know anything more.
> I don't even need to know what's happening
> to this body composed of five elements.
> I am simply going to sing
> the name of Divine Mother and sail
> through this worldly sea singing Your name.
> This is my only desire.
> You can submerge me i
> n the ocean of this world,
> but I won't know anything.
> I only know my devotion to You.
> Day and night I'm swimming
> in the bliss of Your name.
> Durga, Durga, Durga!
> I'm totally immersed day and night
> in the name of Durga,
> but still all the pain has not left me.
> If I go on in this way, oh, Most Beautiful One,
> I shall surely die,
> and there won't be anybody
> to sing the name of Durga.

Ramakrishna sang another song about the Mother of eternal supreme consciousness:

> You're always in ecstasy with Shiva,
> and the two of you only know bliss.
> Though constantly drinking
> this nectar of devotion,
> it never exhausts itself.
> The entire earth is shaking
> under the feet of Shiva.
> He is dancing like a crazy man.
> No shame and no fear can remain.

The devotees listened with rapt attention, completely silent and mesmerized. They sat with one-pointed attention looking at the manifestation of his bhava. Ramakrishna completed his song.

Ramakrishna: I didn't sing that song very well. I have a cold.

Fourth Discussion

It was the evening, and the pujas prescribed for this time of the day had been completed. The reflection of the sky was seen on the water when viewed from the bank of the river. There was a beautiful breeze blowing down from the mountains across the river into the Dakshineswar temple complex. Anyone seeing this beautiful expression of nature would automatically be imbued with a corresponding beatific expression of attitude. It was sunset.

Ramakrishna (with the attitude of a child, thinking): Where has the sun gone? It is now evening. How fantastic! Who made this form? The birds have flown to their nests. Those humans with even a little consciousness are repeating the names of the first and foremost among the poets, that Supreme Divinity that has created all this expression.

He was contemplating as the evening melted into night. The devotees were mesmerized and sat rooted on their asans. Ramakrishna began to sing the names of the Mother with a beautiful voice. Everyone's face reflected the radiance of Thakur as they drank in the sweet nectar pouring forth from him. This was a child calling out to his mother with such intense love and devotion that no one had ever seen anything quite like it before.

The devotees (thinking): What is the necessity of looking at the sky or the mountains or the ocean or the forest?

They felt that their Guru deva, Sri Ramakrishna, was the very embodiment of compassion. He nourished the devotees just like a cow that freely gives its nourishing milk. Everyone that saw Ramakrishna had all their confusions dispelled. Where there had been no bliss, bliss was established. Why is that? The devotees saw the embodiment of peace and bliss in Ramakrishna. Can one begin to imagine the beauty of the form of this embodiment of love, this man established in truth? He is verily the Infinite Supreme Divinity. It was both nourishing and refreshing, just like drinking milk, listening to his nectar-like words or reveling in his attitude in calling the names of God. It was immaterial wondering whether he was an incarnation of God or not.

The minds of the devotees became still in his presence. He was like the North Star to the devotees, an emblem of love and constancy. Look deep within the mirror lake of your heart. Who do you see reflected there? As the devotees were contemplating the beautiful form of Ramakrishna in this way, from Thakur's holy lips flowed the names of God and the names of the Divine Mother. Everyone assembled was deeply appreciative of the opportunity to drink these nectar-like words flowing from Sri Ramakrishna. When he finished

the recitation of the names and qualities of divinity,
Ramakrishna began to pray. He was a shining example of the
Supreme Divinity. For the benefit of all, Ramakrishna had
come to demonstrate true devotion and prayer and the form
that a prayer should take.

Ramakrishna:

> Mother, I am taking refuge
> in those who take refuge in You.
> I have taken refuge in Your lotus feet.
> I don't want any comforts for my body, Mother.
> I don't want any respect from society.
> I don't need the eight siddhis.
> Mother, please give me true devotion
> to Your lotus feet.
>
> Take away all of my selfishness
> and give me true devotion to You.
> You know for a certainty, Mother,
> that Your mesmerizing countenance
> would never be far from me.
> In this world of objects and relationships,
> make it so that I have
> no attraction to desires and attachments.
> Mother, other than You, I have no one.
> I have no capacity to sing Your name,
> I have no sadhana,
> I have no wisdom,
> and I have no devotion.
> Please, Mother, give me Your grace,
> and give me pure devotion to Your lotus feet.

M. (thinking): Whoever will sing Her name at the three
times of prayer, from that mouth pours forth the Ganga.
What need is there for any other type of prayer?

Afterwards, M. understood that Ramakrishna had taken the human form in order to teach humans. In truth he was a yogi in a human form, singing the names of God in order to teach everyone the meaning of a real devotee.

Girish Ghosh invited Ramakrishna to go to the theater with him. Ramakrishna objected that it would be too late in the night. Girish promised that they could leave whenever Ramakrishna desired. Girish said that he had to go to the theater because there was an interesting drama being enacted.

Fifth Discussion

It was nine o'clock in the evening. Ramakrishna desired to eat, so Balaram prepared a meal. Because Ramakrishna was getting ready to go to Girish's house, he asked Balaram to send the food there. Ramakrishna started to descend from the second floor surrounded by Narayan, M., Ram, Chuni, and many other devotees. One of the devotees asked him whom he wanted to accompany him to Girish's house.

Ramakrishna: If one person goes, that will be sufficient.

While descending the stairs, Ramakrishna suddenly became totally transfixed with love for God. This divine bhava intensified until he was completely intoxicated in ecstatic love of God.

Seeing Ramakrishna in this state, Narayan tried to grab his hand to prevent him from falling. Ramakrishna stopped him from doing so. A short while later he sweetly explained to Narayan.

Ramakrishna (to Narayan): If you hold my hand everyone will think I'm either drunk or drugged. Therefore, I will walk by myself.

There are three roads in the little suburb of Bospara.
Ramakrishna crossed them and only had to go a bit further to
reach Girish's house.   Everyone wondered why he was
walking so fast that the devotees had fallen behind.   Then
they began to understand his bhava, the spiritual attitude that
Ramakrishna had assumed. He looked like a crazy man as he
ran across the road. Is that great soul remembering the words
from the Vedas? He is realized as the one who has a pure
mind, a pure soul, and a pure intellect.   Ramakrishna is
completely pure. The devotees are beginning to understand
that Ramakrishna has actually seen God. He has had His
darshan and is seeing Him even now. Whatever That is, That
is what Ramakrishna is.

Ramakrishna: Oh, look, Narendra is coming.   Hey,
Narendra, come here!

He called him and then became quiet. Amazing! After
Ramakrishna called out to Narendra, he went into samadhi.
Awestruck at his sudden silence, everyone must have said to
themselves with wonder, "This is true bhava, God
Consciousness. Is this what Gauranga was like as well? Did
he experience this very same state? Who is able to understand this bhava?"

Ramakrishna came to the entrance of Girish's house. His
devotees had caught up to him by then. He beckoned to
Narendra and asked if he was doing well.

Ramakrishna (to Narendra very sweetly): You see, my
child, I could not speak before.

Every letter that came out of his holy mouth was the
epitome of beauty and compassion. He stood at the front
door.

Ramakrishna (to Narendra): I have something to say. This is one individual body, and that is the whole perceivable universe. When you go into samadhi, you will see that the individual becomes the universe.

Narendra looked at him with astonishment. They exchanged a few more words, words that could have come from the Vedas -- divine words. They had soared to the bank of the infinite ocean and were now standing there in complete wonderment listening to the sound of infinite waves rising and falling upon the infinite expanse of the ocean.

Sixth Discussion

In the Temple with the Devotees and

Reading the Newspaper and Talking to Nityagopal

Girish was standing by the door and invited Ramakrishna into his house. Girish came forward and prostrated completely on the floor. He got up only when he received the word to do so. He held onto the two feet of Ramakrishna and took the dust of his feet. He escorted him to the second floor and into the parlor. The excited devotees followed indoors and took their seats. Everyone wanted to sit next to Ramakrishna and drink the nectar-like words flowing from his mouth. When Ramakrishna was going to sit down, he saw a newspaper near his seat and started to talk about the news in that paper. He said that the newspaper contained worldly gossip which was impure in his eyes. He signaled someone to take the newspaper away. After the newspaper was removed, he took his seat and bowed down to Nityagopal.

Ramakrishna (to Nityagopal): You sit down here.

Nityagopal: I will.

Nityagopal had never been to Dakshineswar. He was not feeling well, and his body was in pain.

Ramakrishna (to Nityagopal): How are you?

Nityagopal: I'm not feeling very good.

Ramakrishna: Nityagopal is a high flier. You should live a little lower.

Nityagopal: I don't like people very much. I fear them. They say so many things. Only one or two times have I had enough courage to stand up to them.

Ramakrishna: That may be so, but what do you fear? Who lives with you?

Nityagopal: A respectable man named Tarak stays with me, although at times I don't like to be with him either.

Ramakrishna: There was a holy sadhu that stayed in Nangta Totapuri's ashram. He used to look at the sky all the time. He left his body while looking at the sky.

While talking thus, Ramakrishna drifted into samadhi. Everyone was amazed with this expression of divine attitude. After a while he said, "Hello, are you here? I am here too. Who will understand that we are both here?"

This was his divine attitude. He was speaking directly to God.

Seventh Discussion

The Avatar is the Perceivable Form of Perfection

Ramakrishna (to M.): I see in reality that He has become all of this. He has become the individual life, and He has become the entire perceivable universe as well. Until we attain to that consciousness, we cannot truly know what consciousness is. Merely speaking these words is not sufficient. I actually see that God has become everything. It is through His grace that you attain to that consciousness and move into samadhi. From time to time you may completely forget that you have a body. You don't have any selfish attachments or desires. You find that you don't enjoy anything except words about the Supreme. It becomes very painful to listen to worldly gossip. At once you get up and leave that place.

Ramakrishna (to Narendra): Kali is the Supreme Divinity. What you call Brahman, I call Kali. When you have attained to that consciousness, then you know truly what consciousness is.

Ramakrishna (to M.): I have seen that if you continue in worldly thoughts, then you get to know Him in some ways. However, if you meditate on Him with one-pointed focus, then you know Him in a different way. When She reveals Herself to you and you become one with Her, you become an avatar. If She shows Her play to you in the form of a human being, you will not think about worldly gossip anymore. You will not have to explain it to anybody. Do you know what it's like? It is like being in a dark place struggling to light a match when suddenly it ignites. When She gives you that sudden flash of illumination, all your doubts are dispelled immediately. Do you think that you can know the infinite just by thinking about it?

Ramakrishna called to Narendra to sit him down beside him. Ramakrishna started to ask him questions in such a loving way that one could literally feel the love pouring out of him.

Narendra (to Ramakrishna): I meditated on Kali for three or four days and nothing happened.

Ramakrishna: It will happen gradually as your worship intensifies. Kali is not separate or different from you. The one who is called Brahman, the Supreme Divinity, is Kali. Brahman and Kali are one and the same. She is the primeval energy or power, Shakti. When there is no activity, we call Her the Supreme Consciousness. When She creates, protects, and transforms this universe, we call Her the divine energy. Who are you calling Kali? Kali is all. All this is Kali. He whom you refer to as the Brahman is Kali to me. There is no distinction between the Supreme Consciousness called Brahman and the Supreme Energy called Mother Kali. When one accepts Kali, one automatically accepts Brahman. They are just like fire and its capacity to burn. If you contemplate fire, you also contemplate its capacity to burn. If you contemplate Kali as the existence of the Divine Mother, then you must contemplate Brahman, the Supreme Divinity. By contemplating on the Supreme Divinity, you will discover the form of Kali. There is no distinction permissible between the Supreme Divinity and His energy. I call Her Shakti, I call Her energy, and I call Her Kali.

It was well into the night.

Girish (to Haripada): Hey, brother, call a carriage for us. I have to go to the theater.

Ramakrishna (laughing, teasing to Haripada): Make sure you bring the carriage.

Haripada (laughing): I am going to bring the carriage, why not?

Attainment of God and Our Karma,

Rama and Karma, God and Desires

Girish (to Ramakrishna): May I leave you and go to the theater?

Ramakrishna: No, you keep me here and you keep me there too. Janaka the King stayed in divine knowledge and ran his kingdom as well and at the same time drank his glass of milk, which means that he was both in the samsara and outside of it. (They all began to laugh.)

Girish: I am going to leave the theater to the next generation.

Ramakrishna: No, you can't! You are doing fine. You are creating a benefit for many people.

Narendra (quietly): You were just discussing avatars and incarnations of God, and now you are going to the theater?

Eighth Discussion

In the Temple of Samadhi

Ramakrishna was sitting in the temple filled with divine bhava. He was next to Narendra and looked at him with one-pointed attention. Suddenly he moved a little closer and exclaimed, "Narendra doesn't believe in avatars. It doesn't really matter. What can you hope for from him?"

Feeling great love for Narendra, Sri Ramakrishna rose higher and higher. Whenever Ramakrishna sees Narendra, he at once becomes filled with love and an attitude of communion.

He put his hand on Narendra's head very lovingly.

Ramakrishna: Whether you believe in incarnations of God or not, I still have great love for you.

Worldly Thoughts and the Attainment of Godliness

Ramakrishna (to Narendra): As long as you are contemplating worldliness, it is impossible to attain to Godliness. I don't like the thoughts that keep going through your mind. For example, say you get an invitation to go visit another person's house. When you're getting ready to eat, there is so much gossip in the room. When everyone sits down and starts to eat their puris and vegetables, the room suddenly becomes silent. All you hear is the sound of chewing. The more food given to eat, the more silent the room becomes, except for the sound of chewing. When yogurt is served at the end, all you hear is slurp, slurp! When you have eaten completely, then you fall sleep. Similarly, the nearer you attain to Godliness, that much your worldly thought is reduced. When you attain to the fullness of God, then you become very silent and enter into samadhi.

Speaking thus, he stroked Narendra's head. He lovingly pinched his chin.

Ramakrishna (to Narendra): Hari Om, Hari Om.

Narendra (thinking): Why is he doing this to me?

Ramakrishna saw that Narendra was in fact Lord Narayana. This is seeing God in human beings. How wonderful it was! He looked at Narendra repeatedly and moved into samadhi. He became completely oblivious to the outside world. As he went deeper and deeper inside, his consciousness was partly inside and partly outside like Gauranga Mahaprabhu.

He put his hands on Narendra's feet, just like Lakshmi massaging the feet of Vishnu. Then He put His hand on Narendra's body. Everyone wondered, "Why is the Guru massaging the body and the feet of the disciple? Is he serving God, or is he giving him energy?"

Ramakrishna went still deeper into samadhi and said loudly to Narendra with folded hands.

Ramakrishna: Sing a song for me. Then I will be fine. Otherwise, how will I be able to get up?

Ramakrishna was in such deep samadhi that he was incapable of rising on his own. After a little bit of time, again he sat transfixed. It was as if he had become a wooden doll. He fell totally silent. Then intoxicated with this bhava, he began to sing again:

> My friends, how far is that forest
> where my beautiful Shyama resides?
> I want to go where I can get
> the scent of my Krishna,
> so I continue to move towards that forest.

By then Ramakrishna had forgotten the perceivable universe completely. He was sitting right beside Narendra and looking at his face, but he didn't recognize the presence of Narendra. His mind had completely merged with the Supreme Lord of Life.

> Swamiji: His mind has been blown and his soul has flown.

Sri Ramakrishna was totally submerged in samadhi. While still somewhat in samadhi, he suddenly stood up and then sat down again.

Ramakrishna: Hey! Can you see there is a light coming? I can't understand from which direction that light is coming.

Narendra started to sing:

> Now You have taken away
> all our pain by giving us darshan.
> I forget the seven worlds when I sit at Your feet.
> Where have I been so many days without You?

Ramakrishna listened while he opened his eyes very slowly like Lord Shiva in the stsate of Shuddha Vidya. He was very still, without any movement, in deep samadhi. He came out of his samadhi.

Ramakrishna (like a small child): Who is going to take me home?

It has become very late in the night. It's the tenth day of the dark fortnight in the month of Falgun, and it is very dark. Ramakrishna left for the Kali temple in Dakshineswar. He stood near the carriage with the devotees surrounding him. With some difficulty the devotees helped push him up into the carriage because he was still in bhava samadhi. The carriage began to move and the devotees dispersed. Om.

Chapter 15

Conversation with Sri Ramakrishna and Joyful

Celebration in Shyampukur House with Dr. Sarkar,

Girish, Ishan and Other Devotees

October 22, 1885

First Discussion

It was the month of Aswin, and it was the fourteenth day of the bright fortnight. Sri Ramakrishna and the devotees had all been celebrating Navaratri with much joy and fanfare. The seventh, eighth, and ninth days of the festival had been increasingly filled with more music and bliss! The tenth day was Vijaya, the victory celebration. This day of celebration had a special quality. Everyone expressed their love by embracing each other.

Doctor Sarkar

Sri Ramakrishna was suffering from throat cancer, so the devotees had moved him to a house in Shyampukur, which was a suburb of Calcutta. The cancer was causing him great physical pain.

When Sri Ramakrishna was staying at Balaram's house, Kaviraj Ganga Prasad, who was an expert in ayurvedic medicine, had been the doctor attending him. He had visited him frequently. On one of those occasions, Ramakrishna had asked him if this disease was a difficult one to get rid of or if it could be easily cured. The doctor had fallen silent. He just didn't have the heart to honestly answer Sri Ramakrishna's question.

Doctors who took a more English approach, trained in the ways of western medicine, had also examined him. They had admitted that the prospects for a cure were doubtful, if not impossible.

Doctor Sarkar was the physician treating Sri Ramakrishna.

It was Thursday the twenty-second of October 1885. Ramakrishna was residing in a two-story house in Shyampukur. He was sitting upon a bed that had been arranged for him. Doctor Sarkar had arrived to examine Sri Ramakrishna. The respected Ishan Chandra Mukhopadhyaya had come along with him. They, along with a number of other devotees, were sitting all around Ramakrishna.

Ishan was an extremely generous man. Though he lived on a small, fixed pension, he always ended up giving it away to those in need. On top of that he borrowed money and gave that away as well. He had a devotional nature, always contemplating God. When he heard of Ramakrishna's pain, he came immediately to see the patient.

Whenever Dr. Sarkar came to see Sri Ramakrishna, he stayed for six or seven hours at a time. He had tremendous faith and devotion towards Sri Ramakrishna. With the greatest of devotion and respect, he attended to Sri Ramakrishna.

It was about seven o'clock in the evening. The moon had risen, and its silvery rays were illuminating the four directions. Inside the room the lights were burning. In the room many people had come to see the great soul, Sri Ramakrishna. Everyone was gazing with one-pointed attention at the embodiment of this great soul. They all wanted to hear what he would say, and they wanted to see what he would do.

Ramakrishna (to Ishan): I am going to tell you the way of success, how you can become free even while living in the midst of all this worldly bondage, how to live in this worldly ocean of samsara without getting wet. The individual who is able to perform his or her functions in the world with their mind and attention focused on the feet of God are blessed and heroic individuals. For example, a man is walking along carrying two mounds (eighty kilos) on top of his head when he sees a groom marching off in a bridal procession on the way to meet his future wife. There is such a heavy load on his head, yet still he is able to see the groom.

If you don't have a lot of energy and determination, you are not going to be successful. You must be like the fish that lives in the mud at the bottom of a pond, yet no mud ever sticks to its body. It's also like a goose that sticks its head into the water to grab a fish. It comes up and shakes, and none of the water sticks to its body.

Ramakrishna (continuing): In order to maintain this type of independence and freedom while living in this ocean of worldliness, it's necessary to perform some sadhana, spiritual discipline. From time to time it is imperative to spend some time alone. Stay for a year, stay for six months, stay for three months, stay for only one month; but in some lonely place, you must perform some spiritual discipline on your own. You must always pray to God with sincerity, with sincere commitment.

You must pray sincerely for greater devotion, while saying to yourself, "I don't have anyone in this ocean of worldliness. Whatever people say to me is mine for only two days. Whatever I call my own, I can only have for two days at most. I have to understand and feel with complete sincerity that I am Yours. I belong to You only. I am Your individual. You are mine and You are my all." You must feel this deeply with all your mind and heart. You have to deeply contemplate, "How am I going to attain You?"

Now after you have attained this type of devotion, then only it becomes possible to act in the world without getting wet. Just as if you first rub your hands with oil before cutting open a jackfruit, your hands won't get sticky. The ocean of worldliness is in the form of water, and man's interaction is in the form of milk. If you put milk in water, the milk will mix with the water and become one. That's why if you want to make cream, you have to keep the milk separate. When you make the cream into butter and then put the butter into a bowl of water, it will not dissolve in it. It will float on top. It will always remain separate.

The members of the Brahmo Samaj asked me, "Do you mean that we should perform our worldly actions in the same way Janaka the King performed his? In the same way that he freed himself from attachment to his worldly affairs, is that how we should perform all of our activities in the world?"

Ramakrishna: I answered them, "It is very difficult to perform your worldly responsibilities without attachment. Just saying so does not make you a King Janaka." He did a headstand for thousands of years, while keeping his feet in the air as a tapasya! Now I am not saying that you have to stand on your heads in order to find God, but you do have to practice some spiritual discipline. It is imperative for you to reside from time to time by yourself. In that kind of aloneness comes the attainment of wisdom.

After you have attained devotion, then go and resume your worldly responsibilities. You have to make the yogurt in a still and quiet place. If you keep shaking, stirring, and mixing it, it won't congeal into yogurt. You won't have the yogurt. Janaka was so unattached that one of his names was Videha, he who resides without a body. He had no consciousness or apprehension of his body. He was so liberated from his worldly interaction that he could perform actions in the world without awareness of his body. He was the perfect example of a jivamukta, one who is liberated in this very life. To rid oneself of body consciousness is a very long process that requires a lot of spiritual discipline. Janaka was an extremely heroic individual. He held on to two swords, one was right action and the other was wisdom.

Wisdom That Comes from the Ocean of Worldliness

and the Wisdom That Comes from Sannyas

Ramakrishna: Someone may wonder if the wisdom gained by a wise individual living in the midst of worldliness and the wisdom gained by an individual living the renounced life of a sannyasi is the same. The answer is that they are both one. There is a wisdom that is performed in the world, and there is a wisdom that is achieved outside of the world. Those that have both wisdom and worldliness have some fear. If you go to live with desires and attachments, you should be afraid. If you go into a house that is filled with soot, you will be afraid that you might get some on you. You will be very careful to avoid the soot.

If you make butter and put it in a new vessel, the butter will not become spoiled. If you put it into a mud pot, you have a doubt. (They all began to laugh.)

When you go to fry flat rice, some of the rice jumps out of the pan. The puffed rice opens up like the petals of a white jasmine flower, and it is stainless. The kernels that remain in the pan don't puff up as much as the ones that jump out, and they retain a small stain. In the same way, if a sannyasi attains wisdom in the world, he becomes stainless like the puffed rice that popped out of the pan. If after achieving that wisdom he goes back to the world, a slight stain will remain on him.

Once a bhairavi, a lady sannyasi worshiper of Shiva, came into the court of Janaka the King. When he saw a woman walking into his court, Janaka hid his eyes in embarrassment. When the bhairavi saw that Janaka was hiding his face from her, she said, "Hey, Janaka, even today you still fear women?" When one has attained pure wisdom, one will have the attitude of a 5-year-old child. One won't understand the difference between a woman and a man. Be that as it may, the stain that remains on an individual who continues to live in samsara after attaining divine wisdom does not do any real harm. There is a spot on the moon, but it doesn't diminish its light.

After Attaining Wisdom Comes

the Ability to Uplift Humanity

Ramakrishna: After wisdom comes action in order to uplift and unite humanity. Some individuals, after achieving wisdom, come to teach others, like Janaka and Narada. In order to teach individuals, you must have Shakti, spiritual energy. The rishis used to roam in search of their own wisdom. They were very heroic individuals. If a reed lands in the water and a bird lands on it, both the bird and the reed will sink. If you have a very solid piece of wood sitting on the water, a person can float on it, a cow, or even an elephant, and it will remain afloat. The steamboat crosses the river carrying not only itself, but also many passengers along with it. Narada and other such teachers were like the wood that was solidly made into a steamboat.

One person eats a bellyful of food and then with his towel wipes away all traces of his meal, so no one will see that he has eaten. (Everyone laughed.) There is another type of individual who, having for his meal only one piece of fruit, still cuts it into as many pieces as there are people in the vicinity. He shares his fruit with everyone he can, taking only what remains after everyone else has been fed, even if he himself must go without. In this same selfless way after attaining knowledge, Narada and others went to share the prasad of their great devotion.

Second Discussion

Ramakrishna: In this period of time we are now living in, it is most appropriate to practice jnana yoga, the path of wisdom, and bhakti yoga, the path of devotion.

Doctor: When you attain wisdom, it is astounding. Your eyes close, and pour forth great streams of tears. Then the need for devotion becomes very important.

Ramakrishna: Devotion is a female and that is why she can go inside. Wisdom can go up only as far as the guest room. (Everyone began to laugh.)

Doctor: You mean they don't allow wisdom to go all the way inside the inner rooms of the house? Not all women are able to go into the inner rooms. A prostitute can't! She needs wisdom to find her way inside. So this shows that wisdom is needed along with devotion.

Ramakrishna: If you don't know the right path, have devotion and a sincere desire to know her. In this way people can attain to Godliness.

There was once a great devotee who went on a pilgrimage to Jagannath Puri. He didn't know the way to Puri. He went in the wrong direction and got lost. He was really sincere and in that sincerity he asked everyone he met, "Where is the path to Puri?" Everybody he asked said, "It is not this way, it is that way." Finally, he arrived in Puri and had the darshan of Jagannath. So even if you don't know the path, someone is going to tell you how to get there.

Doctor: He started in the wrong way?

Ramakrishna: Yes, that is true, but ultimately he found his goal.

One person asked: Is God with form or without form?

Ramakrishna: She is with form and again without form. A sannyasi went on a pilgrimage to Jagannath. When he had the darshan of the deity of Jagannath, a doubt arose in his mind, "Is God with form or without form?" He was holding a stick in his hand. He started to wave it to find out if God was real. Does the stick hit the body of the deity? He took the stick and waved it where the deity was and it didn't touch anything. So he waved it back, and it still didn't touch anything. It was as though there was no deity at all, so he decided that God did not have form. Then he moved closer towards the deity and waved the stick again. This time it hit the deity. So he decided that God has form.

Then he understood that God is both with form and without form. It is very difficult to understand this contemplation. How is it possible that She who is beyond all form again takes a form? How is that possible? This doubt arose in his mind, "If She is with form, how does She have so many forms?"

Doctor: She who made the infinite is beyond form, yet if She so wills, She can take form. It is She who created the mind, and it is She who takes away the mind. She who is beyond everything can indeed become everything.

Ramakrishna: Unless you have attained to the highest realization of God, this is very difficult to understand. For the benefits of sadhus, She assumes different forms. There was once a man who had a pot of dye. Many people came to the dyer to have their cloths colored. One person came and the dyer asked, "What color do you want to dye your cloth?" The person replied, "I want my cloth to become red-colored." The dyer took the customer's cloth, dipped it in the pot, pulled out the cloth, and said, "Take your red-colored cloth." Another person came and said, "I want my cloth to be yellow-colored." The dyer took the cloth, dipped it in the pot, and said, "Here, take your yellow-colored cloth." Another customer wanted a blue-colored cloth, and the dyer dipped the cloth into the same pot and said, "Here, take your blue cloth." Many people came to the dyer to have their cloths dyed in different colors. He used the same pot of dye and colored everyone's cloth to the color of his or her desire.

One man was standing and watching this entire wonderful event. He asked the dyer, "What is going on here?" The dyer asked him, "What color would you like your cloth dyed?" The customer said, "My brother, I want the cloth dyed the color that is in the pot!"

Swamiji: Another story.

Ramakrishna: One individual went to answer the call of nature. He saw a beautiful animal sitting in a tree. He told another person of that event. He said, "My brother, in a certain tree I saw a red-colored animal." That person replied, "I have also seen that animal, but why are you calling him red? He was green!" Another person said, "No, no! How are you calling him green? He was yellow!" In this way, many people gave their opinions. "He was purple. He was blue. He was black." Ultimately, they began to fight. Finally, they went to the foot of the tree. There was somebody sitting there. They asked him if he knew of the animal, and he replied, "I stay at the foot of this tree. I know that animal very well. You are all correct. Sometimes he is red, sometimes he is green, sometimes he is yellow, and sometimes he is blue. He becomes many different colors. Sometimes you see him without any color at all. He is called a chameleon."

That individual who is always in contemplation of God is able to know the intrinsic nature of divinity. That individual knows that God shows Herself in various forms and attitudes. She is with qualities, and She is without qualities. Those who sit at the foot of the tree know that the chameleon has many colors and sometimes no color at all. Others only debate and get into difficulties. She is with form, and She is beyond form. Do you know how that is possible?

Ramakrishna: Suppose in the ocean of Truth - Consciousness - Bliss, there is no bank or no shore. With the cold of devotion, the water of this infinite ocean congeals, and in this way, the formless is able to present a solid form to the devotee. This means that because of the sincere devotion of the devotees, She sometimes removes Herself from the infinite expanse of formlessness and assumes a form to demonstrate and show Herself. Again, when the sun of wisdom rises, the ice melts, and She once again becomes formless.

Doctor: You mean when the sun rises, the ice melts, and it becomes one with the ocean again? Sometimes the water evaporates and rises as vapor.

Ramakrishna: It means that Brahman, the Supreme Divinity, is the true existence, and the perceivable universe is transitory. When you contemplate in this way, that the Supreme Divinity is the true reality and the perceivable world is transitory, then you move into samadhi. In this samadhi all forms dissolve. Then there is no consciousness to call upon God with form. What She is, you cannot speak from your mouth. Who is there to speak? Who could say anything when the individual is no longer there himself? Neither is there a speaker nor a listener. At that time, I can no longer find even my own "I". Who is there left to search? Then that Supreme Divinity is beyond all qualities. She is at that moment beyond all knowledge, unknowable. You cannot immediately understand through your mind or through your intellect. That is why it is said that devotion is the moon and wisdom is the sun.

I have heard that there are great oceans to the very north and to the very south, but it is so cold that the water congeals and becomes ice, continents of ice. A ship can't go there. If a ship were to try to cross, it would get stuck in the ice.

Doctor: In the path of devotion, human beings sometimes do get stuck.

Ramakrishna: Yes, that is true, but there is no difficulty no complexity there. When the Ocean of Satchidananda congeals, it becomes ice. If you contemplate more about it, that the Supreme Divinity is the true reality and the perceivable world is transitory, then there is no difficulty. With the rise of the sun of wisdom, all the ice will melt. Then we will remain in the same ocean of Satchidananda.

Maa: Would you like to read more?

Swamiji: I am not the reader. (Looks at the audience.) Would you like to listen to more?

Audience: Yes!

Swamiji: This is a discussion about the unripe "I" and the ripe "I."

Ramakrishna: There is the "I" of a devotee and the "I" of a child. Ultimately, if you keep contemplating in the way of wisdom, the concept of "I" does not remain. It is very difficult to move into Samadhi so long as "I" remains. The "I" doesn't want to leave me. Because it doesn't want to leave me, it says, "I am going to have to return to the ocean of objects and relationships."

The bullock calls out "Hamba, hamba, I, I," and that is why it is in pain. All day long he has to pull a plough. Even in the rain and in the cold, he has to work. Ultimately, he goes to the butcher. His problems don't end there. They take his skin and make shoes out of it. They take his nerves and veins and make cords out of it using the cords to fluff up cotton.

Swamiji: They puff up the cotton with the innards of cows and bulls.

Ramakrishna: When the cotton is being puffed up, the cord makes the sound "Tu hu, tu hu, you, you." Then the bullock is quiet. At last he is at peace.

When a living being says, "Oh, God, You are the Doer. I am the servant. You are the Lord." When this is realized, there is peace. Then there is liberation.

Doctor: We all want to surrender to the person who puffs the cotton. (They laughed.)

> Swamiji: We are in need cotton puffer-uppers here in Napa.

Ramakrishna: If my "I" refuses to go, if I can't get it to sit still in solitude, then I will say, "Stupid idiot, you be a servant then!" (All laugh.)

> Swamiji: If I can't make my "I" stay quiet, then at least make him a servant.

After attaining to samadhi, some individuals keep a little bit of the "I" with them. They keep the servant "I" and the devotee "I." Sankaracharya kept the knowledgeable "I" in order to teach others. This kind of "I" -- the servant "I," the devotee "I," and the knowledge "I" -- these are the ripe kinds of "I."

Ramakrishna: Do you know the unripe "I?" "I am the doer, I am the son of an important person, I am knowledge-able, I am wealthy." These are the words or ideas arising from an unripe "I." If someone steals something from a house and the thief is captured by the occupants, the first thing that is done is to take back all of their stolen items. Then they begin to beat the thief. After that they give him to the police and say, "We don't know whose house he stole from, but we know he is a thief."

When you have attained to the wisdom of God, you get the intrinsic nature of a 5-year-old child. The "I" of a 5-year-old child is very, very pure. It is ripe. The child has not accepted any quality as his own. He is beyond the three gunas. He is beyond the sattva, rajas, and tamas gunas.

Swamiji: The child has no particular propensity towards any one quality.

Ramakrishna: Look, the children are not afflicted by tamas. Even if they just fought, they hug each other and play together happily moments later. The child is not even afflicted by raja guna. He has so many wonderful toys that capture his attention, and he seems to be so attached to them. However, the next moment he drops them in a heap and runs into the arms of his mother. Sometimes a child is dressed beautifully in a new silk cloth and goes outside with his or her family. Then suddenly without notice they just remove the cloth wherever they happen to be.

Swamiji: No attachment.

Ramakrishna: They forget entirely about the cloth. They put the cloth under their armpits and walk around naked. You may ask, "Whose cloth is it that you are carrying around under your armpit?" He will say, "This is my cloth. My father gave it to me." You may say nicely, "You are a wealthy child. Will you give me the cloth?" He will say, "No! This is my cloth. My father gave it to me. I won't give it to you." Later on, if you distract him with a toy to play with, he may give you the cloth and leave it without even a second thought.

This 5-year-old child is not bound by sattva guna either. He has a sense of affinity with all the children of the neighborhood and feels badly if he doesn't see them every day, but if he moves to a new place with his mother and father, he finds new friends immediately. He gives them all his love and affection and forgets his old friends completely. He has no attachment. If his mother tells him, "This is your elder brother," he believes her without a doubt.

One child may be the son of a brahmin, and another perhaps is the child of a leather maker. Yet they both sit on the same path eating rice together, maybe even from the same plate. They have no concept of purity or impurity. They have no modesty or shame in front of others. Two children went to the toilet at the same time and they didn't even wash up afterwards, but then they went to eat. They have no concept of purity or impurity. (The doctor began to laugh.)

> Swamiji: The children have no attachment to the conventions of society.

Ramakrishna: The older and respectable people are bound in various ways. They are bound by their concept of birth, attachments, shame, modesty, aversion, attraction, and their fears. They have worldly attachments. They are deceitful and have scheming conniving natures. The knowledgeable people have great egos, and others have the egotism that comes from being wealthy. This older "I," this worldly "I" is a very unripe "I."

Who Cannot Gain Wisdom?

Ramakrishna (to the doctor): There are a few kinds of people that don't get wisdom. Those who have the egotism of knowledge or the egotism of a lot of learning or the egotism of wealth -- these people never get wisdom. If you say to these types of people, "There is a sadhu in a certain place. Will you go to meet him?" They will invariably reply, "No, I won't go." In their minds they are thinking, "I am such an important person. Why should I go and see a sadhu?"

> Swamiji: There are three qualities. Through the quality of truth or sattva, we can attain to Godliness.

How to Be Successful Controlling the Senses

Ramakrishna: The intrinsic nature of the quality of tamas is egotism. Egotism is born of ignorance. It is born of the quality of tamas, darkness. In the Puranas, it is written that Ravana had the quality of rajas, tremendous activity. Kumbakarna had the quality of tamas. Vibhishana had the quality of sattva, truth. That is why Vibhishana was able to attain Rama.

There is another definition or symbol that demonstrates the presence of tamas, anger. When you are angry, wherever you look there is no wisdom. Hanuman burned Lanka, but he didn't think that Sita's hut would be destroyed too.

Girendra Ghosh of Pathuraghat was sitting on top of a rock, and he said, "I still cannot get rid of all the ripus, all the limitations of kama, krodha, moha, lobha, modha, matsarya. Turn them away and make them flee. I should desire only God. I should be pursuing the realization of Satchidananda, and if the anger doesn't leave, at least give me devotion. I have said the name of Durga. Won't I be taken across this ocean of worldliness? What kind of sin do I have? What kind of bondage do I have?"

Ramakrishna: Get greedy for the realization of God. Become intoxicated with a form of God. Think of yourself as the servant of God and say, "I am the child of God." If you have to have an ego, then have a nice ego. In this way, you have to send the six limitations of ego packing.

Doctor: It is very difficult to control my senses. When you hitch the horse to the horse cart, you have to put a cover over his eyes. Sometimes you have to completely cover the eyes of the horse.

Ramakrishna: Those six limitations of the ego can't touch you once She bestows Her grace upon you. Once you have Her vision and experience, being submerged in Her reality, you need have no more fear.

Swamiji: Remember the six limitations are kama, krodha, moha, lobha, modha, and matsarya. Kama is desire, krodha is anger, moha is ignorant attachments, lobha is greed, modha is foolishness, and matsarya is jealousy.

Ramakrishna: Narada and Prahlada and such beings were eternally liberated souls that came to the earth. When these great beings incarnate in the body, they don't have to put blinders on their eyes. For example, that little boy who grabs his father's hand when they start across the field must not let go, for he could easily trip and fall down. When the father grabs onto the child's hand, then there is no more danger of the child falling.

Doctor: It is not appropriate for the father to always hold the hand of the son.

Ramakrishna: No, that is not true. The great souls have the intrinsic nature of a child. They are always children in front of God. They have no sense of egotism whatsoever. All their energy comes from God. It is all their Father's energy. They have no capacity whatsoever on their own. This is their firm faith.

Swamiji: This is about the path of worldly contemplations and the path of contemplating bliss and the union through wisdom and the union through devotion.

Doctor: If you don't close the eyes of the horse, the horse won't want to move along the path. If we cannot contain these six limitations of the mind, is it possible that we can attain to Godliness?

Ramakrishna: What you have said, you are saying from contemplating worldliness. Now you are talking about the path of wisdom, and in that path you can find God. The wise people say, "First it is necessary to purify your consciousness and to perform sadhana, and then you will attain wisdom." However, you can also find God through the path of devotion. If you have devotion to the lotus feet of the Lord even once, if you really enjoy singing the names and qualities of God, then you don't have to try and make an effort to control your senses. The limitations of the mind come under control of their own accord. Someone is grieving for their children. When they are in the midst of that grief, will they think of going to argue with their neighbor? Would they think to go and accept an invitation to a party or festival? Would they go walking around with a lot of ego with their head held high up in the air? No, during the time of grief, that kind of behavior is not possible. When the moth is attracted to the light, will they go towards the darkness? No.

Doctor (laughing): They would rather die in the light than go to the darkness.

Ramakrishna: No, devotees don't dissolve like moths in a flame. When the devotees see the light, they run towards the light. They understand it is the light of a gem or jewel. The light of the jewel shines very brightly, but it has a cooling effect and is under control. The light of that jewel won't burn your skin. When you see the light of the jewel, you get peace, you get bliss. The path of wisdom is very difficult.

Ramakrishna: If you are contemplating by means of the path of wisdom, then you can attain to Godliness. This path is very difficult. You have to understand that "I am not the body; I am neither the mind nor the intellect. I have no sickness, no grief, and no lack of peace. I am the intrinsic nature of Satchidananda. I am beyond pleasure and pain. I am not controlled by my senses." It is very easy to say all this from your mouth, but it is very difficult to actually perform this behavior and contemplate in this way. If you were to cut your hand by a thorn, and while watching the blood pour forth from the wound, say, "The thorn didn't cut my hand. I am fine." Even though you say this, it is not true. First you have to burn that thorn in the fire of wisdom.

The Knowledge Learned from Books Compared

to Sri Ramakrishna's System of Learning

Ramakrishna: Many people think that if they don't read many books they can't achieve wisdom or get any kind of knowledge. Better than reading books is listening to them. Even better than listening is seeing.   There is a great difference between hearing about Benares, reading about Benares, and actually going to Benares.

There is a chess game. From the audience the viewer can tell better than the player who is a good player of chess. Many people who are steeped in worldliness think, "I am very intelligent," but they are filled with selfishness. They are the players themselves, but they can't understand their own game. They are playing with selfish attachment and therefore can't see the proper moves they should make. Those who have renounced their attachments are free from selfishness in their every action. They are the intelligent ones of this world. Even if they are playing themselves, they can speak correctly because they have no selfishness.

Doctor (to the other devotees): Faraday communed with nature. That is why he could discover such great scientific truths. Mathematical formulae only throw the brain into confusion. If you take too much intellectual knowledge into your brain, you will create a great obstacle on your path of spiritual inquiry. God is the Supreme Wisdom of both learning and knowledge.

Ramakrishna (to the doctor): When I was in the Panchavati grove of five trees, I used to call on the Divine Mother with so much enthusiasm I would fall down. I used to fall down on the ground and call to the Divine Mother. I said to Her, "Maa, show Yourself to me!" Whatever the performers of activity have performed, whatever the yogis have attained by coming into union, whatever the wise people have achieved by attaining to wisdom -- what more can I say, or what more can I add to what they have experienced? What circumstance has befallen me? Saying this, Ramakrishna began to sing:

> When the sleep has gone,
> then who can sleep anymore?
> I am awake in the sacrificial fire of union.
> You bestowed upon me
> this divine yogic sleep
> Where even sleep has been put to sleep.

Ramakrishna: I didn't read any books, but by calling the name of Mother, I have gotten everything. Shambhu Mallick said to me, "You don't have a sword or a shield. You are the most peaceful warrior." (They all began to laugh.)

Girish Ghosh invited the doctor to see the drama about the life of Buddha. He was so filled with bliss to see the drama. The doctor said to Girish, "You are really a bad person. Do I have to go to the theater everyday?"

Ramakrishna (to M.):   I don't understand what this person is saying. What does he mean?

M: He likes the theater and enjoyed the play very much.

Third Discussion

The Relationship between an Incarnation (Avatar)

and the Individual Life Force (Jiva)

Ramakrishna (to Ishan): You haven't said anything. This doctor doesn't believe in incarnations of God.

Ishan: If you order me to speak, I will. But I really don't wish to think or discuss anymore.   I don't like all this thinking and discussion.

Ramakrishna (a little disgusted): Why not? Don't speak like this! You must stand up and speak out for the truth!

Ishan (to the doctor): We have a big ego, and our faith is little. The crow in the Ramayana, Kak Bhushundi, didn't believe in the incarnation or the divinity of Sri Ramachandra in the beginning.   After traveling to the Devalok, the Brahmalok, and circumambulating Mt. Kailash, Kak Bhushundi decided that there was no one greater than Rama. Then he understood and took refuge in Rama. Rama caught hold of Kak Bhushundi and brought him close as his own. The crow understood that he had sat in the tree of Rama. After his ego was pulverized, he understood that even though Rama looked like an ordinary human being, within him he contained the entire egg of creation. Within him he saw the entire ether, sky, earth, stars, sun, oceans, mountains, and all the life upon them, the animals and vegetation, all was within him.

The Limited Intelligence of the Conditioned

Ramakrishna (to the doctor): It is very difficult to understand this. He is very small, and he is very great. Who is the Eternal Being? It is Her drama. How can that individual become a human being? What can we with our little intelligence say about the manifestations of God? It is very difficult for us who have very, very small intelligence to describe the manifestations of divinity. If you have a pot that can contain one kilo, can you pour four kilos of contents into it? That is why you have to believe the words of those sadhus and great souls who have attained to Godliness. The sadhus live in the thoughts and contemplations of God. Just like the lawyer dwells in the courtroom and can't get the law out of his head. Do you believe in this crow, Kak Bhushundi?

Doctor: I have faith in whatever good he spoke. There is no confusion that remains once I have faith in something. But if I try to contemplate it all, I am going to sink. How can I say that Rama is an incarnation? First of all, he killed Vali. Like a thief, he hid himself and struck Vali with an arrow. Isn't this the work of man and not God?

Girish Ghosh: Oh, Sir, God can also do this work!

Doctor: Thèn look at Sita. How did she get lost?

Girish: Oh, Sir, this work too God can do. Humans cannot.

> Swamiji: Now we are going to describe the relationship between science or worldly knowledge and the statements of the great souls.

Ishan (to the doctor): Why don't you believe in the incarnations of God? You just said, Doctor, that He who is beyond manifestation has also assumed a form. You thought that He was without form. You just said that anything could be done by God. All is possible.

Ramakrishna (laughing): God can assume a human form. These kinds of statements are not found in science, and they are not in the English books of knowledge. So how can you believe in that? (They all began to laugh.)

Listen to a story. One person said, "Hey, I saw a house fall down in my neighborhood." The other person was a well learned man in the English language, and he said, "Wait, let me see if it is in the newspaper." He read the newspaper, and he saw that there was nothing written about the destruction of the house. Then he said, "I don't believe in what you are saying. It is not in the newspaper, so it must be false." (They all began to laugh.)

   Swamiji: If you didn't see it on TV, it cannot be true.

Girish (to the doctor): You have to believe in the incarnation of Sri Krishna. I won't allow you to believe that He was just a human being.

Faith in God and Being Simple

Ramakrishna: If you are not simple, it is very difficult to have faith in God. God remains very far from worldly contemplations. When you have various worldly contemplations, you have great attachments to objects and relationships in your paradigm of reality. Then you have various forms of egotism that crop up. The egotism of a very learned person, the egotism of being a wealthy individual, and all that. The doctor here is very simple.

Girish (to the doctor): Oh, Sir, what are you saying? Can these crippled deficient beings be considered wise?

Doctor: If you say the name of Rama, it is possible.

Ramakrishna: Keshab Sen was so simple. One day he went to Rani Rasmani's house. It was about four o'clock in the afternoon, and he went to the guesthouse and asked, "Won't you serve some food to this crippled guest?"

>   Swamiji: The queen's palace used to feed the
>   poor every day.

Ramakrishna: As long as you have faith, then your wisdom will increase. The cow that eats here and there splashes milk everywhere. The cow that eats in one place gives a pure stream of milk. (They all began to laugh.) If you don't have faith like a child, you can't get to God. The mother says to the child, "This is your big brother." The child believes that he has a big brother. The mother says, "That is a ghost," and the child believes it completely. Seeing the form of the faith of a child, God has compassion. You can't get to God with a worldly cleverness.

Doctor (to the devotees): If the cow eats from various sources of food, it doesn't give good milk. I had one cow and let her eat whatever she felt like eating. Ultimately, my house was in sickness. Then I thought, "What's the cause of this?" I searched very thoroughly and finally understood that this cow wasn't eating right. Then I had to go to Lucknow, and I had to spend a lot of money! (They all began to laugh.) You can't say what effects come from which source. In one neighborhood, there was a 7-year-old girl who fell ill with whooping cough. I went to see her, but I couldn't understand any cause for her disease. Ultimately, I came to learn that the girl had drunk the milk from a wet donkey. (They all began to laugh again.)

Ramakrishna: What did you say? One day my carriage went by a tamarind tree, and I started to belch a sour flavor.

(They laughed again.)

Doctor (laughing hard): The captain of a ship got a great headache. The doctor came to cure him and put a poultice on the side of ship. (They all began to laugh again.)

Swamiji: They cured the captain's headache by administering to the ship.

Associating with Sadhus and Renouncing

Attachments to the Enjoyments of the World

Ramakrishna (to the doctor): It is always important for you to associate with sadhus. Everyone has disease, so one should listen to what the sadhus say. However, if you only listen to what the sadhus say, will you have any benefit? You have to take the medicine. You have to eat a diet in keeping with your health.

Doctor: If you control your diet, then all the illness will flee.

Ramakrishna: There are three kinds of doctors: the best doctor, the middle-of-the-road doctor, and the bad doctor. There is a doctor that comes and takes your pulse and says, "You better take your medicine!" Then he leaves. He is a bad doctor. He didn't find out if the patient took the medicine or not. The doctor that explains to the patient the necessity and advocacy of taking the medicine in a timely and efficient manner and says very sweetly, "How will you get well if you don't take the medicine? You have to eat the right food. I am preparing this medicine myself for you to take." This is the middle-of-the-road doctor. Finally, there is the doctor who sees that the patient has not taken the medicine. He pushes his knee down on his chest, forces open his mouth, puts the medicine in, and makes him swallow it. That is the best doctor of all.

Doctor: There are some medicines for which you don't have to restrain the person's chest in order to make him take it.

Ramakrishna: There is no fear if the great doctor knees you in the chest. Just like doctors, there are different kinds of teachers. That teacher who gives great lectures to his disciples, but doesn't see if they are following them, that is a poor teacher. That teacher who again and again explains to the disciples very sweetly and nicely why they should follow the teachings, explaining to them with logic and feeling and with a lot of love why they should follow the teachings, that is the middle kind of doctor. That teacher who forcefully instructs the students to follow the teachings and even reprimands or punishes them for failure to practice, that is the best teacher.

Sannyasis will not even look at pictures of women. Do you know what form women take? Just like the tamarind is to the pickle. If you only think about the sour in the pickle, you begin to salivate. You don't have to actually eat the pickle, you just have to think of the sourness of the pickle, and you will get the juices flowing.

Shree Maa : Is it true?

Swamiji : Not so much in American cuisine.
We are not big pickle eaters here.

Ramakrishna (continuing): These words are not for you, Doctor. This is for the sannyasis. For you, as much as you are capable, regard women without selfish attachments. Whenever you get the time, go to a lonely place, and contemplate God. Make sure that no one is around. If you can grab onto the devotion of God, you will, for the most part, be able to live without selfish attachments. Once having had one or two children, a married couple can remain like brother and sister. If you have a kid or two and then live like brother and sister, you will have so much more time for thinking about God. Pray to God that no more physical or sensual desires will come into your minds and that there will be no more children.

Girish (laughing, to the doctor): You have been here three or four hours. Aren't you going to visit the sick?

Doctor: I am both the doctor and the patient. He who has become the Paramahamsa, he has become my all. (They all began to laugh.)

Ramakrishna: Look, there is a river by the name of Destruction of All Activity. If you go to bathe in that river, you will get into a lot of difficulty. All your karmas will be destroyed. You won't be able to perform any more activity in this world. (They all began to laugh.)

Doctor (to M., Girish, and the other devotees): Look, I remain among you as your own kith and kin, but if you fall ill, I will have to resume my role as a doctor. Our relationship will not be the same. As long as I am among you and you regard me as your own, then I am yours.

Ramakrishna (to the doctor): There is something which is called unselfish devotion. It is very good if you get this kind of devotion. Prahlada had it. A devotee expressing this type of devotion might say, "Oh, God, I don't want any wealth or fame. I don't want any pleasures or comforts. I don't want anything. Just give me pure devotion to Your lotus feet."

Doctor: Yes, I see that so many people are bowing down to the feet of Kali, but they are filled with various types of desires -- "Give me some work, give me a cure for my disease" and so on.

Doctor (to Ramakrishna): That disease that is within you, if you talk too much, you will never get better. When I come here from time to time, you can just talk to me. (They all began to laugh.)

Ramakrishna: Hey, you fix my disease. I can't sing the name and qualities of God!

Doctor: It will be enough for you to meditate. You don't have to sing anything.

Ramakrishna: Hey! What are you saying to me? What will happen to me if I sit silently? I want to eat five kinds of fish. I don't want just the soup! Sometimes I belch and get indigestion from too many chilies. Sometimes I want fried food. Sometimes I want to do puja, sometimes japa, sometimes meditation, and sometimes I want to sing Her name. Sometimes I dance when I hear Her songs!

Doctor: I too am not the same all the time.

What Harm Is There in Not
Believing in Incarnations of God?

Ramakrishna (to the doctor): Your son Amrit doesn't believe in the existence of the incarnations of God. Is there any harm in it? By believing in the formless God, one can also attain realization. If you believe in a form of God, you can attain to Godliness as well. If you believe and take refuge, you will attain to God. These are the two things that are absolutely required.

Humans are ignorant. They will make mistakes. Is it possible to put four kilos of milk into a one kilo container? So whatever way you choose, you must call on that form of God with a deep intense sincerity. She is the knower of what is inside you. She will listen to the inner call of every human being. If you have intense sincerity when you call upon God, and if you move along the path with form or without form, you will find God. If you eat sweetbread flat or rolled up, it is still sweet. Your son Amrit is fine.

Doctor: He is your disciple.

Ramakrishna (laughing, to the Doctor):   I have no relations, no children, or disciples. I am everyone's disciple. Everyone is a disciple of God. Everyone is a servant of God. I am also the Son of God and the servant of God. The moon belongs to all.

Everyone is filled with delight and are very happy. Om.

Chapter 16

First Discussion

It was Sunday the tenth day of the month of Kartik. It was the second tithi of the waning fortnight, the twenty-fifth of October 1885.

Ramakrishna was staying at Shyampukur in Calcutta. He was recuperating from throat cancer. Dr. Sarkar visited often to see his patient. Almost everyday M. was sent to the doctor's office to explain the condition of the patient, Sri Ramakrishna.

It was 6:30 in the morning. M. went to Ramakrishna and asked him how he was feeling.

Ramakrishna: You tell the doctor that towards the end of the night, my mouth is full of water. I have a cough and many other things. You ask him if I can take a bath.

About 7:30 in the morning, M. went to Dr. Sarkar's office and explained to him all the circumstances of the patient. The doctor was sitting with his old friend, a teacher, and with two other friends.

The doctor (to his friend): Sir, from 3:30 this morning this Paramahamsa is being a paramahamsa.

Swamiji: Ramakrishna has been in his bhava.

Doctor: He doesn't sleep. He is sick, but he is still a paramahamsa. (Everyone laughed.)

One of the friends (to the doctor): Sir, I heard some people call that Paramahamsa an incarnation. You see him everyday. What do you think?

Doctor: As a man, I have the greatest regard for him.

M: The doctor and his friends earn grace by attending on this patient.

Doctor: He is giving me grace by letting me attend to him.

M: I cannot speak for Ramakrishna, but we are all getting a lot of grace.

Doctor: You don't understand. I am actually sustaining a financial loss by attending on this patient.

Swamiji and Maa (laugh): A non-paying customer!

I have to neglect two or three calls a day to attend to him. I go to your patient's house, and I get no fee at all. How can I take a fee from him?

Mahima Chakravarty: I was once present when the doctor went to see Ramakrishna on a Saturday. I saw the doctor and said to Ramakrishna, "Great Sir (Mahashay), have you have become ill to expand the ego of this doctor?"

M. (to the doctor): This Mahima Chakravarty used to come to see me and attend my science lectures.

Doctor: He is a very tamasic person. Seeing him, I thought he was worthy of respect. Within God all the gunas (sattva, rajas, and tamas) are present, but Mahima Chakravarty was convinced that Ramakrishna became ill in order to expand my ego.

M: Mahima Chakravarty has the full faith that Ramakrishna should heal himself.

Doctor: Oh, is that possible? We are doctors. We know what cancer is like. How is it possible for people to cure themselves? Even the doctors won't be able to cure themselves. How can he? In what way can he heal himself?

Doctor (to his friends): Look. He is beset with illness, and all these devotees are doing seva for him.

Second Discussion

Ramakrishna was sitting with his sevaks. M. had sent word to the doctor, and everyone was awaiting his arrival. It was about three o'clock in the afternoon, and everyone had finished their midday meals. They were waiting for the arrival for the doctor.

Ramakrishna: What happened to him?

M: You are ill in order to expand the ego of these funny doctors. I heard that when I went to see him yesterday.

Ramakrishna: Who said that?

M: Mahima Chakravarty.

Ramakrishna: Then what happened?

M: Mahima Chakravarty is filled with tamo guna. The doctor said that God has all the qualities. Again he told me that he had woken up at three in the morning and started to worry about the you. He said that by eight the paramahamsa was still on his mind.

Ramakrishna began to laugh.

M. (continued): The doctor said that Ramakrishna was full of bhava and wanted to meditate. "It is eight o'clock now, and still he is in his Paramahamsa bhava!" He was ridiculing the patient.

Ramakrishna (laughing greatly): Oh, he studied in English medium schools, and he talks like that because he has the capacity to speak. He doesn't take the time to understand the problem, and that's why he is speaking in this way.

M: The doctor then said, "I have great regard for him as a man." This means he can't think of him as an avatar. He has devotion to Ramakrishna as a man.

Ramakrishna: Were there any other discussions?

M: I asked him, "What shall we do to eradicate this illness?" The doctor replied, "Nothing to do. I have to go again. Now let me see how I should prepare for it."

Ramakrishna (laughing): Don't you know that this doctor is having so much financial loss because of attending to me as his patient. He loses his capacity to visit two or three other paying customers.

Third Discussion

Vijay and other devotees were in a lot of bliss. Vijay Krishna Goswami came to have the darshan of Thakur. Along with him came a few devotees of the Brahmo Samaj. He was in Dacca (present Dhaka, Bangladesh) for several days. After many days of visiting places of pilgrimage, he came to Calcutta. He bowed to Thakur and prostrated completely on the floor. There were many people present -- Narendra, Mahima Chakravarty, Nandagopal, Bhupati, Latu, M., Chota Narendra, and other devotees.

Mahima Chakravarty (to Vijay): Oh, Sir, you have come after visiting several places of pilgrimage. You saw many different places, but what do you see here now?

Vijay: What shall I say? From where I am seated, I see everything is God. Without purpose I wandered alone. In some places there was one anna, in other places two annas, but here all sixteen annas are present.

> Swamiji: There are sixteen annas to a rupee. So according to Vijay, he got only a little from every place, but the full benefit is in the presence of Ramakrishna.

Mahima Chakravarty: You spoke correctly. She makes us wander, and She makes us sit.

Ramakrishna (to Narendra): Look what happened to Vijay. His goal has completely changed. He has become crazy for God. I look at a person's forehead, his body structure, and I can determine who is a paramahamsa, a great soul.

Mahima Chakravarty: Oh, Great Sir (Mahashay), your food intake has been reduced.

Vijay: Ah, yes.

Vijay (to Ramakrishna): We were in Dacca and heard that you were in pain and came quickly to see you.

Ramakrishna: What?

Vijay didn't reply. He sat silently for some time.

Vijay: It's very difficult to stay away from this place. Here all sixteen annas are present.

Ramakrishna: Kedar said that he went to many places but couldn't eat much. He came here and ate until he could eat no more.

Mahima Chakravarty: He ate so much he got indigestion.

Vijay (with folded hands, to Ramakrishna): I understood who you are. I don't have anything more to say.

Vijay: Yes, I understand.

Ramakrishna (full of bhava): If that's the way you feel, then that's the way you will be.

Hearing this, Vijay fell at Ramakrishna's feet and put Ramakrishna's feet on his chest.

Ramakrishna sat in bhava samadhi. This is the emblem of love. Looking at this amazing and wonderful sight, all the devotees present began to cry. Some began to pray. Everyone, with his or her own bhava, began to look at Ramakrishna with one-pointed attention. Some saw him as a great devotee, some as a great sadhu, and some saw him as the incarnation of God. Everybody saw him with his or her own bhava.

Mahimacharan (with a voice choked by tears): Look, look! This is the image of love. You know from time to time Maa gives her darshan. You are actually Satchidananda. You are the one who distinguishes between duality and unity.

Nandagopal was crying, and another devotee began to sing:

> Maa begins to sing the verses a few at a time, and Swamiji translates.

> Victory, victory to the Great Supreme
> Divinity beyond manifestation.
> You have come to us from so far.
> You are the Supreme of the Supreme
> and again greater

You are the truth of life.
You are the manifestation of
love and truth.
You are the root of all welfare.
You serve us with so many
kinds of nectar.
You contain such deep emotions.
Everywhere your radiance is cooling to
those who perceive.
The great poets and the foremost poets
speak of you as the cooling moon,
as the rise of the sun
and the setting of the sun.
You are the stars.
You are the reflection in the water.
You are wearing a blue form.
The six seasons.

Swamiji: Because of your reflection in the
water.

Mahimacharan is singing, filled with the bliss of comfort
and delight:

You have a garland of flowers,
and You radiate peace.
You are the strength of Brijbasi,
Vrindaban.

Swamiji: Ramakrishna is sitting in bhava.

Your bhava is so deep,
and we are foolish people.
How can we understand where You go?
You are like the waves
that come from time to time.

You give the greatest bliss
when we praise Your lotus feet.
You radiate light like ten million moons
and ten million suns.
All the men and women love to sing
about Your various qualities.
When we see You in this form,
we are mesmerized in wonder,
and we can express our love in tears.
You are the repository
of everyone's welfare.
Give us wisdom.
Give us love.
Give us devotion.
Give us the refuge of Your lotus feet.

    Shree Maa: Jai Maa.   The poem is not
complete.

Bhupati was singing again.

    Shree Maa sings:

In the ocean of the bliss
of consciousness, the waves of
love are flowing.
The drama of divine nectar is in process,
and everybody is in the bhava.
All of the different desires are dissolved
into the nectar of delight
of this illumination.
Everybody has this tremendous bhava,
this attitude of communion.
Somebody is sinking in the ocean,
and somebody is rising up.
Everyone is assuming a new form every
time, singing the name of God.

Hare, Hare!
All the great yogis are all one,
and they are all united.
All the differences, all the distinctions of
time, place, caste, and creed --
all are dissolved.
All are forgotten.
All my desires are fulfilled.
My hopes, my longings are fulfilled,
and all my desires.
All my taste buds are really satiated.
I am intoxicated with bliss.
My two hands are raised.
Raise your hands and sing!
Hare! Hare!
Sing with me!
Hare! Hare!
Hare Bol, Hare Bol!

Bhupati is singing again:

All the different forms of creation,
all the different distinctions of life are all
eradicated by singing the name of God.
Where am I?
Who am I?
And what is God?
He has bound me in love for Him
and stolen away my life.
How did I come to the banks of this
ocean of love?
In this intense, deep attitude
of communion,
my heart has been stolen away in the
waves of love.
I don't know anything more.

My name is the servant of love and I am
saying, "Hey, listen, sadhus!
This is the practical way of life.
There is no fear, no fear, no fear."

Ramakrishna went into a deep communion internally for
a long time. He was in Samadhi.

The Wisdom of the Supreme Divinity

and the Number of Wonders That

Can Be Seen by an Avatar

Ramakrishna (to M.): When I fall into this attitude,
where do I stay? Do I exist, or do I not exist? I don't even
know that. Am I a ghost, or am I a real human being? I am
a little bit ashamed. I don't know where I am. This situation,
this circumstance, doesn't become fixed. When you go to
town, you count "One, seven, eight, and you forget two,
three, four, five, and six." I forget how to count. I just skip
around.

Narendra: It's not at all the same.

Ramakrishna: No, this is beyond one and beyond two.

Mahimacharan: Yes. It is the distinction between
duality and non-duality.

Ramakrishna: The account does not remain. You can't
find the love of God through pundits. She is beyond the
scriptures and beyond the Vedas and beyond all learning, way
beyond that. Those who are really filled with wisdom, they
are not really called rajarishis. They don't even know any
distinction or any comprehension of being brahmarishi. Who
becomes Brahman, who becomes one with the Supreme
Divinity, doesn't have any such distinctions.

Ramakrishna (continuing): Do you know the behavior of the scriptures? There was one person who wrote a letter. He said, "Send to me five kilos of sweets and a piece of cloth." The person who received the letter read the letter. Understanding that the need was for five kilos of sweets and one piece of cloth, he threw the letter away. Was there any further need for the letter?

Vijay: If the sweets were actually sent, then we understand.

Ramakrishna: Vijay is always thinking about the sweets. When we take on a human body, then God assumes the form of that body. He is within every atom of existence -- within all existence is His residence. Every object of existence is a residence of God. The desires of men cannot be fulfilled until God assumes the avatar, the incarnation of divinity. Their goals are not completed.

Do you know what it's like? If you touch the cow in any place, you know you've touched the cow. If you touch the horns of the cow, then you say, "I touched the cow." But the milk comes from the udder. (They all started to laugh.)

Mahima: If you need milk from the cow, it will be of no avail to touch the horns. You have to hold onto the udder.

Vijay: But at first the calf goes from side to side.

Ramakrishna (laughing): Some people show the udder to the calf, and then the calf stands still. Then the cow gives milk. (They all laughed.)

So if you want milk from the cow, you don't grab onto the horn. You grab onto the udder. If you want to touch the cow, you can touch it anywhere and say, "I've touched the cow."

Fourth Discussion

The devotees were in the bliss of love. They were talking, and the time came for the doctor to come and look at his patient. The doctor took his seat.

Doctor: Last night at three o'clock in the morning, my sleep fled from me. I was only thinking about you. I was concerned that you would get cold.

Ramakrishna: I had a little cough. Ultimately, I had water in my mouth and a sour taste. There was pain in my throat.

Doctor: Everyone got the news.

Mahimacharan (talking about his tour of India): In Sri Lanka, there is nobody laughing.

Doctor: How can that be? We will have to inquire about that.

They all laughed, and the doctor began to do his work.

The Business of the Doctor and Ramakrishna

Ramakrishna: A doctor's work is a very high work. Everybody knows that it is very important work. If you don't take money and you treat the poor and restore them to good health, then this is the best kind of work. If you take the money and you do this work, then you become devoid of compassion. When you do business, you're always thinking about the stuff of business. It's a much lower kind of work.

Doctor: Well, if we cure them, then the work has been done efficiently. You are speaking with great pride to me when you say that my work is worth less because I take money.

Ramakrishna: Yes, it's very, very great if you can perform your doctor's work and raise others up without selfishness. This is very good. Even still, it's necessary for people in the world from time to time to have association with sadhus. If you have devotion to God, you will find sat sangha with sadhus of your own accord. I am giving you instruction. The people who smoke pot always find other pot smokers. If they see any other type of person, they put their heads down and walk away. They hide. But when a pot smoker sees another pot smoker, he is filled with bliss. They even hug each other and embrace. (They all began to laugh.)

Ramakrishna: A vulture keeps company with other vultures. Sadhus like to keep company with sadhus. The sadhus give compassion to every form of life.

Doctor: When the vulture sees a crow, he gets scared and flees. I say it is incumbent upon every human to perform seva for all other beings. I always give food to the sparrows. I take little bowls of wheat flour and throw the flour to the sparrows. When I throw the food out on my roof, many sparrows and other birds come to eat.

Ramakrishna: This is wonderful! You're quite a man. To feed other souls is the work of a sadhu. A sadhu gives sugar to the ants.

Ramakrishna (to Narendra): Would you sing a song?

Narendra took the tanpura. Other people began to play instruments too.

Narendra sings:

> Your name is so beautiful.
> We are remembering You.
> The nectar of bliss is flowing upon us.

I am hearing Your sound,
and my life is flying to You.
Your name has so much wealth.
It carries the nectar of immortal bliss.
Whoever will say Your name even once
will become immortal.
They just want to sing Your name.
They want to sing kirtan
for the rest of their days.
In that immeasurable nectar of bliss,
all else is dissolved.
When the vibrations of Your name
touch my ears, my heart is filled
with the nectar of sweetness.
Oh, Lord of my heart,
You are the intrinsic nature
of the bliss of consciousness.

Narendra sang some more:

Maa, make me crazy.
I don't want any other ideas
or any other wisdom or any other
thoughts other than You.
Oh, Manifestation of Supreme Divinity,
give me craziness.
Let me become intoxicated
with the bliss of Your name.
Maa, take all the stuff out of my head
and submerge me into the
ocean of devotion.
In this asylum for lunatics, someone is
laughing and someone is singing.
Someone is dancing with bliss.
Jesus and Buddha and Chaitanya,
they were all crazy with Your love.

Hey, Maa, when will I be so fortunate as
to be able to mix with them?
Heaven is a festival for lunatics.
Just as is the guru, so are Her disciples.
Who can understand this play of love?
You are the one who causes everyone to
become crazy with love.
You are the epitome of craziness.
Maa, You are so wealthy.
Give me the blessing of insanity
with love.
I'm begging for Your love
at the ocean of love.
I am the servant of love,
and I'm singing this song to You.

After the song there was a wonderful sight. Everybody was intoxicated with this attitude and this feeling. Even the pundits had left their punditry and the egotism of their knowledge aside.

They sang:

Give me craziness.
I have no more need for all of
this thinking about wisdom.

Vijay was the first to stand up from his asana, and he was intoxicated with bhava. Then Ramakrishna forgot the difficulties of his illness, and he forgot that he was suffering. He was intoxicated with bhava.

Ramakrishna was in front of the doctor, and the doctor stood up too. Nobody had any control. The doctor had no control. Narendra went into bhava samadhi. Latu too went into bhava samadhi. The doctor had studied a lot of science, but he was incredulous to see this wonderful sight.

Fifth Discussion

Along with the devotees of Sri Ramakrishna was an individual named Krotojai. After this experience, everyone slowly sat down. It was about eight o'clock in the evening when they began to speak.

Ramakrishna (to the doctor): Doctor, the bhava, the attitude you just saw, what does your science say about this attitude? How does your science describe a bhava? You consider all of this to be fraudulent?

Doctor (to Ramakrishna): Wherever so many people are affected, there everyone will naturally understand. It has to be true because so many people are infected with the epidemic of devotion. I don't understand it to be a fraud or false at all.

When you were singing earlier:

> Give me insanity.
> Make me crazy with Your love.
> I don't want any more work
> of the intellect.

When you were singing that, I couldn't stay in my seat any more. I myself had to stand up with the bhava. Then with great difficulty, I swallowed that bhava and kept it inside. I thought it was not appropriate to display this reaction.

Ramakrishna (laughing, to the doctor): You have such a deep stillness. You're like Mt. Meru around which the whole cosmos revolves. (Everyone laughs.) You are a very deep soul. No one can understand that you are the form of the eternal attitude if you keep it inside. Don't show it to just anyone.

If an elephant goes into a small pond, the elephant can kick its legs and try to get out. If the elephant goes into a very deep lake, no one can see it. It will just sink. No one would know that the elephant is beneath the water. This doctor is like that. The doctor is as deep as the elephant is in the water. You can't see that his attitude is one of eternal bhava.

Radha said to all her friends, "Friends, you guys are crying so devotedly for the arrival of Krishna. But look. Look how hard I have become. Not even one drop of tears comes from my eyes." Brinda cried, "My friend, you do have water in your eyes! It has a very deep, deep meaning. In your heart, the fire of love is always burning. The water comes to your eyes, but it dries up immediately because of the fire in your heart."

Doctor: I cannot debate with you. Every time I choose a subject, you take it to another level.

Ramakrishna: Here you are describing your own status.

Swamiji: Then they started discussing how to control anger and other limitations of the mind.

Doctor (to Ramakrishna): You fell into the bhava. You went into that deep bhava, that attitude, and some foolish person kicked you with their shoe. I heard that.

Ramakrishna: You must have heard it from Mahendranath Gupta, M. Yes, the person's name was Chandra Haldar. I fell down to the ground intoxicated with the love of God. This Chandra Haldar thought I was faking it and that I had fallen down for other reasons. He had become close to Mathur Babu, and he thought he would expose my fraud. In the darkness of night, he came and started to kick me with his shoes. I even had bruises on my body. Everybody said it was appropriate that we should complain to Mathur Babu, but I stopped them and made them refrain from making such a complaint.

Doctor: This also is the play of God. Many people can learn from this. They can learn how to control their anger. They can learn forgiveness. They will all learn from this episode.

Vijay and Narendra get the vision of the divine form. In the midst of all this, Ramakrishna started talking with Vijay and all the other devotees.

Ramakrishna: Vijay, there's somebody who stays with me all the time and lets me know what's going on in every locality. Even if I stay far away, this friend explains everything to me. This friend is an intuitive feeling, a knowledge that comes from within. He gives me knowledge of what's going on all over the place. Even if I am far away from where it transpires, he tells me what's going on.

Narendra: He is like your guardian angel.

Vijay: I saw one great soul in Dahahr, and I touched his body.

Ramakrishna (laughing): Oh, then there is another one.

Narendra: I also saw him many times.

Narendra (to Vijay): How can I say that I don't have faith in you?

Chapter 17

First Discussion

It is Monday the twenty-sixth of October 1885. It is Krishna pakshe, the third day of the dark fortnight in Sanskrit and the eleventh day of Kartik in Bengali. Ramakrishna has beens staying in a house in Shyampukur with his devotees. With him are Girish, Rakhal, Sarat, Narendra, Suresh, Kali, and many other devotees. Sri Ramakrishna has come to Shyampukur from Calcutta in order to recuperate from his disease. Dr. Sarkar has been the attending physician, and he comes every day. Throughout the day and night, people come back and forth to see Sri Ramakrishna.

It's the autumn season, and several days have passed since the completion of the fall Navaratri and the Durga Puja. The disciples couldn't have much delight in the Durga Puja because Ramakrishna has been suffering from this throat cancer. For the past three months Gurudev has been experiencing extreme pain because of the cancer in his throat. Dr. Sarkar and other doctors have been coming regularly, but it is impossible to cure the pain of this disease.

Many of the disciples are sitting nearby, and they can't restrain their tears at seeing their guru suffering in such a way. The disciples are serving Ramakrishna with their full lives and their full surrender. Narendra and these other young men have renounced their selfishness, and they are serving their guru. They are learning as much as they possibly can.

The guru has so much pain and even still, wave upon wave of people are coming to visit him to have darshan of the great saint. Though he is in pain, the people come to Ramakrishna. They find peace, and they find bliss. He is without a doubt the ocean of grace. He is filled with compassion. He refuses to rest, and he speaks with everyone who comes. His outlook is to give welfare to each and every visitor.

Dr. Sarkar forbids Ramakrishna to engage in any discourse, but the doctor himself comes and sits for six or seven hours at a time. Dr. Sarkar says, "No one should speak with Paramahamsa. You should only talk to me." By drinking the nectar of the wisdom and the immortal bliss of Ramakrishna's words, the doctor becomes completely intoxicated. He just sits there the whole day. Once it was ten o'clock in the night, and Mahendranath Gupta came to show the doctor the door and tried to encourage the doctor to leave. Still the doctor sat there talking with Ramakrishna.

M. arrived at the house on his way to Dr. Sarkar.

Ramakrishna (to M.): This medicine is very light. It's very good medicine. I'm fine. Even though this medicine has that form, still I'm feeling good from taking that medicine. Give me more. I'm going to say that his patient is better. I'm going along with the doctor, and I'm going to follow the doctor's orders. Whatever the doctor says is what we are going to do.

Ramakrishna: Look, there is a devotee who hasn't come for two or three days, and my mind is worried. Kali Babu, you go over and call Purna. (Kali says he'll do it.) The doctor's son is a really nice fellow. You tell him to come sometime, too.

The Second Discussion

When M. got to the doctor's house, the doctor was talking with two or three friends.

Doctor: You said that you would come at ten o'clock. Now you are late. How is Sri Ramakrishna? What happened? You made me worry about him.

Doctor (to one of the friends): Would you sing me that song? The song I heard the other day?

The friend sang.

Shree Maa sings:

As long as I have life in my body,
I will sing Her name.
The light of Her greatness
lights the entire world.
The energy of Her love fills all the
citizens of the world with delight.
No mouth can ever explain the feeling of
seeing that compassionate deity.
All the grief, all the sorrow
will be eradicated for
whoever takes Her prasad.
In the ten directions, in the water,
in the sky and everywhere,
She fills all the directions.
Where can you find the end of Her?
Where can you find the end of Her?
This is the question that confronts us all.
Where can you find the end of Infinity?
When consciousness is filled with the
jewels and the gems of divinity,
Her eyes are jewels
that are extremely expensive.
You see Her once
and you will have no more sorrow.
Where is the end of Her?

Where is Her end?
This is the question that confronts us all.

Doctor: M., this song is very nice. "Where is the end of Her? Where is Her end? This is the question that confronts us all." I like that song a lot.

M: It's a beautiful song. It has this infinite bhava.

Doctor: It's become very late. Have you had anything to eat? I take my food before ten o'clock. Then I go out and do my doctoring. If I don't eat and I go out, then I get very weak. I think one day I'll invite you and the other devotees to come to eat with me.

M: Oh, that will be very great fun, enjoyable.

Doctor (to M.): We can do it here, or we can do it there. It doesn't matter.

M: If you feed us here or feed us there, we will all eat with great delight. (Then they started talking about Kali.)

Doctor: Kali is a village girl. (Everyone started laughing.)

M: Where is that written? Where did you get that?

Doctor: I heard Kali was a village girl. In the old days the respected Vijay Krishna and all the other devotees went into bhava samadhi. I was present, and I saw that. I saw the bhava. Is it good to have so much bhava?

M: Our Great Swan says to us that whoever goes into that bhava, that feeling of thinking about God, there is no difficulty if they go too deep. There is a light that comes from the jewel. The body is attracted by that light, but the body does not burn from the light of the jewel.

Doctor: But the light that comes from the jewel is reflected light.

M: Ramakrishna says if you submerge yourself in the ocean of the nectar of the bliss of immortality, humans don't die.   God is the ocean of immortal nectar.   If humans who submerge themselves in that ocean, have no difficulty. Even human beings become immortal.   Certainly they can if they have faith in the existence of God.

Doctor: Hmm. Yes, I understand.

The doctor took M. in his carriage and went to see two or three other patients before going on to Shyampukur to see Ramakrishna again. Along the way he began to discuss with M. about Mahima Chakravarty.

M: He comes to see the Great Swan regularly.   Even if he does have ego, in a few days he won't have any left. Whoever sits with Ramakrishna, their ego takes flight. Their ego becomes ground to powder. There's no way you can maintain your ego there.   When ego comes to someone devoid of ego, then the ego flees.

M: Look, Vidyasagar was such a well-known citizen, and suddenly he became so humble and modest. Ramakrishna went to see Vidyasagar in his garden. When Ramakrishna left, it was nine o'clock, and Vidyasagar himself came down with a light to show Ramakrishna the way. He showed him great respect and bowed down to him.

Doctor: OK, in this regard, what is Vidyasagar's opinion of this bhava?

M: He had a great deal of devotion. I saw when he was speaking, the bhava that Vaishnavas have is not like the bhava that others have. Vaishnavas don't love with that degree. In a way, he's like you.

Doctor didn't like hearing this. He disliked displays of emotion. He put his head on his feet and said, "I don't like it." He didn't like bowing or touching another's feet with his head.

Doctor: Whoever has a different opinion, let him perform according to his own understanding.

M: You don't like bhava very much, but Ramakrishna said that you have a very, very deep soul, and I understand that you are thinking about this. Even yesterday you were thinking when I was saying that when the elephant enters into a shallow pond, it climbs right out. When the elephant goes into a very deep ocean or deep lake, you don't even see the water ripple. When the elephant goes into the very, very deep soul, he can't see anything else, he can't perform anything else. You have a very deep soul.

Doctor: I don't deserve the compliment. I have devotion and many other feelings. If you have so much, can you hide it?

M: Can anyone give the explanation of what the feelings are? No one can tell what the feelings are. But Great Sir (Mahashay), the feelings of bhava are such a wonderful experience. It's like Stebbing on Darwinism. I saw in the library, Stebbing said, "Whatever comes to the human mind, even if you support the field of evolution or if you believe in God creating the creation, separately they are both wonderful." He gave a great comparison, the theory of light. Whether you know the undulatory, or wave, theory of light or not, in either case light is equally wonderful.

Doctor: Ah, yes. Did you see what Stebbing says about Darwinism? Even if you support evolution or you support God, both are equally wonderful.

Doctor (continues, about Ramakrishna): I see that he is a worshiper of Kali.

M: Do you think his definition of Kali is different? What is said in the Vedas as Parabrahman, the Supreme Divinity, he is calling Kali. What the Muslims are calling "Allah," what the Christians are calling "God," he is calling that Kali. He doesn't see many forms of God. He sees one God. In the olden times those that had the wisdom of Supreme Divinity called it as Brahman. The yogis called it the soul. The devotees called it the manifestation of the form of God. That is what the Paramahamsa Sri Ramakrishna is calling Kali.

I heard from him that there was a man with a bowl full of dye. Anybody who had to dye their cloth went to him. He asked them, "What color do you want to color your cloth?" If someone gave the reply, "I want green cloth, he used to stick the cloth into the pot and return it to them as green. He said to them, "Here, you take your green cloth; I have dyed it for you." If someone said to him, "I want a red-colored cloth," he put the cloth into the same pot and gave it back to the customer and said, "Here is your red cloth." From the same pot of dye, he took out green, red, blue, or yellow cloth. He could dye any cloth any color. When someone saw this amazing thing, the dyer said to the onlooker, "What color would you like to dye your cloth?" The customer replied, "Any color you choose to dye, that color I will accept." In the same way, within Ramakrishna is every bhava, every attitude. Every religion, every sect finds peace with Ramakrishna. They all find bliss. What is his bhava, what is his feeling? Can you understand how deep his situation is? Who can understand how deeply situated he is within his own Self?

Doctor: He is all things to all men. That too is not desirable. Even though St. Paul has said it, "God becomes all things to all men."

M: Who can understand the circumstances of Sri Ramakrishna? I heard from his own mouth, "If you are not a tailor, you won't be able to see the difference between a number forty thread and a number forty-one thread." If you are not a painter you won't understand what art is. The great soul Sri Ramakrishna has a great bhava, a deep feeling, a great attitude. If you haven't attained to the Christ, you cannot understand what the bhava of Christ is. The attitude that Ramakrishna displays is what Christ has described. "Be thou perfect, as your Father in Heaven is perfect."

Doctor: OK, you fellows have to supervise the recovery of my patient.

M: From time to time one person is present. Each day one of the older devotees takes on the duty to supervise. Sometimes Girish does it, sometimes Ram, sometimes Balaram, sometimes Suresh, and sometimes Navagopal or Kali Babu. In this way, one person takes a turn of duty to see that Ramakrishna is taken care of.

Third Discussion

Ramakrishna (sitting with the devotees): What is the value in just being a pandit?

Ramakrishna was recuperating from his illness in a house at Shyampukur, a town outside Calcutta. This was the topic of discussion among the devotees there. The doctor's car came right in front of that house and stopped there. It was about one o'clock in the afternoon. Ramakrishna was sitting on the second floor of the house. There were a lot of devotees assembled there. Among the devotees, there were

Girish Ghosh, little Narendra, and Sarat.

Everyone's perception was focused on the embodiment of that pure bliss of consciousness, the Great Swan, Sri Ramakrishna. Everybody was waiting on his every word, leaning on the edge of their seats knowing that something wonderful was going to be expressed from his consciousness. Just like the bride's friends were waiting for the groom to arrive at the house, in the same way, everybody was waiting to hear what was going to come from Ramakrishna.

The doctor and M. arrived. They bowed down to Ramakrishna and took their seats. Seeing the arrival of the doctor, Ramakrishna began to laugh.

Ramakrishna: Oh, today I am very good because, along with the devotees, we have been talking about God all day long.

> Swamiji: The doctor had told Ramakrishna to sit down and shut up, not to say a word, because of the throat cancer. So Ramakrishna told the doctor, "Today I am feeling fine because I have been talking about God all day long." The doctor had also given instructions to Ramakrishna, "If you have to talk to anybody, you save it all until I come, and then you talk to me." Smart doctor.

Dr. Ramnarayan and Bankim Chandra Ghosh

Ramakrishna: Will you attain anything by being a pandit? If you don't have discrimination, you don't have renunciation. What value is all learning? When I think of the lotus feet of the Divine Lord, I go into a state. My cloth opens up of its own accord. I can't even keep my dhoti tied on. I feel a trembling, tingling sensation from my feet to the top of my head. I understand that everything is so small and insignificant. If a pandit doesn't have discrimination, if he doesn't have real, sincere, deep, intense love for God, I think it's like a piece of dry grass.

Swamiji: Pandits, they are all dry.

Ramakrishna: Ramnarayan was a doctor, and he was debating with me. We were in the midst of the debate, and I got the same bhava. I said to him, "What are you saying? Can you find that Supreme Divinity by debate? Who can understand the nature of creation? You become a bitter intellectual." He saw my condition, and he began to cry. Then he began to massage my feet.

Doctor: Dr. Ramnarayan is a Hindu. He puts sandal paste all over his forehead. He is an orthodox Hindu.

Swamiji: Dr. Sarkar was conducting the interview.

Doctor: I am not the kind of Hindu that blows the conch shell and rings the bell.

Ramakrishna (to the doctor): Bankim is a pandit. When I saw him, I asked, "What is the duty of a human being?" He said, "To eat and sleep and make babies." When I heard this, I was disgusted! I said to him, "What kind of words do you speak? You are a very dirty person. You do such work day and night. You think about it day and night, and even still it comes out of your mouth. When you eat radishes, you belch radish." Thereafter I began to speak about God. There was a great kirtan in the house, and I began to dance. Then he said, "Great Sir (Mahashay), you come and visit us sometime." I said to him in reply, "That depends on the will of God." He said, "If you come to visit us, many devotees will come to see you." I laughed and said, "What kind of devotees assemble at your place? Like Gopal, Gopal? Are they the kind of devotees that say "Gopal, Gopal" all day long?"

Doctor: What do you mean? What kind of expression is that to say "Gopal, Gopal" all day long?

Ramakrishna (laughing): There was a goldsmith who had a store. He was a great devotee, a great Vaishnav. He had a mala around his neck and a tilak on his forehead. On the wrist he wore a mala with the name of God. Everybody had faith in him. They all felt that he was a great devotee. Certainly he was an honest man. When a group of customers came to the store, one of the workers there said, "Keshava, Keshava." Another one of the workers said, "Gopal, Gopal." In another part of the store, another worker replied, "Hari, Hari." Someone else said, "Hara, Hara." The customer, seeing the devotion of all the workers, thought, "These are very wonderful, highly evolved souls." But do you know what the real truth of the matter was? The one who said "Keshava, Keshava" was actually thinking "customers, customers." Those who said "Gopal, Gopal" were saying "I see that they are actually a bunch of cows and donkeys." The one who said "Hari, Hari" was thinking "If they are really a bunch of cows and donkeys, I am going to fleece them." And the big boss who said "Hara, Hara" said, "Rip 'em off. They are only a bunch of cows and donkeys." (They all began to laugh.)

Ramakrishna (continuing): I went to another place with Mathur Babu. A lot of pandits came to discuss with me. You all know I am a fool. (They all began to laugh.)

Ramakrishna: When they all saw my condition, they said to me, "Oh, Great Sir (Mahashay), all that I have read, all that I memorized, all that I have learned, I look at you, and it's all worthless. Now I have understood. If you get the grace from God, you have no lack of wisdom, even if you are a fool. Even a fool, even a mute can speak." That's why I am saying to you. If you read a book, it's no value to become a pandit.

>   Shree Maa: Is it not true? She starts singing "Bhavile Bhaver Uday Hoi."

>   Swamiji: Just as is your attitude, just so is your gain. The root is your idea. It won't happen from reading books.

The First Samadhi

How Saraswati Came to Sit in the Throat of a Fool

Ramakrishna: When you get Her grace, there is no lack of wisdom. Look at me. I am a fool, and I don't know anything. But who is speaking all these words? The feast of Her wisdom is bounteous. In the village they stack the grain. Those who stack the grain say the name of Rama as they stack the grain. There was one man who was stacking grain and just when he got to the last bundle of grain another cartload came. He continued stacking the grain. That was his karma all day long. No matter how many times he emptied out each stack, another bundle came. I am also in a similar predicament. The words that I speak, just so many times as I empty my supply, She gives me a new supply. I am also a worker bee in the feast of her nectar. I keep emptying my store, but she gives me more.

>   Swamiji: When Ramakrishna was young, he found this store of wisdom. He was 11 years old at that time.

Ramakrishna: When I was 11 years old, I was walking in the field and what did I see? Everyone said that I fainted and became unconscious. There was no breath at all coming from me. From that time I have become a different kind of person.

I began to see within me a new person. When I went to do the worship, I tried to extend my hand towards the deity but many times it ended up on my own head, and I gave the flower to my own head. There was one boy who used to do seva for me, and he used to say to me, "I see a light emanating from your face, and I fear to get too close to you." He wouldn't come near me at that time.

> Shree Maa: Ramakrishna is talking about faith. When you have true faith, all the debating societies seem to dissolve from your presence. The debates are very far away. With faith you find it all.

Fourth Discussion

Free Will or God's Will

Ramakrishna: I am a fool, and I don't know anything. But who says all this? I say, "Maa, I am the tool, You are the Craftsman. I am the house, and you are the Master of the house. I am the conveyance, and You are the Driver. Just as You make me do, just so I do. Just as You make me speak, just so I speak. Just as You drive, just so I run. Not me, not me! You, You!"

> Swamiji: Maa wants to tell a story.

> Shree Maa: Trailinga Swami was a great devotee. He closed his door and sat inside for three days. One of his devotees was standing outside the door and wondered, "What's going on here?" He went and knocked on the door. Trailinga Swami asked, "Who's there?" He replied, "I am, Guruji, I am." Trailinga Swami did not make any move at all. He sat silently in his room. The disciple was thinking, "What happened to my Guru? He is sitting inside. Before he was always happy to see me, and now he is not

replying at all." He sat outside and began to think, "What happened to the Guru?" The next day he came again and knocked on the door. Trailinga Swami said, "Who is there?" The disciple once again replied, "I am, Guruji." Trailinga Swami kept silent. All the day and all the night, the Guru did not open the door, and the disciple was sitting outside. The disciple sat through the whole night in meditation wondering why the Guru didn't open the door. On the third day he went and knocked on the door. Guruji asked, "Who's there?" The disciple replied, "You are." And the Guru opened the door.

Swamiji: It's not me, it's not me! It's You, it's You!

Ramakrishna: I am merely a tool in Her hands. When Radha was carrying a pitcher of water on her head, not one drop of water spilled from the pot. Everyone began to praise Radha. "She has so much devotion, so much focus, so much stillness, she didn't spill a drop." Then Radha replied, "Why are you praising me? Praise Krishna. I am merely His servant."

Ramakrishna: Once when I was in bhava samadhi, I put my foot on Vijay's chest. I had so much respect for Vijay, yet I put my foot right on Vijay's body. What do you say to that?

Doctor (to Ramakrishna): You'd better be careful.

Ramakrishna (bowed down with folded hands): What shall I do? When that bhava comes to me, I become unconscious. What I do, I don't know at all.

Doctor: It is best that you be careful. If you fold your hands and pray, don't you think that's enough? Be careful.

Ramakrishna: Do you think I can do something to control myself? What do you think is my condition? If you think that this is a fraud or a play, then your science will dissolve into ashes.

Doctor: Great Sir (Mahashay), do you think that I would come so frequently if I thought you were pretending? Look, I left all my other work, and I came here to be with you. There are many patients I couldn't visit because I sit here for six or seven hours everyday.

God Was the Doer and Arjuna Was the Instrument

Ramakrishna: I said to Mathur Babu, "Don't mind. You are a big person. I am indebted to you because you believe in me. But whether you believe in me or you don't believe in me, I want to tell you one thing. What will human beings do while they are here? She must agree. It's all up to Her. Before the power of God, human beings are just a little piece of straw."

Doctor: What do you think? Just because somebody believes in you, I will believe in you? But I do give you my highest respect. I regard you very highly. Just like a very respectable human being.

Ramakrishna: Did I ever tell you to believe in me?

Girish: Did he tell you to believe in him?

Doctor (to Ramakrishna): What are you saying? That this is all God's desire?

Ramakrishna: What else am I saying? Before the power of God, what else can human beings do? When Arjuna was going to battle in Kurukshetra, he said, "I can't fight. I can't destroy my own family." Krishna said to him "Arjuna, you have to fight. This is your nature. Your very nature will make you fight." Sri Krishna showed him everything. Every one of the enemies had already perished. Later He showed Arjuna His universal form.

A group of Sikhs came to visit Sri Ramakrishna, and they had the opinion that the leaves on the banyan tree were swaying in the wind because of the desire of God. Without God's desire, not one leaf on the tree can sway in the breeze.

Liberty or Necessity

Doctor: If everything is God's desire, then why are you scolding us? If everything is God's desire, why are you teaching us so much wisdom?

Ramakrishna: She is making me speak, and that's why I am speaking. I am the tool, and she is the craftsperson.

Doctor: You say that you are the tool. That's why you are talking. Otherwise sit there silently. Everyone is God.

Girish: Sir, what are you thinking? She is making us act and that's why we are acting.

Doctor: She gave us a free will. If I want to, I can think about God, and if I don't want to, I don't have to.

Girish: You think about God or any other work or any other subject because you like to. Your inner intrinsic nature is going to force you to act.

Doctor: Why? I do my duty.

Girish: You chose your duty because you like it.

Doctor: A child has fallen near the fire. I think it is my duty to save the child from burning himself.

Girish Chandra Ghosh

Girish: Do you get bliss from saving the child? Is that why you go into the fire to take the child out? The desire for bliss takes you into the fire. Just like people who eat bhang, who take it because of their desire. It becomes blissful.

Knowledge, the Knower, and the Known

Three Distinguishable Portions of the

Consciousness of All Actions

Ramakrishna: If you want to do some action, first you have to have the faith. You have to feel that you are going to get some bliss from performing that action. That's why people engage themselves in action. There is a golden coin hidden under the dirt. First you need the knowledge and the understanding, and then you need the faith. When you start to dig, you get bliss. You are digging. You hear the sound of metal on metal, and your heart jumps with delight. Then you see that it is actually the golden coin that you have uncovered. In this way step by step, the bliss grows and grows. I myself was standing on the verandah\ of the temple. There was a sadhu who was making a chillum of ganja. He had such a look of delight in his face as he was preparing the ganja to smoke.

Doctor: The fire burns and the light gives illumination. With the illumination of the light, you can see. But the heat of the flame could burn you. When you do your duty, it is not just that you have bliss. You have to put in some effort.

M: (to Girish): You fill up your stomach and you get a backache. You have the bliss of a full stomach, but your back hurts. There is a bliss that comes along with the pain.

Girish (to the doctor): Duty is extremely dry.

Doctor: Why?

Girish: Then you have your own nectar. (Everyone began to laugh.)

M: From your greed, your own desire, you eat your own medicine.

Girish (to the doctor): Your duty has a lot of nectar. It has a lot of juice. If it didn't, why would you do your duty?

Doctor: They say that this is the inclination of the mind.

M. (to Girish): The intrinsic nature of the mind will pull them in the direction they are going. (They all began to laugh.)

M: Once you have seen Her, then where is your free will?

Doctor: I can't say that you are completely free. The cow is bound to the stake. For as long as the rope goes, to that extent the cow is free. As soon as he pulls the rope taut, then he is no longer free anymore.

Free Will, *continued*

Ramakrishna: Jadu Mallick gave the same comparison.

Ramakrishna (to the doctor): Listen. God is doing it all. He is the wielder of the tool, and I am the tool. If somebody has this faith, they are liberated in this life. You do your work. People say, "I am doing." Do you know how it works? There is a comparison in Vedanta philosophy. There was some rice left in the pot. They added all of the potatoes and all of the eggplant to the rice. The potatoes and eggplant were boiling. After a few minutes they were boiling and going "blub, blub, blub." They were extremely proud and full of ego and said, "Look at me, I am dancing and jumping." The little children were looking at it and thinking, "The potatoes and the eggplant are all alive. Look at them inside the pot. They are dancing." The elders explained to the children that the potatoes and the eggplant are not alive. They are just cooking. They are not jumping of their own accord. Beneath the pot the fire is burning, and that's why they are jumping. If we take the logs out of the fire, they won't jump anymore. The individuals who say "I am the doer" say so from their own ignorance. Everyone is empowered to do work because of God's energy. As soon as you take the burning log out of the fire, everyone is silent. The puppets dance as long as the puppeteers pull the strings. If the puppeteer lets the strings fall from his hands, then the puppets don't dance anymore. Just so long as you don't have the vision of God, just so long as you have not touched the gemstone that yields all desires, for as long as we think "I am the doer," this mistake, this error of judgment will remain. As long as we think "I am doing true work," or we think "I think I am doing untrue work," this type of discrimination will remain. This discrimination is called maya. In order to make this samsara (this ocean of worldliness) work, we have to have this type of attachment. If you leave the refuge of this maya and grab onto the truth, then you can attain to Godliness. Who has attained to Godliness, who has seen the actual vision of God, they move across that ocean of maya. She alone is the one doer. I am the witness. Who has this faith, that individual is liberated while living in this world. I told this all to Keshab Sen.

Girish: How do you know that free will exists?

Doctor: Not by reason. I feel it.

Girish: I feel it to be reversed. You feel you are doing everything out of your own free will. I feel that She is doing everything to me. We understand it to be in reverse. We are the effects of Her cause. (They all began to laugh.)

Doctor: There are two parts to duty. One part is what is incumbent upon me to perform.

Shree Maa speaks.

Swamiji: Mother had a great devotee named Vasishta. He was the only son of his family. He said that he wanted to be a sadhu, he didn't want to get married. At that time he was employed in the railways, and used to drive the local trains. His mother said, "You are going to have to get married. Who is going to take care of me in my old age?" Vasishta fled from the house. A true sadhu. He ran away into the jungle. Everyone began to look for him. They called the police. A British officer found him in the jungle and brought him back to his mother. His mother took him to the family guru. Vasishta said that he didn't want to marry or have a job or be bound by the world and its relationships. The guru looked at him and said that it was his life, his fate to get married. Vasishta was very sad. The guru said, "I am going to give you a blessing. You are going to get married and live in the world, but you are going to live like a potato."

Shree Maa: Everyone loves potatoes, no? There is no place they don't eat potatoes.

Girish: You know how free will is demonstrated?

Doctor: Reason is something you don't think about. You feel it.

Girish: Then I and others feel it to be reversed. I feel that the opposite is true. We are feeling it is opposite. We are beyond the tantra. (They all began to laugh.)

Doctor: There are two constituent elements that comprise duty. The first element is saying that we are performing those activities that are incumbent upon us. The second one says after performing the duties that are incumbent upon us, we feel a delight. Ultimately we find that there is no delight that comes from the completion of the activity. When I was a child, I noticed that the devotees had offered many sweets to the deities. The pujari is reciting the mantras, and he is thinking about the sweets. At first he had a great delight, "Ah, look at all the sweets that are going to be offered." Then the ants started to come and eat the sweets. The pujari is thinking that the ants are going to be eating the sweets. Now he has lost all his bliss.

M: Whether he gets bliss or not is very difficult to say. When you make a great effort in the pursuit of your goal, you get bliss. That's where the bliss comes from, the great effort. The bliss doesn't come from the sweets or from the ants or from eating the sweets.

Fifth Discussion

With all of his devotion, Sri Ramakrishna has assumed the attitude of a servant.

Ramakrishna: What the doctor was saying, it is called motivated devotion. I don't want anything from Mahendra Sarkar. He has no need from me. I enjoy seeing him. This is the type of devotion that has no motivation. It is not attached. If there is some delight there, that's what I will do. Ahalya said, "Hey, Rama, I have no difficulty to take birth from the womb of a pig, but give me pure devotion to Your lotus feet. I don't want anything else." Even in order to destroy Ravana, Narada went to Ayodhya to see Rama. He saw Sita and Rama, and he began to sing a hymn of praise. When Rama heard this song of praise, he said, "Narada, I am pleased by hearing the song that you have sung for me. Choose from me a boon." Narada gave the reply, "If you will give me a one boon, then give the boon of eternal devotion to Your lotus feet. And please give me along with that the boon that I will not become mesmerized or intoxicated with maya or the illusion of worldly attachments." Rama said, "You take another boon." Narada replied, "I don't want anything else. I only want pure devotion to Your lotus feet. I only want pure devotion to God. I only want to see God and I only want to be with God and I don't want any wealth or any status or any position or worldly goods." This is called pure devotion. If you have some bliss ultimately, but you don't have any bliss that comes from worldly thoughts, you get bliss from the love and devotion which is pure.

Ramakrishna: I used to go to Sambhu Mallick's house. Sambhu used to say, "Master, you come and see me. You feel a great delight in being in my presence." That's why I have the bliss. When devotees have pure devotion, then the Guru feels bliss.

Swamiji: Like you (pointing to Maa). When
Mother used to see a sadhu, she used to sit
silently. They would dissolve in the bhava of
bhakti. Whoever has pure devotion, the souls
unite. There are no words to explain. There is no
capacity to explain devotion and love of
communion. When there is any selfish motivation,
there is no possibility for the souls to unite. That's
Mother's experience.

Ramakrishna: There is another circumstance that
prevails. He goes along like a child. There is no way to
predict his next move.

Ramakrishna (to the devotees): Did you understand the
attitude of the doctor's mind? He is in constant prayer to
God. "Hey, God, give me pure desires that I don't even go
close to untruthful activities," this is what my feeling was.
This is what they call a servant bhava. I said "Maa, Maa,
Maa" and cried in such a way that people used to stand up.
They saw what my circumstance was. They thought I was
crazy. In order to chase away my craziness, they brought me
a healer, an exorcist.

Shree Maa: It happens in India a lot. Here in
the United States, they will give an electric shock.

Ramakrishna: I cried, "Maa, Maa, Maa," and he fled
from the house. I called to Haladhari, "Look who has come
to the house." Haladhari came to the house and I said to all
the people, I was crying "Maa, Maa, Maa." I said, "Mother,
please protect me, please protect me. You come close to me
and be with me. You keep me in the path of truth and don't
let me go to untruth."

Ramakrishna (to the doctor): Your attitude is very
clearly the attitude of a servant.

Swamiji: This is about how to perform for the welfare of the world and for ordinary people and how to act without attachment and with pure truth.

Ramakrishna: If anybody has submerged themselves in the bhava, in the attitude of pure truth, they only think about God. They don't like anything else. Some pure souls from their prarabdha karma, from their previous births, have from their births an innate sense of truth. Even without desires, they try to perform the activities in the world. Ultimately they attain to the pure truth. When you mix your sattva with rajas, according to the ways of the world, your mind goes in various arenas. Then you get the egotistical concept that you are going to be a benefactor to society. In order to perform work for the welfare of the world, it is very difficult for such a little person like us to be a big benefactor to the world. But if someone has freedom from desires and still they act for the benefit of others, they have no fault. This is what is known as activity without attachment. If we try to act in this way, it is very, very good. But everyone is not so capable because it is very difficult. Everyone has to perform activities. A very few individuals are able to renounce their attachment to activity. Very few people are empowered to see pure truth in action. By performing this way, acting without desires and without attachment for selfish gain, the raja guna that was mixed with sattva becomes purer and purer until it becomes pure sattva. When you have the quality of pure truth, then you get the vision of God.

Normal people or ordinary people are not even able to comprehend what is this pure truth. Hem said to me, "Only Mr. Bhattacharjee, after attaining to the respect of the world, he contemplated what is the status of a human being."

Chapter 18

Tuesday, October 27, 1885

It is about half past five in the afternoon, and several devotees are blissfully enjoying the words emanating from the holy lips of Sri Ramakrishna. They are singing devotional songs and enjoying a very deep, blissful samadhi-like state. Among the devotees are Narendra, Dr. Sarkar, Girish Chandra Ghosh, Shyam Basu, Dr. Dukari, Naren the younger, Rakhal, and several others.

Dr. Sarkar feels Sri Ramakrishna's pulse and makes arrangements for his medicine to be administered. After Ramakrishna and the doctor discuss many of the pains and difficulties that Ramakrishna is experiencing, the doctor watches to make sure Sri Ramakrishna takes the medicine.

Dr. Sarkar: You can talk with Shyam Basu now as I must be leaving, but I will come back another time.

Ramakrishna and another devotee quickly stood up and asked if the doctor would like to listen to a song.

Doctor (to Sri Ramakrishna): You express too much emotion when you sing and enter into bhava samadhi. It aggravates your disease. You may sing, but please try to control your bhava. After saying that, the doctor sat back down.

Then with a very melodious voice, Narendra began to sing. He played the tanpura while another devotee played on the mridanga, a drum.

He started to sing:

> You made such an amazing creation!
> You fill this entire creation

with Your radiance.
The stars glitter and shine in the sky
like jewels and gems
in a vast treasure chest.
Countless are the moons and suns.
Mother Earth contains
an amazing wealth
that no one can define.
She offers a bountiful feast to everyone.
Oh, Lord Shiva, vast amounts of people
praise you again and again   ·
singing, "Oh, what a wonderful creation
You have made!"

Now Narendra sings another heartfelt song:

Your infinite expansive peace
is like a magnet pulling us to You
filling us with the love of God.
That's why yogis sit in meditation
within the dark mountain
cave of their hearts
joyfully floating on the
infinite expanse of Your lap.
It is within that great expanse
in that great beyond
where the infinite peace
of Nirvana is attained.
There is no way on earth
the tongue can express that peace.
Ever focused on Maha Kali's holy name,
the yogis clothe themselves
in Her garment of Love.
In this temple of samadhi,
there is only One.
For You alone, Maa, are all that exists.
Treading this path of oneness,

victory of Love expresses itself
freeing us from all fear.
Seeing us set free,
Her shining face smiles, and She laughs
with infinite delight.

Doctor: This type of singing is dangerous and inappropriate for Sri Ramakrishna. If he goes into bhava samadhi, who knows when he'll come back. It will be disastrous for us all.

Ramakrishna (to M.): What's he saying?

M: The doctor is fearful, lest you go into bhava samadhi.

While M. was talking in this way, Ramakrishna started experiencing bhava. He then looked into the face of the doctor, folded his hands in the namaste gesture, and said, "No, no, no. Why shall I go into bhava?" But while he was saying that, he went into a very deep state of samadhi. His body became as still as a statue, and his eyes did not move.

Everyone was astounded by Sri Ramakrishna's bhava. He looked like a wooden doll sitting there. His breath was still, and he had no consciousness of the outside world. All his mind, his intellect, and ego were completely still and turned inward. He wasn't the same human being any longer.

Narendra continued to sing in his melodious, harmonious voice. Looking at Ramakrishna, he sang:

Look at this beautiful radiance!
Look at this delightful face
that I'm seeing.
The King of my heart
has entered my home
where there is a festival of love going on.
Master of my heart, please tell me what

could I possibly give to You?
Take my life, my heart, and my soul.
Whatever I have, You take it.
What more can I possibly say?

Narendra then sang another song:

There can be no delight, comfort,
or pleasure in this life
unless I keep the bee of my mind
constantly intoxicated at Your lotus feet.
All these external forms of wealth,
what value are they to me?
Why shall I be greedy for the external
world
when I have been given the privilege of
devotion to Your lotus feet?
I fear I will get bound by maya
unless I always see Your beautiful,
radiant moon-like face
shining within this samsara.
As I look at the deep radiant light
of the moon,
I realize that it would appear completely
dark without Your moon-like face
shining in that moonlight.
When Your love shines within the chaste
heart of a loving wife
that love will forever remain
pure and stainless.
All of my doubts are creating
a faith-destroying poison
diluting my devotion for Your feet.
Bless me with Your grace and keep me
always attached to You.
Then all my doubts will cease.
What else can I say to You, my Lord?

You are the Priceless Jewel and the
Precious Gem of my heart.
You are my Holy Abode of Peace and
Bliss.

Hearing the part about "Your love within the chaste heart
of a loving wife," tears came to the eyes of the doctor, and he
stood up and said, "Ahh, ahh!"

Then Narendra sang another song:

How long will this feast of love continue?
Before all the work is finished,
everyone sing the name of God!
Let the tears of love flow from your eyes.
When will I achieve that
pure consciousness within my mind?
When will I go to the forest of delight
filled with love?
When will all the bonds
of worldly attachment disappear?
When, oh, when will my eyes look
through the eyes of wisdom?
The philosopher's touchstone turns
everything into gold.
When will You, oh, Lord,
with Your divine touch
turn this iron body of mine into gold?
Manifestation of God,
give me Your darshan.
I offer You all of my devotion.
Come, take it from me!
When will all this karma and
dharma let me alone?
When will this burden of family
and the distinctions of birth, caste,
and creed, oh, when, when will

those illusions cease to be?
When will the maya of fear, shame, and
modesty leave me?

When shall I sip with the palms of my
heart the divine nectar of Thy name?
I am taking the dust from the path that
the devotees have tread upon.
I am rubbing this dust of devotion all
over my body,
and I am filling my bag
with the mud of renunciation.
And then I'm going to circumambulate all
of the pilgrimage places
and with both hands, I am going to drink
from the Fountain of Love.
And I will toss handfuls of flowers into
the River of Love.
Intoxicated with love,
I'm going to weep and laugh
and submerge myself
in the Ocean of Satchidananda.
Maddened with the love of God,
I'm going to make every one else crazy, too!
I'm going to ceaselessly sing the name of God
and eternally travel in Godliness. Om.

Second Discussion

The Application of Wisdom and Knowledge

and the Vision of the Supreme Divinity

Now that the song was completed, Ramakrishna slowly regained his external consciousness. Everyone, from the illiterate to the most learned of the pandits, everyone present, was mesmerized by Ramakrishna's countenance. The assembly was silent and looked at Ramakrishna. He had been suffering such pain a while ago, and now where did the pain go? His face looked just like a blossoming lotus, and there was a divine radiance shining from his countenance.

Ramakrishna (with great respect to the doctor): Renounce your shame and call on God. What shame could there possibly be in calling out the names of God? Shame, aversion, and fear -- these three cannot remain. You are thinking that you are such an important person, so how could you possibly sing out the name of God and dance? You are thinking, "What will other important people say if they heard that I sing and dance with the devotees of God?" What will they say? They might say with great disdain, "Did you hear that Doctor Sarkar was dancing and singing Hari, Hari?"

Ramakrishna: Doctor, you have to renounce that feeling.

Doctor: I have no attachment to that feeling. I don't care what people will say about it.

Ramakrishna: That is very good. (They all began to laugh.)

Ramakrishna: Look, by means of wisdom, you can cross over the ocean of ignorance, but you can't get to know that Great Being by various forms of worldly knowledge. Worldly knowledge only leads to egotism and ignorance. The egotism of the pandits is ignorance.

One Supreme Divinity resides within all of creation. The certain comprehension of this fact is called wisdom. If you know the Supreme Divinity in a special form, that is called the application of wisdom to life. If you get a thorn stuck in your foot, you need a second thorn to remove it. After you dig out the first thorn, you throw them both away. In the first instance, in order to remove the thorn of ignorance, you have to use the thorn of knowledge. Then you take the thorns of ignorance and knowledge and throw them both away because the Supreme Divinity is beyond wisdom and ignorance.

Ramakrishna: Lakshmana said, "Rama, this is indeed wonderful. Vasishta was such a wise man, yet he was immersed in sorrow due to the loss of his son." Rama answered Lakshmana by saying, "Hey, Brother, whoever has wisdom also has ignorance. He who has one kind of wisdom has various other kinds of wisdom as well. Who knows the light also knows the darkness. The Supreme Divinity is beyond both wisdom and ignorance. He is beyond sin and merit, and He is beyond dharma and adharma. He is beyond purity and impurity."

Speaking thus, Ramakrishna began to sing a song composed by Ramprasad:

> Hey, mind, would you like to go on tour ?
> Go to the tree of Kali that satiates every desire,
> and you will find the four satisfying fruits (the
> objectives of manifesting in a human body.)
>
> Swamiji: Those four objectives are: dharma, the ideal of perfection; artha, the resources needed for the attainment of that ideal; kama, the satiation or freedom from all other desires; and moksha or self-realization.
>
> Shree Maa sings: Hey, mind, do you want to go on a tour?

Shyam Basu: After you throw away the two thorns, what remains?

Ramakrishna: You can't explain the intrinsic nature of Supreme Divinity, the eternal, pure, knowledge of the intrinsic nature. How can I explain what that means? If anyone asks me, "What is the taste of ghee like?" How will I

explain it? Can you explain the flavor of ghee? Ghee is like
-- ghee.

Ramakrishna (continuing):   One young girl asked her
friend, "What kind of joyful feeling do you get when your
husband comes home?" The lady replied, "Only after you are
married will you be able to understand. How can I explain to
you the exquisite delight I feel when my husband arrives until
you are married yourself?"

The Puranas say that when Parvati took birth in the
Himalayas, She gave darshan to Her father, King Himalaya,
in Her various forms. When Himalaya, the king of the
mountains, saw His daughter in these many divine forms, He
said to Her, addressing Her as the Mother of the Universe,
"Maa, now may I have darshan of the Formless One spoken
of in the Vedas as the Supreme Divinity?"

Parvati said, "Father, if you want to see the Supreme
Divinity, then keep company with sadhus."

Sri Ramakrishna: What Brahman is can't be conveyed
through the mouth. Someone has said, "Everything becomes
impure by the tongue's touch, but Brahman, the Supreme
Divinity, is never impure." This means that the Vedas,
Puranas, Tantras, and all other scriptures are somewhat
impure because they are chanted with the tongue. All that
you can speak is impure. Just what the Supreme Divinity is,
can only be experienced. No one has been able to express
with their mouth exactly what the Supreme Divinity is. That
is why the Supreme Divinity remains completely pure. What
is it like to experience the bliss of Brahman? Only he or she
who has had the experience understands, and these true
knowers will always say that it is impossible to express.

Swamiji: The words talk about God. They
can't express God Herself.

Third Discussion.

The Egotism of Pandits and Sin and Merit

Ramakrishna (to the doctor with great respect): Until you have dissolved your egotism, you can't achieve wisdom. The day "I" leave is the day I take liberation. Both "I" and "mine" are born out of ignorance. You and Yours are wisdom. A real and true devotee says, "Hey, God, You are the doer. It is You who does everything. I am only the tool. Just as you make me perform, that's just how I perform. This is all Your gift. You are imperishable. You are the perceivable universe. You are the house. You are the insiders and the outsiders. I have nothing of my own. I am Your servant. Just as You order, just so I am authorized to serve You.

Shree Maa: Beautiful!

Ramakrishna (continues): Those who have read a few books, their egotism grows and grows. These are the people who have not achieved to the imperishable nature of God. I said to someone, "He has gone to Delhi." That person said, "I have also visited Delhi," and he makes a very big statement. The person who is of authority will say, "I have great authority."

Swamiji: So Ramakrishna is saying that those who have a little knowledge say, "Oh, I know that. I don't have to learn that from you because I already know that." We call those people a know-it-all or a brahmarakshasa, a demon so proud of his learning. Their learning made the ego greater rather than making it smaller. Whenever we have the idea that we know it all, then we have fallen.

Shyam Basu: They have great faith in you.

Ramakrishna: Oh, what should I say? There was a servant in Dakshineswar who had a great ego. She had two or three ornaments on her body. One day she was coming along the path. There were two or three men walking on the other side, and the servant lady said to them, "Hey, get off my path!" What shall we speak of other people's egotism?

Swamiji: She was a servant lady, but she had a couple of pieces of gold ornaments on her body, and so she thought she was very important.

Shyam Basu: There is a punishment for sins. God is doing everything. What kind of words are these? How do we reconcile them?

Ramakrishna: What? You do not understand correctly.

Narendra (to Shyam Basu): Your mind is always calculating.

Ramakrishna: Go eat the mango. There are so many hundreds of trees in the grove. There are so many thousands of branches. There are hundreds of thousands of leaves. What do you have to do with so much calculation? Go eat the mango. Don't count the trees. You came to eat the mango. Go eat the mango, and your hunger is satisfied. You have a human body in this lifetime to realize God. Try to gain devotion to the feet of God. That is what you should be making an effort towards. Why do you need to make such an account? What will happen if you contemplate all the branches of philosophy? Look, if you have just a little bit of liquor, you can get intoxicated. You can listen to how many bottles there are in the store, but of what practical use will that be to you?

Swamiji: What is the value of knowing how many bottles of liquor are in the store if you just need one for yourself? Your work is complete.

Doctor: God has an infinite amount of liquor. There is no end to the intoxication that one gets from contemplating God.

Ramakrishna (to Shyam Basu): Give it all to God. You give Him all your authority. If sincere and honest people give Him total authority, will He behave badly with you? Will He give you punishment for your sins? Whether He gives you or not, He will understand.

Doctor: How does He calculate? How does He know the accounts of all men? He is beyond all accounts.

Ramakrishna (to Shyam Basu): He is One. All you people from Calcutta say that God is a businessman, that sometimes He makes one person happy and comfortable, and sometimes He makes another person pained and sorrowful. Whatever is within the individual, the same thing is seen within God.

Is the Objective of Life to

Attain Respect from Others?

Ramakrishna: Hem used to visit Dakshineswar. Whenever he would see me, he would say with hands folded, "Respected Bhattacharya, how are you?" You see, Hem thought that the most important thing in this universe is respect. Very few people understand that the attainment of God is the true objective of human manifestation. Very few people understand that.

Fourth Discussion

The Gross Body, the Subtle Body,

the Causal Body and That Which Is Beyond

Shyam Basu (to Ramakrishna): Is it possible for anyone to show us the subtle body? In order to see it, you have to go beyond it, and if you go beyond it, how can you see it?

Ramakrishna: For one who is a true devotee, is it of any necessity to see the subtle body? If somebody sees it or not, what is the necessity? He really doesn't care. A true devotee doesn't have any inclination to impress others by demonstrating any type of powers. He doesn't need to impress or make friends with some big fellow.

Shyam Basu: Ok, what is the difference between the gross body and the subtle body?

Ramakrishna: This physical body, which is composed of five elements, is known as the gross body. Mind, intellect, all recollection, and the ego are known as the subtle body. The body that has attained to supreme divinity and unites with that divinity is called the causal body.

In the Tantras it is said, "The body is a manifestation of the infinite energy. It is the unconditional Great Cause which is beyond all thought and description. What it is can only be experienced. You can't express it with your mouth. You can know what it is by practicing some form of sadhana."

God desires us to do a little sadhana whereby we can develop sincere devotion. If you only listen, will that produce any fruit? You have to do something to get the spiritual fruit. You must nurture and water the seeds that have been planted. If you simply say "Ganja, ganja," will that be enough to get you intoxicated? Do you get stoned just by talking about marijuana? If you rub your body with ganja, will you get stoned? I don't think so. You have to eat it.

Ramakrishna (continuing): Which is the number forty-one grade thread and which is the number forty grade thread? If you are not in the business of dealing in threads, you can't tell the distinction between them. Unless you are in the thread business, you will not be able to tell that subtle difference. But if you are in the thread business, it is not difficult for you to tell the difference between all of the many grades of thread or sizes of needles. That is why I am saying you must do some sadhana. Then you will know the gross body, the subtle body, the causal body, and that which is beyond. Then you will know what they are talking about.

First pray to God with sincerity with all your heart. Then with tremendous devotion fall at the lotus feet of your chosen deity.

After Ahalya was freed from her curse, Ramachandra said to her, "You may choose a boon from me." Ahalya replied, "If Rama will give me a boon, then give me the boon that even if I take birth in the womb of a pig, I will have no difficulty because I have had the darshan of Rama. But, Rama, please bless me that my mind will always stay devoted to Your lotus feet."

Ramakrishna: I only want devotion from the Divine Mother. I was offering flowers to the lotus feet of the Divine Mother, and I asked Her for only that one thing. I prayed, "Mother, take your ignorance, take your wisdom. Give me pure devotion. Here is purity, here is impurity. Give me pure devotion. Here is sin, here is merit. Give me pure devotion. Here is good, here is bad. Give me pure devotion. Here is dharma, here is adharma. Give me pure devotion."

Whatever dharma you perform, you will receive the opposite as well. If you go to take merits, you will get sin. Every time you take wisdom, you will get ignorance. Every time you take purity, you will get impurity. If you understand there is a light illuminated, then you will understand that there is a darkness as well. Who knows only one thing, they know a lot. Who knows the good things, they know the bad things as well. But if anyone eats the meat of a pig, and they have pure devotion to the lotus feet of God, that individual is blessed. If they are eating the pure food of puja, but have a selfish attachment to their samsara, then...

Doctor: Who is the lowest? Now I am going to tell you something. Buddha did eat the meat of a pig, and he always had a pain in his stomach, so he used to eat opium. Do you know what Nirvana and all that is? He used to eat opium and would become fully sedated yet full of knowledge. He would lose all outer consciousness of the external world. That was the nature of his Nirvana.

Hearing the doctor's definition of the Buddha's Nirvana, everybody laughed and laughed! After composing themselves, the discussions resumed.

Fifth Discussion

The Householder's Life and

Activities Free from Attachment

Ramakrishna (to Shyam Basu): There is no fault in protecting your dharma in the samsara, but keep your mind at the lotus feet of God. Try to perform your duties without selfish desire. Sometimes you may have seen that if someone has a cyst on his back, they will continue to talk with everybody. Perhaps they will even perform their work, but their mind remains with the cyst on their back.

You do your samsara like a married woman. A married woman's mind stays with her husband, but she does all the work of the house.

Ramakrishna (to the doctor): Do you understand?

Doctor: Without having this attitude, how can I understand?

Shyam Basu (to the doctor): You understand -- at least a little bit. (They all began to laugh.)

Ramakrishna (laughing heartily): He has been doing this doctor business for a long time. Isn't that so? (They all began to laugh again.)

Shyam Basu: Sir, what do you think about Theosophy?

Ramakrishna: The main issue is this. Those who make disciples and at the same time wish to acquire siddhis (powers) are of a lower nature. Those who have become adepts want various forms of energy or powers. For example, if someone wishes to walk upon the Ganga, that requires energy, the power to walk on water. To hear what other people are saying in distant places, that is also an energy, or power. It is very difficult for people who concentrate on these external powers to have pure devotion to God.

Shyam Basu: But they are trying, according to their capacity, to establish Hindu dharma.

Ramakrishna: I don't know their qualifications or situations very well.

Shyam Basu: After death where does the individual soul go? Does he go to the moon, stars, or any place else? The Theosophists like to explain these things.

Ramakrishna: Yes, that is possibly their attitude. Let it be that way. Do you know what my attitude is? One person asked Hanuman, "What day is today?" Hanuman replied, "I don't know the day or the month. I don't know where the stars or planets are. I only think of Rama." I have that same attitude.

Shyam Basu: They say all the mahatmas, adepts, are spiritually advanced souls. What is your faith?

Ramakrishna: You leave all those thoughts right now. Wait until my disease leaves me, and then you may come back. I will answer all your questions. If you believe in me, that is enough. You will find a way to understand. I don't take any money. I don't take any cloth. I don't have any attachments. That is why so many people come to see me. (All laugh.)

Ramakrishna (to the doctor): Don't get angry with all these things I have been saying to you. I know you have done all of these things -- earning money, giving lectures, etc. Now it is time for you to give your mind to God. Occasionally you come here. Just listening to the word of God, you will get advancement.

Then after a short time, the doctor got ready to leave. About that time Girish Chandra Ghosh arrived. He took the dust of Ramakrishna's lotus feet and sat down. When the doctor saw Girish, he was filled with delight and sat back down again.

Doctor (humorously pointing to Girish): When I was here, he wasn't. Then when I thought I would go, he arrives. (All laugh.)

The doctor engaged Girish in conversation about the Science Association.

Ramakrishna: One day you will take me to the Science Association.

Doctor: If you go there, you will faint. If you see the amazing drama of God there, you will go unconscious.

Ramakrishna: Is that true?

Sixth Discussion

Worshiping the Guru

Doctor (to Girish): Do whatever you choose, but don't worship him (Ramakrishna) as God. Don't call him God and do puja to him. You trouble this good man enough as it is.

Girish: Great Sir (Mahashay), what are you saying? That individual who takes us across this ocean of worldliness, what else shall I do with him? Is it because his poo looks the same as everyone else's?

Shree Maa laughs: Slang language.

Doctor: It doesn't happen because of the poo. I don't have any aversion. One shopkeeper's son came. He made poo right there. Everyone closed their noses with their cloth. I sat with that child for half an hour, but I didn't put the cloth over my nose until the sweeper came and cleaned up everything. I didn't need to put a cloth over my nose. I understood that what he is, that also I am. Why should I feel aversion? Can't I take the dust from my guru's feet? Look, I am taking. (He took the dust of Sri Ramakrishna's feet and put it on his forehead.)

Girish: In this situation, everyone is receiving blessings.

Doctor: Is that something wonderful, to take the dust from the guru's feet? I can take the dust from everyone's feet. Give me your dust. (He took the dust from everyone's feet.)

Narendra (to the doctor):   We understand Sri Ramakrishna to be God- like. You understand what I mean? Just like in the vegetable and animal creations, from time to time there are living things that you can't tell whether they are plants or animals. It is very difficult to distinguish. This man is living in both the human world and in God's world, or somewhere in between. That is his position. It is very difficult to say whether he lives in God's world or man's world. Is this individual a human being, or is this individual a god?

Doctor: You can't give examples of God's world.

Narendra: I am not talking about God. I am talking about a person who is like God.

Doctor: You have to control your individual attitude. It is not good for you to publicize it. No one will understand. Even those who claim to be my closest friends think of me as having no compassion whatsoever. Perhaps all of you will beat me with your shoes.

Ramakrishna (to the doctor): What is this? They love and respect you with such sincerity. When they hear that you are coming, they set everything up and keep everything ready.

Girish: Everyone has great faith in you, Doctor.

Doctor: Even my wife thinks of me as having an empty heart without any love or attachment because I have this one fault. I don't publicize my attitude in front of others.

Girish: Then, Great Sir (Mahashay), it will be very good of you to open up your heart and speak your mind. Have some compassion for your friends, and show your grace.

Doctor: When I am with all of you, I also get emotional and go into bhava.

Doctor (to Narendra): I shed tears when I am alone.

Final Discussion

Great Individuals Accept the Sins of Individuals, the Avatars, and Narendra

Doctor (to Ramakrishna): When you go into bhava, you sometimes put your foot on somebody's body. That is not appropriate.

Ramakrishna: Do you think I understand when I do that? Upon whose body do I put my foot?

Doctor: That is not good. You have to have a little discrimination.

Ramakrishna: When I go into this bhava, how can I explain to you how or what I am? After my bhava is over and I return to my normal consciousness, then I think that the reason I am suffering from this disease is because of doing things like that. I become crazy for God when I am in this bhava. So many unorthodox things I do when I am in that craziness. What can I do?

Doctor: God understands what your attitude is.

Doctor (looking at the devotees): He expresses regret for what he does. At least he knows those actions are sinful.

Ramakrishna (to Narendra): You are very truthful and your words are quite penetrating. Why don't you explain to him? Try and make him understand.

Girish (to the doctor): Sir, you understand incorrectly. He is not pained by all that. His body is pure. He has no sin. He touches people for their own welfare. If he didn't take away their sins, it wouldn't be possible for him to experience this disease. That is why he sometimes experiences feeling this way.

When you had colic, didn't you regret that you had stayed up many nights studying your books? Were you doing anything wrong by staying up late in the night? You regret it because it was the primary cause of your getting ill. Is it incorrect for one individual to touch another when he has nothing but the best of intentions for that person's welfare?

Doctor (disgusted and fed up with Girish): You win! Go ahead and give me the dust of your feet.

Doctor (to Narendra): I have no further debate with that intellectual powerhouse. I have to concede.

Narendra (to the doctor): There is another side of the issue. For scientific discovery, Doctor, you may risk your health with the intensity of your research. This is beyond science. He also has risked his health and everything else for the Divine Science, the Worship and Realization of God. In the intensity of his bhava, he pays little attention to the discomforts of his body or his disease.

Girish (to the doctor): Sir, you have the same fault. You have a great ego. The fault that he has, you also have. Who has a fault, will always see that particular fault in others. (The doctor is silent.)

Narendra (to the doctor): By worshiping him, we are worshiping God, and God is coming very close to us.

Ramakrishna began to laugh with great delight.

Shree Maa: Narendra is saying there is no difference between worshiping God and worshiping the Guru.

Jai Sri Ramakrishna! Jai Maa! Om.

Ramakrishna's Last Rites